RECONSTRUCTION

RECONSTRUCTION

A REFERENCE GUIDE

Paul E. Teed
and
Melissa Ladd Teed

Guides to Historic Events in America
Randall M. Miller, Series Editor

ABC-CLIO™

An Imprint of ABC-CLIO, LLC
Santa Barbara, California • Denver, Colorado

Library of Congress Cataloging-in-Publication Data

Teed, Paul E.
  Reconstruction : a reference guide / Paul E. Teed and Melissa Ladd Teed.
    pages cm. — (Guides to historic events in America)
  Includes bibliographical references and index.
    ISBN 978–1–61069–532–9 (hard copy : alkaline paper) — ISBN 978–1–61069–533–6 (ebook) 1. Reconstruction (U.S. history, 1865–1877) I. Teed, Melissa Ladd. II. Title.
E668.T28   2015
973.8—dc23   2015012223

ISBN: 978–1–61069–532–9
EISBN: 978–1–61069–533–6

19 18 17 16 15   1 2 3 4 5

This book is also available on the World Wide Web as an eBook.
Visit www.abc-clio.com for details.

ABC-CLIO
An Imprint of ABC-CLIO, LLC

ABC-CLIO, LLC
130 Cremona Drive, P.O. Box 1911
Santa Barbara, California 93116-1911

This book is printed on acid-free paper ∞

Manufactured in the United States of America

For Emilia and Lucy

CONTENTS

Biographical Essays

LIST OF ILLUSTRATIONS

Series Foreword

P erhaps no people have been more difficult to comprehend than the Americans. As J. Hector St. Jean de Crèvecoeur asked during the American Revolution, countless others have echoed ever after—"What then is this American, this new man?" What, indeed? Americans then and after have been, and remain, a people in the process of becoming. They have been, and are, a people in motion, whether coming from a distant shore, crossing the mighty Mississippi, or packing off to the suburbs, and all the while following the promise of an American dream of realizing life, liberty, and happiness. The directions of such movement have changed, and sometimes the trajectory has taken a downward arc in terms of civil war and economic depression, but always the process has continued.

Making sense of that American experience demands attention to critical moments—events—that reflected and affected American ideas and identities. Although Americans have constructed an almost linear narrative of progress from the days of George Washington to today in relating their common history, they also have marked that history by recognizing particular events as pivotal in explaining who and why they believed and acted as they did at particular times and over time. Such events have forced Americans to consider closely their true interests. They also have challenged their commitment to professed beliefs of freedom and liberty, equality and opportunity, tolerance and generosity. Whether fighting for independence or empire, drafting and implementing a frame of government, reconstructing a nation divided by civil war, struggling for basic rights and the franchise, creating a mass-mediated culture, standing up for capitalism and democracy and against communism, to name several critical developments, Americans have understood that historic events are more than just moments. They are processes of change made clear through particular events but not bound to a single moment or instance. Such thinking about the character and consequence of American history informs this new series of Guides to Historic Events in America.

Drawing on the latest and best literature, and bringing together narrative overviews and critical chapters of important historic events, the books in the series function as both reference guides and informed analyses to critical events that have shaped American life, culture, society, economy, and politics and fixed America's place in the world. The books do not promise a comprehensive reading and rendering of American history. Such is not yet, if ever, possible for any single work or series. Nor do they chart a single interpretive line, though they share common concerns and methods of inquiry. Each book stands alone, resting on the expertise of the author and the strength of the evidence. At the same time, taken together the books in this new series will provide a dynamic portrait of that on-going work-in-progress, America itself.

Each book follows a common format, with a chronology, historical overview, topical chapters on aspects of the historical event under examination, a set of biographies of key figures, selected essential primary documents, and an annotated bibliography. As such, each book holds many uses for students, teachers, and the general public wanting and needing to know the principal issues and the pertinent arguments and evidence on significant events in American history. The combination of historical description and analysis, biographies, and primary documents also moves readers to approach each historic event from multiple perspectives and with a critical eye. Each book in its structure and content invites students and teachers, in and out of the classroom, to consider and debate the character and consequence(s) of the historic event in question. Such debate invariably will bring readers back to that most critical and never-ending question of what was/is "the American" and what does, and must, "America" mean.

Randall M. Miller
Saint Joseph's University, Philadelphia

PREFACE

The Reconstruction era is one of the most important and dramatic periods in American history. Though less well understood than the military events of the Civil War, the intense political conflicts, social upheavals, and far-reaching constitutional revisions of Reconstruction nevertheless shaped the kind of nation the United States became in the twentieth century. The national Union had been preserved, but the terrible destruction wrought by four years of civil war and the revolutionary implications of slavery's abolition presented Americans with serious challenges, all of which generated passionate and often violent disagreement. The sectional antagonisms that had caused the war remained an enduring fault line in American life as did the deep racism that had so blighted the promise of American democracy. This book examines the ways in which Reconstruction-era Americans confronted these burning issues and it explores the sharp conflicts resulting from them. While acknowledging that Reconstruction ultimately failed to achieve the far-reaching egalitarian goals that its strongest advocates had envisioned, the book suggests that the period witnessed an extraordinary biracial struggle for equality and left an important legacy for the future expansion of American democracy.

While paying close attention to the political debates over Reconstruction, both at the federal and state level, this book offers a broadly inclusive approach to the period that builds on recent works by social and cultural historians. Issues such as work, religion, and gender roles receive considerable attention here, and the political conflicts of the period are presented in light of their impact on the daily lives of the ordinary and extraordinary men and women who lived through Reconstruction. The book also goes beyond the mythic portrayals of evil carpetbaggers and scalawags that once dominated the literature on the post-Civil War South. Instead, it presents a more careful and nuanced analysis of the origins and motives of contending groups and offers a more accurate but no less dramatic picture of the struggles over racial equality, political rights, and sectional interests that make up the history of this remarkable period.

After a chronology of the major events of Reconstruction, the book's prologue sets up the Reconstruction period by exploring the questions about American life that were generated by the searing experience of the Civil War. Chapter One examines the wartime planning for Reconstruction, including free labor and educational experiments with former slaves, and Chapter Two details the controversial and ultimately ill-fated attempts by President Andrew Johnson to restore the ex-Confederate states to the Union. Chapter Three shows that the intensifying conflict between the president and Congress for control of Reconstruction policy took place at a time when former slaves were struggling to preserve their freedom against increasingly coercive policies in the southern states. Focusing on the implementation of and conflict over Congressional Reconstruction policy, Chapter Four examines the political reorganization of ex-Confederate states and the political mobilization of the African American population of the South. In Chapter Five, the political, social, and economic ramifications of Congressional Reconstruction are explored with a special emphasis on the new realities of family and work that confronted Southerners of all backgrounds. This chapter also offers an assessment of the Republican-dominated state governments organized under congressional Reconstruction policy. It highlights the role of African American leaders in these governments and details their vulnerability to accelerating levels of white supremacist violence. The subject of Chapter Six is the defeat of Reconstruction through orchestrated campaigns of violence and fraud and the return of white southern Democrats to power through campaigns of "redemption."

Four additional sections of the book follow the narrative chapters. The first includes a series of essays, each of which employs a distinct analytical method to highlight important aspects of the Reconstruction era. One uses a counterfactual approach to consider the impact of Abraham Lincoln's death on the larger history of the period. A second essay points to the passage of southern black codes as a defining moment in the early history of Reconstruction from which much of the political and social conflict of the period stemmed. The next essay contains a detailed analysis of the Fourteenth Amendment, explaining its many complex provisions in the context of partisan and sectional battles over race, citizenship, and political power. The essay section concludes with an analytical perspective on the repeated claim, made by contemporaries and some historians, that the policies of Congressional Reconstruction constituted a truly radical program of change. The essay section is followed by a wide-ranging collection of primary sources from the period, including laws, speeches, work contracts, and congressional testimony from former slaves among many other documents. Each document is preceded by a brief introduction explaining the character of the document and placing it in the broader context of the period. These sources are followed by brief biographies of 23 individuals who either made a significant impact on Reconstruction or whose lives represent important themes of the period. The book concludes with an annotated bibliography that will be useful to those considering further exploration of this period. It contains detailed descriptions and brief evaluations of key works on the history of Reconstruction.

****

We would like to thank several individuals for their help on this project. Randall Miller, the series editor, has placed his deep knowledge of this subject at our disposal and his comments on our manuscript have improved it in many ways. Michael Millman and his staff at ABC-CLIO have worked with us at every stage and we are grateful for their patience and professionalism. Melissa Ladd Teed would like to thank Saginaw Valley State University for a sabbatical leave, which helped make this book possible and we are both grateful to the many students whose interests and questions shaped aspects of the book. We would also like to thank our daughters, Emilia and Lucy, for the exuberance and joyful noise that accompanied the writing of this book.

CHRONOLOGY

1863

January 1   Emancipation Proclamation issued.

December   Lincoln issues Proclamation of Amnesty and Reconstruction (Ten Percent Plan).

1864

July   Wade-Davis Bill passes Congress; Lincoln uses the pocket veto.

1865–67   Presidential Reconstruction.

1865

January   General William T. Sherman issues Special Field Order 15.

March   Freedmen's Bureau created.

April   Assassination of Abraham Lincoln; Andrew Johnson becomes the 17th president.

May   President Johnson presents his plan for Reconstruction.

Summer   Johnson orders the return of confiscated land to the original owners.

November and   Black Codes passed in Mississippi and South Carolina.
December

| December | Ratification of the 13th Amendment; Congress refuses to recognize state governments reconstructed under Johnson's plan and refuses to seat the representatives elected in the former Confederacy. |

1866

April	Civil Rights Act of 1866 passed over Johnson's veto.
May	Race riot in Memphis.
July	New Orleans race riot.
July	Readmission of Tennessee to the Union.
Fall	Congressional elections result in major gains for Republicans. In the next Congress they would hold more than a two-thirds majority.
1867–77	Congressional Reconstruction.

1867

March	Congress enacts Tenure of Office Act.
March–July	Congress enacts three Military Reconstruction Acts.
Summer	President Johnson removes Edwin Stanton as Secretary of War.
1867–1869	Southern constitutional conventions held.

1868:

March–May	Impeachment and trial of President Andrew Johnson.
June–July	Readmission of Alabama, Arkansas, Florida, Louisiana, North Carolina, and South Carolina to the Union.
July	Ratification of the 14th Amendment.
September	Georgia state legislature refuses to seat the African Americans who had been elected.
November	Ulysses S. Grant elected president.

1869

| February | Congress passes Fifteenth Amendment. |

| March | Inauguration of Ulysses S. Grant as president. |

1870:

January–July	Readmission of Georgia, Mississippi, Texas, and Virginia to the Union.
February	Ratification of the Fifteenth Amendment.
February	The Senate votes to seat Hiram Revels of Mississippi, the first African American to serve in the U.S. Senate.
May	Passage of the Enforcement Act of May 31, 1870.

1871

| April | Passage of the Ku Klux Act. |
| October | In response to Klan violence, President Grant declares martial law and suspend the writ of habeas corpus in nine counties in South Carolina. |

1872:

May	Liberal Republicans hold convention in Cincinnati and nominate Horace Greeley for president.
June	Republicans nominate U.S. Grant for president.
June	Freedmen's Bureau closed down.
July	Democrats nominate Horace Greeley.
November	Grant reelected president.

1873

| April | Colfax Massacre in Louisiana. |
| September | Panic of 1873 begins. |

1874

| June | Failure of Freedmen's Savings and Trust Company (founded 1865). |

Fall	Democrats win control of both houses of Congress, first time since before the Civil War.

1875

March	Congress passes the Civil Rights Act of 1875.
Fall	Redeemer government elected in Mississippi.

1876

March	*U.S. v. Cruickshank.*
November	Disputed presidential election between Rutherford B. Hayes (R) and Samuel Tilden (D).

1877

March	Inauguration of Rutherford B. Hayes.
April	President Hayes orders the remaining federal troops in the southern states back to barracks. Reconstruction officially ends.

SLAVERY, WAR, AND EMANCIPATION

I n a speech delivered in the House of Representatives in December 1865, Republican representative Thaddeus Stevens of Pennsylvania warned his congressional colleagues that momentous decisions about the nation's future lay before them. The war, he reminded them, had turned loose nearly four million slaves who had neither "a hut to shelter them [n]or a cent in their pockets," and who had been denied the most basic education by the "infernal laws of slavery." The dire condition of freedpeople and the terrible oppression they had experienced at the hands of their former owners, Stevens insisted, required active and sustained intervention in the social and political life of the defeated South. "This Congress is bound to provide for them until they can take care of themselves," he contended. With homesteads to ensure their economic independence and political representation to protect them from the hostile intentions of southern whites, former slaves had a chance to realize a robust form of freedom and the nation had a chance to realize its egalitarian ideals. Convinced that justice for former slaves was essential if the nation was to redeem the staggering losses inflicted by four years of bloody civil war, Stevens advised Congress to consider the consequences of shirking their political and moral responsibility to the poor and oppressed. "If we fail in this great duty now, when we have the power," he told them, "we shall deserve and receive the execration of history and of all future ages."[1]

Stevens believed that Reconstruction-era politicians would be condemned by history if they did too little for former slaves, but in an ironic twist, condemnation has come more often from those who have believed they did too much. In the early twentieth century, for example, historians such as William Dunning and John Burgess established an extremely negative view of Reconstruction that dominated historical writing about and popular understandings of Reconstruction for more than half a century. Arguing that former slaves were incapable of exercising the rights and privileges that radical Republicans like Stevens attempted to confer upon them, these writers regarded postwar economic and political reforms as failures that subjected the South to a generation of corruption, economic stagnation, and misrule. This tradition of interpretation, which is often called the "Dunning School" in American historiography, was permeated by racism and at least indirectly justified the system of racial violence and legally enforced segregation that came to dominate the South in the years after Reconstruction. Even as late as the 1960s, educated Americans were taught to see Reconstruction as a stain of the nation's honor, a "tragic era" when "carpetbaggers" and "scalawags" looted a defeated, but noble, South by manipulating ignorant and racially inferior blacks. Such views had been immortalized by D. W. Griffith's famous silent film, *Birth of Nation* (1915), which depicted the Ku Klux Klan as a noble brotherhood devoted to the protection of white women and the "redemption" of the South from the excesses of Reconstruction. After sitting through a private screening at the White House, President Woodrow Wilson, himself a white Southerner and ardent segregationist, said that the film was "like writing history with lightning" and lamented the fact that it was "so terribly true."[2]

Yet even as these views of the Reconstruction era became dominant, Thaddeus Stevens's vision of Reconstruction as a period of great egalitarian promise was kept alive by dissenting writers who challenged the Dunning School both for its racism and for the weakness of the evidence supporting it. In his 1935 book *Black Reconstruction in America*, for example, the pioneering African American sociologist W. E. B. Du Bois refuted the notion that former slaves were ignorant pawns of the carpetbaggers and showed that the political activism of Reconstruction-era blacks was a natural extension of both their resistance to slavery and their role as soldiers in the Civil War. In the 1950s and 1960s, moreover, Du Bois's insights were developed by scholars such as Kenneth Stampp, John Hope Franklin, and Joel Williamson. These historians demonstrated that if Reconstruction-era politics was not immune from corruption, neither was it bereft of idealism. Indeed, they showed that the political alliance of former slaves and white

Republican politicians produced some of the period's most notable accomplishments, including the passage of the nation's first civil rights legislation, the ratification of the Fourteenth and Fifteenth Amendments to the Constitution, and the creation of public school systems in southern states. The final blow against the Dunning School was the publication of historian Eric Foner's *Reconstruction: America's Unfinished Revolution* (1988), a work that brilliantly synthesized previous scholarship while presenting new evidence of the period's enormous, if unrealized, potential to revolutionize American society and politics. While it took more than a hundred years, historians have at last come to understand what Thaddeus Stevens was saying on that cold December day in 1865.

What Stevens had understood is that although Confederate armies had been defeated on the battlefield and the permanent secession of southern states prevented, the Civil War was far from over. Its central issue had not yet been resolved. At the core of the sectional conflict that had led to the war was, of course, the institution of slavery, a system that had reduced millions of Americans to a form of human bondage that was among the most brutal in human history. Since its inception in the tobacco economy of colonial Virginia, chattel slavery had proven enormously profitable to planters in the American South, and especially so as the region converted to cotton production in the early nineteenth century. Access to highly fertile cotton lands in the Mississippi River valley and in the new lands west of the river was among the most important forces motivating American expansion in the years before the Civil War. Determined to protect their enormous investment in slave property, southern planters had wielded disproportionate political influence both within southern states and in national politics. During the 72 years between 1789 and 1861, for example, a southern slaveholder had held the presidency for 49 of them, and the Supreme Court had a southern majority for the whole period. Twenty-three of the thirty-six speakers of the House had been from southern states during the same years, as had twenty of the thirty-five presidents pro tempore of the Senate. All of this had occurred during a period when the population of northern states was not only substantially larger than that of the South, but also growing at a more rapid rate.[3]

But slaveholders in the South had never felt entirely secure in their ability to control the slave population, and as the documents issued at the time of secession attest, their decision to create a separate southern confederacy was driven by fear that their rights to slave property were being eroded under the old Union. Part of this anxiety resulted from the actions of the slaves themselves, who resisted enslavement in both ordinary and dramatic ways. Whether breaking tools, stealing food, fleeing from cruel masters, or joining rebellions like the one led by Nat Turner in 1831, enslaved Southerners demonstrated that the slaveowners' power was not absolute and would face constant challenges from within. Added to this worry was the crusading zeal of northern abolitionism, a small but vocal movement of social activists who condemned the slave system as sinful and called for immediate abolition. Although abolitionists were not popular, even in the North, the talent of their leaders and the adept use of petitions, lectures, and the steam-powered press gave them a voice that was difficult to ignore. Leading antislavery politicians, including Charles Sumner, Thaddeus Stevens, and even to some extent Abraham Lincoln, were deeply influenced by the abolitionists' critique of slavery and their description of southern society as violent and immoral. Searing accounts of slavery written by former slaves like Frederick Douglass and Solomon Northup were critical in providing abolitionists with compelling evidence for the view that southern society was fundamentally flawed and morally bankrupt.

Abolitionists sought to challenge slavery on moral grounds, but it was the economic and political dimensions of the slavery debate that had led the nation to civil war. Fraught with racism and economic anxiety, working-class Northerners were vocal opponents of the abolitionists and generally supported proslavery Democrats at the polls. But by the mid-1850s, white Northerners felt increasingly threatened by the South's aggressive insistence on spreading slavery into western lands, a region that many working people hoped would provide a solution to their own growing dependency on wage labor. For others, the dynamic growth of the northern manufacturing system demonstrated the superiority of "free labor" to the slave system of the South, and they too opposed the spread of slavery into new lands in the West. These sentiments stoked growing anger over what some in the North regarded as antidemocratic sentiment in the South. The brutal caning of Massachusetts's antislavery senator Charles Sumner on the floor of the Senate by South Carolina's Preston Brooks simply confirmed the image of a violent, repressive South.

Antislavery forces increasingly made the argument that the slaveholding South represented a powerful but utterly corrupt element in American political life that was prepared to sacrifice the rights of white citizens in order to protect and extend the institution of slavery. Ohio congressman Joshua Giddings, for example, argued that the southern "slave power" had "invaded the sanctity of our Post Office, degraded our patriotism, taxed the free labor of the North, frightened our Statesmen, and controlled the nation."[4] Pointing to the congressional Gag Rule that suppressed antislavery petitions, the repeated mob attacks on abolitionist newspapers, and attempts to prevent the circulation of antislavery literature through the mails, leaders like Giddings warned their constituents that compromises with an aggressive and hostile South might come at the cost of their own freedom. The passage of the Fugitive Slave of 1850 seemed to confirm these fears as the law required that northern communities assist federal officials in recapturing escaped slaves and returning them to southern masters. Increasingly resentful that they could now be legally compelled to serve the interests of slaveholders, northerners became more receptive to abolitionist images of the South as arrogant and corrupt. Harriet Beecher Stowe's popular novel *Uncle Tom's Cabin*, which was published after the passage of the Fugitive Slave Act, powerfully dramatized the ways in which the law forced northern citizens to make painful choices between the duties of citizenship and the claims of conscience.

By the late 1850s, the new Republican Party began to harness this growing antislavery and antisouthern sentiment, and Republican activists issued urgent calls for the restriction of slavery to the states where it already existed and hoped that the system would die out in two or three generations. Most Republicans, including Abraham Lincoln, publically rejected any association with the abolitionists and pledged not to interfere with slavery in the South where it was protected by the U.S. Constitution. Nonetheless Lincoln's election in 1860 convinced the slaveholding South that a crisis had arrived. "A geographical line has been drawn across the Union," the South Carolina secessionists insisted just after Lincoln's victory. "[A]ll the States north of that line have united in the election of a man . . . whose opinions and purposes are hostile to slavery."[5]

Perhaps one of the most profound ironies of this period is that in attempting to protect slavery by seceding from the Union, southern states created the only legal context—that of civil war—in which the institution could be directly attacked. Yet if southern slaveholders could not see this, Union leaders were also slow to accept it. Committed to preserving the Union and convinced that any attack on slavery would lead border slave states like Kentucky to join the rebellion, Lincoln's early war policies scrupulously avoided the slavery issue and he initially refused to consider the enlistment of blacks in the army. Appointing George B. McClellan, a conservative, proslavery Democrat as his general in chief, Lincoln ignored abolitionist demands for antislavery policies and either reprimanded or removed military commanders who attempted to emancipate or arm slaves in occupied regions of the South. Yet two factors ultimately led the president to reconsider his policy and pushed him toward emancipation as a wartime strategy. First, the failure of Union armies to win decisive battles against Confederate forces generated growing congressional pressure on the president to adopt harsher policies toward southern civilians and their property. By the summer of 1862 when Union forces under McClellan were suffering defeat after defeat in Virginia, it became difficult to ignore the arguments of more radical Republicans, such as Zachariah Chandler of Michigan, who insisted that attacking slavery was necessary to weaken the Confederate economic and social structure. At the same time, a second argument came from the slaves themselves who were fleeing the Confederacy in increasing numbers and seeking refuge behind Union lines. Although General McClellan insisted on returning escaped slaves, even to rebel owners, this policy seemed more and more at variance with common sense as black refugees offered valuable military intelligence, cheap labor for the army, and, if they were men, potentially more soldiers in uniform.

These pragmatic considerations made the Emancipation Proclamation possible, but at the same time ensured that important questions about the place of African Americans in American society would have to be answered in the Reconstruction period. On the one hand, the proclamation represented a radical departure from the consistent proslavery character of the United States government since the time of the Revolution. In areas that remained in rebellion at the time of the proclamation's issue, military forces were now directed to enforce the freedom of slaves who fled from their masters to Union lines. As the *New York Times* put it two days after Lincoln signed the Emancipation Proclamation: "Hitherto Slavery has been under the protection of the government; henceforth it is under its ban."[6] In addition, African American men were now eligible to serve in the federal army, a policy which black leader Frederick Douglass believed would provide a strong argument for equal citizenship following the war. "Once let the black man get upon his person the brass letters U.S.," he told a crowd in Philadelphia in July 1863, "and there is no power on earth . . . which can deny that he has earned the right of citizenship in the United States."[7]

Yet for all its "revolutionary" character, the Emancipation Proclamation was in other respects an extremely conservative form of emancipation policy. Lincoln described it as a "military necessity," he carefully excluded border state slavery from the proclamation's scope, and he made no reference at all to the citizenship of those freed by the new policy. Had the government dealt slavery a fatal blow, or was emancipation a temporary expediency that might be reversed when the war ended? Northern Democrats clearly believed the latter, saying that the proclamation merely provided a legal framework under which slaves might sue for their freedom following the war and predicting that the Supreme Court "will declare the proclamation void."[8]

Although the Thirteenth Amendment would eventually prevent court challenges to emancipation and outlaw slavery nationally, the status of those freed by the Emancipation Proclamation was fraught with deep ambiguity for the final two years of the Civil War. Nor was there greater clarity for those nearly 200,000 black men who were serving their country as soldiers in the Union army. Black troops fought with great effectiveness on battlefields from Virginia to Mississippi, thereby disproving racial prejudices that had disparaged their courage and tenacity. But even as these soldiers provided critical manpower to the Union cause, the discriminatory treatment they received undercut the connection between military service and citizenship. Fighting in segregated units led exclusively by white officers, African American troops endured unequal and late pay, poor rations, shoddy uniforms, and only sporadic training in battlefield formation and the use of firearms. White officers of black regiments often shared the racial stereotypes of the period and subjected their men to much higher levels of coercion and discipline than white troops experienced. As one historian has put it, the discriminatory treatment of black soldiers replicated many of the conditions of slavery and as a result "belied the rhetoric of liberation."[9]

Yet if white Americans looked upon emancipated slaves with deeply ambivalent eyes, black Americans sought to transform the vague promises of the Emancipation Proclamation into a robust affirmation of freedom, which they carried into the Reconstruction period. Even before the government's adoption of an emancipation policy, for example, southern slaves recognized that the war represented a critical moment in which they might challenge the power of their masters and topple the system of slavery. Drawing inspiration from the biblical story of the Exodus, enslaved people regarded the war as a divine judgment on the slaveholders of the South and thus fled from plantations across the region whenever Union troops were present. Although the numbers of refugees from slavery were small at the beginning of the war, the Emancipation Proclamation encouraged this exodus from slavery and historians now estimate that as many as 500,000 slaves escaped to Union lines during the course of the war.[10]

In a pattern that would repeat itself many times during Reconstruction, black Americans refused to wait for the government to affirm their rights to freedom before asserting them. Instead, their growing physical presence within Union lines forced the authorities to clarify official policies toward refugees and pushed the government toward formal emancipation policies. At the same time, by removing their labor power from the Confederacy and, in many cases, transferring it to the Union cause, blacks weakened the rebellion and hastened the end of the slave system. This understanding of the value of their own labor power was yet another valuable asset that former slaves took into the postwar period. As one former slave put it, "If every mother's son of a black had thrown 'way his hoe and took up a gun to fight for his own freedom[,] . . . the war'd been over before it began."[11]

But the most overt assertions of citizenship and equality during the Civil War came from black soldiers who, despite the trying circumstances of their military service, found ways to express their vision of manhood and freedom. In response to unequal pay, for example, an anonymous soldier in the 54th Massachusetts Regiment demanded that the authorities treat members of his unit "in all respects like white soldiers, our bounties, rations and emoluments being the same." To ask black soldiers to accept unequal pay, he argued, would "degrade us, and mark us as inferior soldiers, and would be a complete annihilation of every vestige of our manhood."[12] For those African Americans who had joined the army immediately after gaining their freedom, the war sometimes offered remarkable chances to target the very people who had abused them or their families as slaves. In one extraordinary letter, black soldier Spotswood Rice warned the white Missouri woman who owned his daughter Mary that he would not hesitate to use his new status as a soldier to obtain the release of his child from bondage. "My children [are] my own and I expect to get them," he told her. "When I get ready to come after Mary I will have … a power and authority to bring her away and to execute vengeance on them that holds my Child."[13] Rice spoke with both moral indignation and a confidence that "this whole Government" would sustain his right to reclaim his daughter. To many black soldiers, the uniform they wore and the weapon they carried were symbols of a new racial order that, despite the ambiguous government policies and military discrimination, might follow the terrible sacrifice of the war. In a powerful example of the perceived change, a uniformed former slave who encountered his old master among a group of Confederate prisoners smiled and said "Hello, massa; bottom rail top dis time!"[14]

For white Southerners, however, such encounters represented the realization of the deep anxieties that had led them to undertake a proslavery war of independence in the first place. Worried about slave rebellion and convinced that the Republican Party would undermine the white supremacist order in the South, Confederate leaders like Vice President Alexander Stephens had described the new southern government as founded "upon the great truth, that the negro is not the equal to the white man; that slavery – subordination to the superior race – is his natural and normal condition."[15] But in the later years of the war, slave flight, legal emancipation, the advent of black troops, and the decline of Confederate military power reignited southern white fears of racial revolution. Always alert to signs of insubordination among their slaves, white Southerners recognized that the absence of white men on the home front was undermining white authority throughout the region.

The weakening of white authority in the wartime South was manifested in countless personal encounters in which blacks violated the traditional rules of racial deference. Susanna Clay, for example, a plantation mistress from northern Alabama, struggled to manage the family's 70 slaves during her husband's illness and her son's service in the Confederate army. "The negroes are worse than free," she told her son. "We cannot exert any authority." In a scene that drew upon the deep anxieties over race and sexuality in the South, Clay said that one of her slaves had entered the house with a Union officer and demanded to speak to her in her bedroom. "I was undressed," she recounted with horror, "and . . . they looked at me while I threw on a Robe."[16] Although Clay did not suffer any physical harm, stories like this one were deeply disturbing to white Southerners for whom the protection of white women against imagined threats from black men was a central aspect of personal honor and social order. During Reconstruction, the determination to restore white authority over African Americans was inseparable from these concerns.

Not surprisingly then, the appearance of armed black soldiers in the South represented an overt threat to the traditional racial order, and it elicited violent responses that continued well into Reconstruction. One Confederate soldier who was released from a Union prison at the end of the war and who encountered black troops for the first time could barely contain his disgust, saying that "If I could have my way, I'd have a rope around every nigger's neck, and hang 'em, or dam up this Mississippi River with them."[17] During the fighting itself, Confederate forces who saw black troops on the battlefield were overcome with rage and refused to deal with them on the same terms as white prisoners. Officially, the Confederate government classified black soldiers as slave rebels and required their military forces to turn them over to state officials who would bring them before state courts on charges of insurrection. But at times, outraged Confederate troops simply refused to accept the surrender of black soldiers at all and instead massacred them on the battlefield. At the notorious battle of Fort Pillow, Tennessee, for example, as many as 200 captured black troops were murdered by Confederate troops under the command of future Ku Klux Klan leader Nathan Bedford Forrest. At the end of the Civil War, demobilized black soldiers were often targets of white violence, especially if they insisted upon wearing their uniforms in public places. The most violent race riot during Reconstruction occurred in Memphis, Tennessee, in 1866, when white rioters attacked black Union army veterans whose "offense" against local order consisted of their determination to walk the city's streets in their uniforms.

Yet if white Southerners were determined to preserve white supremacy against the political and legal changes wrought by the war, they were also unwilling to relinquish control of black labor power. After all, the slave system of the South was predominantly designed to produce the enormously lucrative cotton crop, a resource that had created and sustained the dominant plantation class of the region. The widespread economic devastation that had resulted from the war made it imperative that agricultural production be resumed as quickly as possible. But having insisted that African Americans would not labor without the coercive inducement of slavery, white Southerners entered Reconstruction unwilling to embrace the wage labor system that so many in the North urged them to adopt. Describing blacks as having "foolish and extravagant notions of freedom," many former slaveholders clung to the view that African Americans were naturally "restless – indolent, discontented."[18]

Belying these judgments, however, was a deep frustration among planters that freedpeople seemed to possess a shrewd awareness of their importance as laborers and a willingness to bargain quite aggressively for compensation and improved working conditions. David Harris, a planter and Confederate veteran, was clearly annoyed that his own notions of what constituted a fair wage for agricultural work were not always shared by freedpeople. "I have much trouble hiring free Negroes," he wrote in his diary in early 1866. "They are not disposed to work for fair wages but soon get tired and want to try some other place."[19] The right to withhold labor and to seek higher wages or better conditions in a broader labor market was, of course, a hallmark of the free labor system of the North, but it was a radical departure from the system that had dominated the South for generations. Thus, at the beginning of Reconstruction, the conflict between white demands for coercive power over black workers and African Americans' equally strong desire for economic independence and self-ownership constituted yet another battleground upon which a new war was to be waged.

Focusing on the history of slavery, emancipation, and citizenship as central to the issues of the Reconstruction era is important because it cuts across the traditional ways in which historians of the United States have conceptualized the period. Even among those scholars who have done so much to refute the Dunning School's distorted image of Reconstruction, there has been a tendency to create an artificial delineation between the Civil War itself and the postwar reconstruction of the United States. Part of the reason for this has to do with historians' disproportionate focus on the political and military events of the period. Elections and battles have clear beginnings and ends, even if their causes and meanings do not, and

Union military victory and the assassination of Abraham Lincoln made 1865 seem a logical dividing line for a period in which politicians and generals had taken center stage. Yet a closer look at the struggles over race and slavery suggests a high degree of continuity between the debates of the Civil War and Reconstruction years. The South's institution of slavery, the larger nation's culture of white racial supremacy, and the violent defense of both systems remained central to the crisis that beset the United States in the entire period between 1850 and 1877. The end of the Civil War's military conflict in 1865, therefore, should no longer be understood as a bright line demarcating one period from another, but rather as a shift in the context in which the dominant issues of the time were worked out. As an extension of the Civil War's struggle over race, citizenship, and power, the Reconstruction era witnessed extraordinary outbursts of violence that reminded participants of the battlefields of a conflict that was supposed to be over.[20]

NOTES

1. *Congressional Globe*, 39th Congress, 1st Session, 74 (December 18, 1865).

2. Douglas R. Egerton, *The Wars of Reconstruction: The Brief, Violent History of America's Most Progressive Era* (New York: Bloomsbury Press, 2014), 331.

3. James M. McPherson and James K. Hogue, *Ordeal By Fire: The Civil War and Reconstruction* (New York: McGraw Hill, 2010), 145.

4. Leonard L. Richards, *The Slave Power: The Free North and Southern Domination, 1780–1860* (Baton Rouge: Louisiana State University Press, 2000), 24.

5. *Declaration of Causes which Induce and Justify the Secession of South Carolina from the Federal Union* (Charleston: Evans & Cogswell, 1860), 9.

6. "The President's Proclamation," *The New York Times* (January 3, 1863), 4.

7. "Speech of Frederick Douglass," *The Liberator* (July 24, 1863), 118.

8. *New York World*, January 3, 1863, in *The Civil War and Reconstruction: A Documentary Collection*, ed. William E. Gienapp (New York: W. W. Norton, 2001), 168.

9. Carole Emberton, " 'Only Murder Makes Men': Reconsidering the Black Military Experience," *The Journal of the Civil War Era* 2 (September 2012), 387.

10. Michael Fellman, Lesley Gordon, and Daniel Sutherland, eds., *This Terrible War: The Civil War and its Aftermath* (New York: Longman, 2003), 143.

11. Leon F. Litwack, *Been in the Storm So Long: The Aftermath of Slavery* (New York: Vintage, 1979), 46.

12. Anonymous letter of a 54th Massachusetts soldier, April 10, 1864, in *The Civil War and Reconstruction*, ed. Gienapp, 228.

13. Spotswood Rice to Kitty Diggs, [September 3, 1864] in *The Civil War and Reconstruction*, ed. Gienapp, 229. The spelling in this letter has been standardized.

14. Litwack, *Been in the Storm So Long*, 102.

15. Alexander H. Stephens, "Cornerstone Speech," March 21, 1861, in *The Civil War and Reconstruction: A Documentary Reader*, ed. Stanley Harrold (Malden, MA: Blackwell Publishing, 2008), 61.

16. Susanna Clay to Clement C. Clay, September 5, 1863, in *The Civil War and Reconstruction*, ed. Gienapp, 224.

17. Litwack, *Been in the Storm So Long*, 103.

18. Glenn M. Linden, ed., *Voices of the Reconstruction Years, 1865–1877* (New York: Harcourt Brace, 1999), 13, 18.

19. Linden, *Voices*, 16–17.

20. For essays that explore the continuity between the Civil War and Reconstruction, see Paul A. Cimbala and Randall M. Miller, eds., *The Great Task Remaining Before Us: Reconstruction as America's Continuing Civil War* (New York: Fordham University Press, 2010).

CHAPTER 1

WARTIME EXPERIMENTS AND THE MEANING OF FREEDOM

T he political debate over the shape of a postwar United States began in Washington long before the final surrender of Robert E. Lee's army at Appomattox courthouse in 1865, and the struggle to define the government's Reconstruction policies produced some of the most contentious disputes in the capital. Perhaps most significant to the subsequent history of the period were the emerging differences within the ruling Republican Party over questions of Reconstruction. The secession of southern states and the withdrawal of their congressional representatives had left the Republican Party with significant majorities in the House and Senate as well as control of the presidency and the Supreme Court. But during the final two years of the war, Lincoln and his party were internally divided over Reconstruction and unable to forge a unified policy. The significance of this failure was enormous, especially after the assassination of the president removed perhaps the only national Republican leader capable of assembling a compromise over what were highly contentious but momentous issues. Instead, the failure of wartime reconstruction left these issues to the discretion of Lincoln's combative and often erratic successor, Andrew Johnson, whose policies undermined the basic gains of the war and led him into a full-scale confrontation with Congress.

Abraham Lincoln's views on Reconstruction policy have long been debated by historians who have searched through his private and official papers for clues as to how he might have led the nation in the postwar period. The problem with such speculation is that Lincoln's thoughts and actions on Reconstruction policy were all formulated in a wartime context in which the defeat of the southern rebellion dominated nearly everything

Abraham Lincoln's approach to Reconstruction
was structured by specific wartime considerations.
(Library of Congress)

the president considered. In December 1863, for example, Lincoln issued
a General Proclamation of Amnesty and Reconstruction, which offered
lenient terms to Confederates in order to lure them back into the Union.
Operating on the premise that the president, rather than Congress,
should determine wartime reconstruction policy, Lincoln held out
amnesty to all but a few white Southerners willing to take an oath of
future allegiance to the United States. Among those exempted from the
amnesty were official members of the Confederate government, high-
ranking members of the Confederate army and navy, as well as any
southern politician who had resigned his seat in the U.S. Congress at
the time of secession. For those who took the oath, the proclamation
restored them to full citizenship, including voting rights, and allowed
them to recover any property that had been confiscated by federal forces
during the war, with the notable exception of slave property. In order to
avoid any misunderstanding about the slavery issue, Lincoln included

language in the oath that equated loyalty with faithful support for all "proclamations of the President made during the existing rebellion having reference to slaves."[1]

Lincoln's wartime offer of amnesty to rank-and-file Confederates was an important precedent for Reconstruction, but at the time it was specifically designed to create a population of loyal southern voters who might return seceded states to the Union and thereby weaken the rebellion. For well over a year before issuing the amnesty proclamation, in fact, Lincoln had been working with white southern Unionists in occupied regions of states like Louisiana, Arkansas, and Tennessee to create loyal governments. Many of these areas had been exempted from the Emancipation Proclamation in part due to Lincoln's concern that they would hesitate to rejoin the Union if they had to relinquish their slaves. Now, the General Proclamation of Amnesty and Reconstruction established a clear process by which these states could form loyal governments and move toward full restoration to the Union. The proclamation stated that once 10 percent of the 1860 voting population of each state had taken an oath of allegiance to the Union, a new state government could be formed and would be recognized "as the true government of the State." Commonly referred to as the Ten Percent Plan, Lincoln's wartime reconstruction formula was extremely vague on the question of the black population. While he generally encouraged the new state governments organized under his plan to "recognize and declare their permanent freedom" and "provide for their education," there was no requirement that they do so.[2] To a wartime president focused above all else on the defeat of the Confederate rebellion, the immediate organization of loyal governments in the South was simply a higher priority than guaranteeing the rights of freedpeople. The Ten Percent Plan was in many respects a conciliatory approach. As historian John C. Rodrigue has argued, it "based loyalty on future rather than past acts; and it dealt with reconstruction as a practical and not a theoretical problem."[3]

The congressional response to Lincoln's wartime reconstruction plan was mixed and indicated the serious factional divisions emerging within the Republican Party. The radical wing of the party was shocked by the leniency of the Ten Percent Plan, especially the easy terms of the amnesty. Radicals like Charles Sumner and Thaddeus Stevens had long believed that Southern society was fundamentally corrupt and they were determined to use Reconstruction policy to accomplish root-and-branch reform. They feared that by allowing ex-Confederates to regain power through loyalty oaths without checking their power through the enfranchisement of blacks, Lincoln's plan would prevent meaningful change. With close ties to the northern abolitionist movement, radicals believed that the region was ruled by a brutal, antidemocratic oligarchy whose economic and political power must be permanently ended in order to make way for a new, more just society. Reconstruction policy must "revolutionize Southern institutions, habits and manners," wrote Stevens. "The foundations of their institutions . . . must be broken up and re-laid, or all our blood and treasure have been spent in vain."[4] But more moderate Republicans were unwilling to endorse such a revolutionary approach to the issue. They feared that radical policies would prolong the war and, even in the event of a Union victory, produce a backlash against Union authority. Moderates were also uncomfortable with the expansion in federal power that radical policies would require, instead hoping to work with southern Unionists to establish loyal governments in the ex-Confederate states. Since moderates made up the bulk of the party in Congress, Lincoln's plan was allowed to go forward despite the obvious discomfort of the radicals.

By the spring of 1864, however, the controversy surrounding the implementation of the Ten Percent Plan in Louisiana led to a direct challenge to Lincoln's Reconstruction policy. In that state, where the requisite number of voters had taken the oath of future loyalty, Union General Nathaniel Banks was attempting to oversee the creation of a new government that met the requirements of the president's proclamation. Like the United States Congress, however, Louisiana's new Republican Party was sharply divided between radicals and moderates. In early 1864, the radical faction included a large number of free black people from the New Orleans area who called for a state constitutional convention to consider establishing black voting rights. Fearing that such a step would delay the reconstruction of the state, Lincoln instructed General Banks to disregard the radicals' demands and to hold an election under Louisiana's prewar constitution. With the support they received from Union military forces who oversaw the election, moderates were able to carry the state, including the governorship. Although Lincoln urged Louisiana's new leaders to consider at least limited voting rights for African Americans, they did not immediately do so. As a result, congressional Republicans refused to seat Louisiana representatives elected under the new government. A confrontation between the president and Congress over Reconstruction policy now seemed inevitable.

The complexity of the issues surrounding wartime reconstruction deepened in the summer of 1864 as congressional Republicans passed their own plan for the political reorganization of the South. The Wade-Davis Bill, named for Congressman Henry Winter Davis of Maryland and Senator Benjamin Wade of Ohio, represented not only a complete repudiation of the specific details of Lincoln's approach but also an assertion of congressional supremacy over most matters pertaining to Reconstruction. Convinced that 10 percent was far too small a number upon which to build a loyal state government, the Wade-Davis Bill required that at least 50 percent of a state's voting population swear oaths of future loyalty to the Union. Even more demanding was the bill's insistence that the political reorganization of southern states would be conducted only by those who could take an oath of past as well as future loyalty. This stipulation meant that political power would be limited to southern Unionists, those who had resisted secession and refused to take any voluntary part in supporting the Confederacy. In addition, the legislation required that any new state constitutions organized under the law contain provisions abolishing slavery, repudiating any debts incurred by rebel state governments, and disenfranchising anyone who had held office in the Confederate government or held high rank in the Confederate military. By avoiding any promise to return confiscated land to ex-rebels; moreover, the Wade-Davis Bill preserved the possibility of distributing at least some of it to former slaves. But at the same time, the legislation did not require reorganized states to establish voting rights for freedpeople.

Not surprisingly, President Lincoln regarded the bill as a challenge to his authority and a direct threat to his ongoing efforts to reconstruct Louisiana, Arkansas, and Tennessee. With the war entering its final and most bloody phase, the president desperately wanted to present the northern public with some evidence that his efforts to preserve the Union were paying off. Hesitant to outright veto a measure passed by leading members of his own party just months before a presidential election, Lincoln simply refused to sign it within 10 days after the expiration of a congressional term, a tactic known as a "pocket veto." Radicals were furious and the bill's sponsors issued a stinging indictment of what they believed was the president's disregard of congressional prerogatives. Using hyperbolic language that would resurface later in the conflicts between congressional Republicans and Andrew Johnson, Wade and Davis condemned Lincoln for "dictatorial usurpation" and instructed him to "confine himself to his executive duties – to obey and execute, not make the laws – to suppress by arms, armed rebellion, and leave political reorganization to Congress."[5] Lincoln, of course, regarded his authority over Reconstruction as an extension of his responsibility as commander in chief in time of armed rebellion. He also believed that his accelerated Reconstruction policies in Louisiana and elsewhere were weakening the South's internal unity. Yet the exchange over the Ten Percent Plan and the Wade-Davis Bill had resulted in a stalemate, and the contentious political struggle over Reconstruction would not resume until after Lincoln's reelection in November 1864.

By that time, however, the context for the debate had changed, as the war was nearly over and the need for a more comprehensive postwar policy was obvious to everyone. But before Lincoln could respond to that need, it was critical to deal with the larger question of slavery itself. Although the Emancipation Proclamation had fundamentally weakened the institution of slavery, it remained legal in large areas of the United States. Achieving clarity on the nation's social, political, or economic future would be difficult unless the place of slavery in American life was settled. When Republicans attempted to pass a constitutional amendment abolishing slavery in 1864, the measure easily cleared the Senate but failed in the House. Key Senate Democrats like Reverdy Johnson came out in support of the amendment, but House Democrats had remained united in their opposition. Endorsed by the Republican Party and Abraham Lincoln, the abolition amendment became a campaign issue in the 1864 election, and many interpreted Republican electoral successes as evidence of a pro-amendment mandate. Lincoln, who had said little in support of the abolition amendment during the House debate in the summer of 1864, became actively engaged after the presidential election. Lobbying on behalf of the Thirteenth Amendment during the lame-duck session of Congress beginning in December 1864, Lincoln pressured northern Democrats to join a bipartisan effort to end an institution that had brought the nation to the brink of destruction. As historian Michael Vorenberg has argued, "No piece of legislation during Lincoln's presidency received more of his attention than the Thirteenth Amendment."[6] Deep political differences remained over questions of racial equality and the federal government's authority to guarantee suffrage, but the passage of the amendment signaled the beginning of the "struggle to define constitutional freedom" that would remain at the center of Reconstruction.[7] Although not ratified until December 1865, the Thirteenth Amendment meant that debates over Reconstruction could at least begin upon the foundation of legal freedom for all former slaves.

As the war ended, there were signs that Lincoln and the congressional Republicans might resolve some of their differences over Reconstruction policy. In March 1865, for example, Lincoln signed a bill creating the Bureau of Refugees, Freedmen, and Abandoned Lands, a federal agency better known as the Freedmen's Bureau. The bureau was given the authority to "adjust and determine all questions concerning persons of African descent," and included a passage authorizing it to oversee the establishment of tenant farms for freedpeople carved out of land that had been abandoned by white Confederates or seized by the government for tax delinquency.[8] Although it was unclear whether black or white refugees would ever receive formal legal title to such property, radicals were increasingly aligning themselves behind the idea that independent property ownership for freedpeople was an essential aspect of their emancipation policy. Lincoln did not endorse the radical view on this issue, but his signature on the Freedmen's Bureau Bill left some room for a possible compromise between moderate and radical Republicans on what would be a critical problem during Reconstruction.

Just two days after the surrender of Lee's forces at Appomattox, moreover, the president made an important speech on postwar issues that hinted he was moving in the direction of voting rights for African Americans. Speaking at the White House to a mostly joyous crowd, Lincoln acknowledged that the subject of Reconstruction was highly complex and "fraught with great difficulty." He reminded the nation that he had already offered a plan in his General Proclamation of Amnesty, but conceded that "this was not the only plan which might possibly be acceptable." He fully accepted that Congress would always be the final authority on "whether members [from ex-rebel states] should be admitted to seats in Congress." Turning to the question of Louisiana's provisional state government, Lincoln urged his Republican colleagues to recognize the new state, not because its constitution was perfect, but because the state had already ratified the Thirteenth Amendment and was moving toward progressive reforms that would be stalled if an entirely new government had to be created. More importantly, he went on record saying that he strongly supported enfranchising "very intelligent" blacks as well as "those who serve our cause as soldiers," a position that moderate Republicans had already endorsed in several congressional debates.[9] To modern ears, Lincoln's recommendation hardly sounds like a ringing affirmation of egalitarianism, but he had clearly moved to the left on the issue and promised that a more comprehensive speech on the subject was coming soon. "By simply mentioning that black men desired the right to vote," writes one historian of the speech, "Lincoln was publicly acknowledging that their views were a legitimate part of the political equation – something no sitting president had ever done."[10] And at least one member of the crowd saw the president's position as unacceptably radical. John Wilkes Booth, who stood just a short distance from Lincoln that night, vowed that Lincoln's speech would be the "last speech he will ever make."[11] Booth's assassination of Lincoln just three days later was the first of what was to become a tradition of violent responses to the possibility of political equality for former slaves.

The political debates of wartime Washington were only one aspect of the larger discourse about postwar realities. Equally important were attempts by military officials, former slaves, and northern reformers to demonstrate the capacity of freedpeople to live and work under free conditions, a critical point for those who hoped to reform the South through the creation of a free labor economy. It is important to recall that a key element in prewar northern hostility to the South was the widespread belief that free or wage labor was economically superior to slavery because it offered both compensation and the promise of upward mobility. Republican politicians had opposed the spread of slavery into the western territories in part because they believed that the free labor system fostered efficiency, innovation, and social mobility. In contrast, Republicans argued that the southern economy was blighted by a labor system that benefited only a small number of aristocratic planters who invested their profits in purchasing more slaves or in propping up their own opulent lifestyles. Unwilling to fully acknowledge the coercion and inequity that existed in the system of wage labor, antebellum northerners tended to see the South as oligarchic and backward, and they regarded the slave labor system as the cause. After traveling for several months in the South during the 1850s, Hartford, Connecticut, journalist Frederick Law Olmsted came away convinced that slavery was a curse on the social and economic life of the South. "The total increase in the wealth of the population during the last twenty years shows for almost nothing," he argued. "Ask the cotton planter for them and ... he will point to his negroes."[12]

As emancipation emerged as a central strategy in the Union war effort, then, hopes for an economically transformed, free-labor South hinged on the ability of freedpeople to make the transition from slavery to wage work. Unfortunately, widespread racism on both sides of the Mason-Dixon line generated enormous skepticism about the possibility of such a system. Southern whites, for example, had long maintained that blacks were naturally idle and improvident, insisting that they were incapable of responding to the same incentives for profit and economic advancement that drove white workers to efficient and productive work. Slavery was justified, they had argued, precisely because blacks could not function as free laborers and would never respond to opportunities for self-improvement. "They are not controlled by the same motives as white men," insisted one southern planter. "Unless you have the power to compel them, they'll only work when they can't beg or steal enough to keep from starving."[13] Nor were such sentiments limited to southern slaveholders, for many in the North shared these racist doubts about the work ethic of African Americans. When black refugees in the South refused to submit to the labor demands of Union General Thomas W. Sherman, for example, he immediately resorted to explanations that were eerily reminiscent of southern proslavery rhetoric. "They are naturally slothful and indolent," he told his superior in December 1861. "A sudden change of condition from servitude to apparent freedom is more than their intellects can stand, and ... it is a very serious question what is to be done with the Negroes who will hereafter be found on conquered soil."[14] The final comment in the general's statement was especially ominous in that it left open the possibility that the army would resort to direct coercion in securing access to black labor.

Union refugee policy, however, was not left to Thomas Sherman, and his sentiments were not universally shared in the North. As Union forces captured strategic positions along the southern coastline early in the war, for example, northern missionaries and reformers sought to build communities of free black laborers that might be used as models for the larger South once the war was over. Perhaps the most famous of them was established at Port Royal, South Carolina, one of the Sea Islands near Charleston seized by Union forces in the fall of 1861. In March 1862, 53 young missionaries, sponsored by the New York-based National Freedmen's Relief Association, arrived at Port Royal hoping to aid the approximately 10,000 blacks who had been left on the island by their fleeing Confederate masters. Drawing inspiration from the biblical story of Gideon, whose tiny band of Israelites had conquered a much larger foe, these new "Gideonites" intended to do battle against slavery, prejudice, and ignorance. They would provide the freedpeople of the Sea Islands with material relief, medical treatment, basic education, and other forms of instruction that would ensure their successful transition from slavery to free labor. As the sons and daughters of abolitionist parents, the Port Royal reformers were idealists who believed that they could demonstrate that widespread doubts about the former slaves' aptitude for free labor were misplaced. They were certain that education and training could overcome any deficiencies that might have resulted from generations of enslavement. If freedpeople did not always seem as hard working as whites, insisted Port Royal teacher Laura Towne, this could only be the result of a system that had deprived blacks of any compensation for their labor. "The negro can see plainly enough," she wrote, "that the proceeds of the cotton will never get into black pockets."[15]

As a public challenge to those who disparaged African Americans' capacity for freedom, the Port Royal "experiment" was a success. Through their contacts in the northern press, for example, the Gideonites were able to provide the northern public with poignant examples of the freedpeople's eagerness for education and their willingness to work for wages. In July 1862, the *Hartford Evening Press*, a Republican daily with radical leanings, printed a private letter from a teacher on Edisto Island that described the almost insatiable appetite for literacy among adult former slaves. She reported that there were "some on this plantation that, with book in hand, way lay me at every nook and cranny to obtain my assistance in learning the letters or spelling short words."[16] Six months later, the same paper printed a letter written by a Union army officer stationed at Hilton Head Island claiming not only that a system of labor for wages had been

A Freedmen's School on Edisto Island, South
Carolina, where northern reformers offered free
schooling to emancipated slaves during the Civil
War. (Library of Congress)

effectively established on the island but also that "the government has
undoubtedly got a great deal of work done by the negroes at a moderate cost."
He rejected the view that former slaves would become dependent on the
government. "In my judgment," the officer argued, "equal laws faithfully
administered would enable the negroes to take their place in society, as a
laboring class, with a fair prospect of self-support and progress."[17] After generations in which the planter class had largely controlled visual images and
printed accounts of southern black labor, here was an important counter-
point for those who wished to see the South remade in the image of the free
labor North.

But the Port Royal experiment was meant to be more than an exercise
in publicity, and day-to-day realities in the Sea Islands reveal what historian Eric Foner has called the "ambiguities" of the free labor ideals
espoused by so many in the North. In 1863, the U.S. Treasury Department
used recently enacted tax laws to confiscate many of the Sea Island

plantations and proceeded to auction them off to the highest bidder in allotments of no more than 320 acres. Since the freedpeople possessed little or no cash, the vast majority of the land was purchased by northern business interests who were intent on hiring blacks as laborers in order to produce the island's valuable crop of high-grade cotton. Among the largest of the new landlords was Edward Philbrick, a Massachusetts railroad executive who believed that the application of the free labor system would simultaneously produce a large profit and assist the freedpeople in adjusting to their new roles as wage employees and consumers. But in order to achieve their goals, highly paternalistic capitalists like Philbrick intended to reform the work habits of the Sea Island blacks, enforcing rules of punctuality, demanding regular daily work hours, and insisting that freedpeople devote their time to wage-producing occupations rather than the production of their own food. When former slaves left the fields before the end of the day, Philbrick regarded their actions as "chaos and insubordination" and at one point threatened that he would "report them to Massa Lincoln as too lazy to be free."[18]

To the freedpeople of the Sea Islands, "free labor" did not always seem like the unqualified blessing that northern whites so often claimed. First, they were deeply disappointed that the land their families had worked on for generations without compensation could so easily be transferred from one white owner to another. A full year after the land sales had begun, ex-slaves had been able to acquire less than 4 percent of nearly 80,000 acres of arable land in the Sea Islands, and reformer-entrepreneurs like Philbrick were convinced that selling valuable land to freedpeople for less than its competitive value would undermine their transition from slaves to free workers. Dependency upon wages was, therefore, the reality for the vast majority of freedpeople. Ironically, the new system of hourly labor, with its insistence upon universally enforced hours of work, seemed to African Americans as a step back from the somewhat more flexible system they had negotiated with planters in the antebellum period. Laboring under what historians of slavery have called a "task system," enslaved people in the lowcountry of South Carolina, including the Sea Islands, had been assigned daily tasks that, if completed in less than a full day of work, allowed for other forms of economic activity. Under this system, slave families often raised domesticated animals, practiced forms of craft production, and cultivated their own "provision grounds" that supplied them with food throughout the year. By the end of the antebellum period, many enslaved people regarded this varied and more flexible arrangement of work as essential to their survival and deeply important to their well-being as families and communities. Therefore, despite all the benefits that northern reformers attached to hourly wage work, many former slaves regarded it as a radical departure from the only labor system that had given them any control of their lives.[19]

The conflict between the kind of freedom offered by northern reformers and the freedom desired by freedpeople became apparent in the final years of the Port Royal experiment. Although Edward Philbrick insisted that employers had the authority to control the "time and manner of doing the work," freedpeople resisted the imposition of factory-style labor management on their work patterns.[20] Others insisted on working together in the fields as families rather than as separate employees, thereby fulfilling their obligations to work for a specified period in a collective rather than individual method. Additionally, many freedpeople sought to ensure that the new system did not produce noticeable inequality among members of the black community, dividing work roles and rotating access to prime cotton lands so that no one would be denied a basic subsistence.[21]

To northern reformers who were determined to teach former slaves that individual, hourly labor was essential to survival and economic advancement, freedpeople's resistance to aspects of the free labor regime seemed like ingratitude. They blamed the relatively modest profits from wartime cotton production on the persistence of poor work habits among Sea Island blacks. What reformers did not recognize, however, was that freedpeople had their own understanding of freedom forged in the fires of slavery, which required resistance to external forces that threatened the limited gains wrung from reluctant antebellum slaveholders. The lesson freedpeople learned at Port Royal was that achieving full freedom would be a struggle almost as monumental as the one waged against slavery.

Despite its high-profile reputation at the time, Port Royal was not the only experiment in wartime reconstruction, and other examples provided contemporaries with a range of possible models for postwar social arrangements. At Davis Bend, Mississippi, former slaves responded somewhat differently to the imposition of the wage labor system. The Davis family, which included the president of the Confederacy, had been somewhat unusual among antebellum southern slaveholders in their willingness to

Former slaves preparing cotton in Union-occupied Port Royal, South Carolina, the site of an important wartime experiment in free labor and African American education. (Library of Congress)

explore alterations to the traditional plantation system of slave management. During the 1820s, Joseph Davis had met British utopian socialist Robert Dale Owen and came to believe that Owen's model of cooperative communities could be established among the more than 300 enslaved people on the Davis Bend plantation. As a result, conditions for slaves on the plantation were among the best in the South, and they enjoyed remarkably high levels of personal autonomy, even to the point of enforcing their own systems of justice and work discipline. When Davis abandoned the plantation in advance of the Union seizure in 1862, former slaves assumed control over its day-to-day operations, and it soon became a magnet for other black refugees fleeing plantations along the Mississippi River. Under the leadership of Benjamin Montgomery, a freedman who had served as Joseph Davis's most trusted slave before the Union occupation, the Davis Bend community continued to function smoothly and formed a cooperative relationship with Union forces in the region. General Ulysses

S. Grant believed that communities like Davis Bend could be a solution to the growing black refugee problem and appointed John Eaton, a moderate New England reformer, as superintendent of contraband in the region.[22]

Eaton was less motivated by evangelical Christian zeal than the Sea Island Gideonites, and his plans for Davis Bend were profoundly shaped by the economic ethos that dominated the thinking of northern Republicans. The work habits of former slaves, he insisted, could only be rehabilitated by a rigorous application of free labor principles, especially hourly wage work, and he was opposed to any forms of charity that would undermine the principle of "self-help." But Eaton also believed that if the South's "old and corrupt civilization" was to be replaced by one more consistent with "the genius of our free institutions," blacks must be given the opportunity to engage in independent farming.[23] The effect, he argued, would be to quicken their "enterprise" and prepare them for life in a competitive postwar society. He told a sympathetic northern correspondent that with the assistance of "some worthy friend of this race," who could provide access to good supplies at reasonable rates, individual black families could then be placed on small to medium-sized holdings.[24] This policy resulted in the leasing of land to approximately 65 families in allotments ranging from 20 to 150 acres, and farmers who owned the largest tracts were allowed to hire wage laborers to assist them. Over the next 2 years, Davis Bend emerged as a powerhouse of cotton production, producing almost 2,000 bales and generating $160,000 in profit.[25] What was most remarkable to Eaton was that, in comparison with the wage employees, the independent farmers were far more efficient, productive, and profitable. "The independent Negro cultivator," Eaton wrote triumphantly after the 1864 cotton crop had been harvested, "was without doubt the most successful."[26]

The success of the Davis Bend experiment in black landholding represents an important element in the wartime debate over the future of the South, and its economic success suggests that former slaves vastly preferred it to the wage labor system. But unlike General Grant and Superintendent Eaton, authorities in other parts of the occupied South responded to the growing population of black refugees with far less creativity or concern for the views of freedpeople. Immediately following the April 1862 Union capture of New Orleans, Louisiana, for example, Union General Benjamin Butler had to make a series of quick decisions about the status of African Americans who fled to his lines and about how to respond to Unionist slaveholders who reported growing rebelliousness on their plantations outside the city. General Butler was a conservative northern Democrat, but his views on slavery had altered during the first year of the war. As the first Union commander to use the term "contraband" to describe slaves who escaped from rebel-held territory, Butler had made an important contribution to the evolution of emancipation policy. But in the spring of 1862, the Emancipation Proclamation was still many months off, and Butler did not have the authorization from Washington to interfere with the rights of loyal masters nor any desire to redesign social and economic life in the South. Instead, the general began a system that combined the most coercive aspects of the northern free labor system with many holdovers from the antebellum slave regime. African Americans were required to remain as plantation laborers, organized into traditional field gangs and subjected to military discipline in cases of vagrancy or insubordination. Plantation laborers would be paid wages, often distributed collectively as one-twentieth of the cotton crop, but this kind of "freedom" seemed little different from slavery. As the *New York Times* commented, in the Louisiana system "freedom and slavery have . . . got so jumbled up . . . that it is difficult to tell which is boss."[27]

Although President Lincoln regarded General Butler's system as a "temporary" arrangement, he was willing to tolerate it because Unionist planters were the backbone of his strategy of reconstructing the state under the Ten Percent Plan. Following the Emancipation Proclamation when General Butler was replaced by Nathaniel P. Banks, moreover, this highly compromised understanding of black freedom became widespread throughout the state of Louisiana. Concerned far more with the maintenance of order and the production of cotton than with the concerns or aspirations of the plantation labor force, Banks was prepared to force blacks to work, with the threat of military force if necessary, in exchange for the meager compensation of $1 per month for women and $2 per month for men. Interacting far more often with the white Louisiana elite than with African Americans, Banks heard a constant drumbeat of complaints from planters that former slaves would not work unless compelled by the threat of the lash. Although the general was not willing to restore the power of landowners to inflict physical punishment on rebellious workers, neither was he willing to consider any form of independence, economic or otherwise, for freedpeople.[28]

While the limitations placed on black freedom in wartime Louisiana are striking, so too are the instances of African American resistance to such limits. As historian John Rodrigue has shown, freedpeople in the sugar parishes of Louisiana flagrantly flouted the plantation regulations, especially limits placed on their mobility and any interference with their family life. While they remained willing to work cultivating and refining sugar, they refused to accept that nothing had changed in their relationships to whites. One of Banks's subordinates complained that "the planters and overseers do not sufficiently appreciate ... the change that has taken place," and that blacks would no longer accept "the same treatment, the same customs and rules – the same language – that they have heretofore quietly submitted to."[29]

Although quiet submission was hardly an accurate picture of how slaves had responded to the antebellum plantation system, it is clear that the war was a tipping point from which the old regime could never fully recover. Reports of insubordination came from all over the state, including one plantation where the laborers thoroughly reshaped the traditional work regime by refusing to labor at critical points in the sugar production process. Planter William Minor complained that his workers would no longer work at night or on Sundays, and that the elderly and young children were no longer willing to work at all. As a result of the resistance to what he considered his prerogatives, Minor expressed anger when he had to shut down his sugar mill because three-quarters of his laborers complained of "violent pains in their back." Frustrated that he could not simply compel them to work, Minor concluded that "A man had as well be in purgatory, as attempt to work a sugar plantation under existing circumstances."[30] Aware of the value of their own labor and acutely conscious that Minor's power to use physical force against them was limited by the Union military presence, black Louisianans asserted themselves against the new regime of halfway freedom.

The problems that emerged at Port Royal and the heavy restraints placed on freedpeople on Deep South plantations during the war provide an opportunity to examine emancipation in the United States in a hemispheric, rather than a purely national, context. Nearly all discussions of emancipation during this period, for example, took place in the shadow of the Haitian Revolution of the 1790s, an event that filled the minds of white Southerners with lurid images of black revolutionary violence and economic devastation. Insisting that immediate emancipation had destroyed what had been a spectacularly productive sugar economy in Haiti, southern whites warned that the rapid introduction of free labor in their own region would produce similar results. In other regions of the Americas where emancipation occurred during the nineteenth century, moreover, the process was generally done in ways that denied full freedom to former slaves. Entertaining the very same racial fears that prompted reformers in the United States to "experiment" with free black labor in South, the slaveholding regimes in the Caribbean and South America strictly curtailed the rights of the emancipated. In 1833, for example, the British Parliament had passed an emancipation bill that ended legal slavery in the British Caribbean but also imposed an apprenticeship system that sharply limited the ability of supposedly free people to choose their work and personal destiny for at least six years. On the French sugar island of Guadeloupe and on the Danish colony of Santa Cruz, emancipation was a protracted process. Various forms of contract labor and indentured servitude were introduced to protect the economic interests of the planters and to compensate for the supposedly poor work habits of formerly enslaved Afro-Caribbean peoples. In none of these societies did widespread landholding emerge among former slaves. As a result, they were "freed from the lash and other evils of inhuman bondage, but sank to the lowest levels of a stratified society."[31] While Davis Bend offered a somewhat different possibility, the more widely known free labor experiments in the South Carolina Sea Islands and the sugar parishes of Louisiana suggested that this would be the likely outcome in the United States.

At the very end of the war, however, an alternative would emerge, less from the intentional planning of reformers or politicians than from the practical exigencies of a prolonged and destructive conflict. In late 1864, as his Army of the Tennessee plowed through the heart of Georgia on its way to the sea, General William Tecumseh Sherman struggled to deal with the thousands of escaped slaves who trailed closely behind his lines. Neither Sherman nor most of the men in his army of largely western veterans were particularly well disposed toward freedpeople, although they were happy to enforce the terms of the Emancipation Proclamation if it would weaken and punish the hated plantation elite. Without a regular supply line, moreover, the army was living off the confiscated property of local whites, and they feared that black refugees would deplete the bounty of the land and attract the unwanted attention of Confederate guerrilla forces. Thus, when Sherman arrived in Savannah, he consulted with Secretary of War Edwin Stanton and a group of free black leaders from Georgia about how to handle the refugee problem, demanding to know the basic aspirations of the recently emancipated. He received a startlingly clear answer from Rev. George Frazier, a former slave-turned-Baptist preacher, who told him that what freedpeople desired most was "to have land, and turn it and till it by our own labor." Only with property of their own, Frazier insisted, could freedpeople "reap the fruit of our own labor."[32] Deeply anxious about the racial hatred that would be arrayed against southern blacks in the postwar nation, Frazier believed that property ownership might become the basis for self-contained communities that could wield political and economic power independent of whites.

It is unlikely that Sherman understood the full import of Frazier's perspective, but with large sections of the southern coastline recently abandoned by whites fearing Union invasion, he saw an opportunity to solve his refugee dilemma. On January 16, 1865, Sherman issued Special Field Order No. 15, a military decree designating 400,000 acres of abandoned coastal and sea island lands between northern Florida and Charleston, South Carolina, as reserved for freedpeople in tracts of no more than 40 acres per family. The pioneers among the some 40,000 freedpeople who settled the mainland sections of what became known as the "Sherman Reserve" were often targets of white militia violence and soon faced threats from returning white landowners who refused to recognize the legality of Sherman's military order. But the expectation that the end of the war would entitle freedpeople to "40 acres and mule" formed one of the key definitions of freedom that African Americans brought into the Reconstruction period. These expectations were encouraged by General Rufus Saxton, a reform-minded brigadier general from Massachusetts who Sherman chose to oversee the refugee land program under the title Inspector of Settlements and Plantations. Saxton had played a major role in the Port Royal experiment, but he was now in charge of an enterprise four times larger and with the capacity to create a radical precedent for postwar economic and social conditions. He told a large gathering of black settlers that the government would grant them "possession of lands, upon which they might locate their families and work out for themselves a living and a respectability."[33] Like the Emancipation Proclamation, Sherman's field order was the product of military necessity rather than an abstract commitment to egalitarianism. In offering former slaves the possibility that freedom might mean economic and social independence as well as emancipation from chattel bondage, the order became an important symbol for those who hoped to radically remake the South.

Although the war years had generated an array of political and economic blueprints for Reconstruction, little was settled as the conflict ended in April 1865. Lincoln and the congressional Republicans had grown closer on postwar policy than they had been after the contentious debates over the Wade-Davis Bill. But questions about black suffrage, about conditions for the readmission of ex-rebel states to the federal Union, and about the social and economic reorganization of the South remained unanswered. Reformers had made a strong case that racist stereotypes of indolent and dependent southern blacks were false, but wartime experiments with free labor had yielded mixed results. By the war's end, free black people in the South were working under vastly different systems, some deeply coercive and others containing the promise that a far more democratic nation might be born from a republic riven by racism and slavery. With the surrender of Confederate armies and the assassination of Abraham Lincoln, however, two new political forces would enter the debate with voices calling for strict limitations on change. In President Andrew Johnson and the resurgent political power of the white South, the vision of a nation remade in the spirit of its highest egalitarian ideals would find its most implacable opponents.

NOTES

1. Abraham Lincoln, "Proclamation of Amnesty and Reconstruction," December 8, 1863, in *The Collected Works of Abraham Lincoln*, volume 7, ed. Roy P. Basler (New Brunswick, NJ: Rutgers University Press, 1953), 54; John C. Rodrigue, *Lincoln and Reconstruction* (Carbondale: Southern Illinois University Press, 2013), 66–68.

2. Lincoln, "Proclamation of Amnesty," 55.

3. Rodrigue, *Lincoln and Reconstruction*, 71.

4. James M. McPherson and James K. Hogue, *Ordeal by Fire: The Civil War and Reconstruction* (New York: McGraw Hill, 2010), 436.

5. Benjamin Wade and Henry Winter Davis, "To the Supporters of the Government," *The New-York Daily Tribune* (August 5, 1864), 5.

6. Michael Vorenberg, *Final Freedom: The Civil War, the Abolition of Slavery and the Thirteenth Amendment* (New York: Cambridge University Press, 2001), 180.

7. Ibid., 210.

8. Phillip Shaw Paludan, *The Presidency of Abraham Lincoln* (Lawrence: University of Kansas Press, 1994), 309.

9. Abraham Lincoln, "Last Public Address," April 11, 1865, in *The Collected Works of Abraham Lincoln*, vol. 8, 400, 401–402, 403.

10. Rodrigue, *Lincoln and Reconstruction*, 140.

11. Ibid., 141.

12. Frederick Law Olmsted, *The Cotton Kingdom: A Traveller's Observation on Cotton and Slavery in the American Slave States*, vol. 1 (New York: Mason Brothers, 1861), 26.

13. Leon Litwack, *Been in the Storm So Long: The Aftermath of Slavery* (New York: Vintage, 1979), 365.

14. Gen. T.W. Sherman to Gen. L. Thomas December 1861, in *Freedom: A Documentary History of Emancipation, 1861–1867*, series 1, volume 3, *The Wartime Genesis of Free Labor: The Lower South*, ed. Ira Berlin (New York: Cambridge University Press, 1990), 118–119.

15. Rupert S. Holland, ed., *The Letters and Diary of Laura M. Towne: Written from the Sea Islands of South Carolina 1862–1884* (Cambridge: The Riverside Press, 1912), 20.

16. *Hartford Evening Press*, July 18, 1862.

17. *Hartford Evening Press*, January 30, 1863.

18. Willie Lee Rose, *Rehearsal for Reconstruction: The Port Royal Experiment* (New York: Oxford University Press, 1964), 81–82.

19. Julie Saville, *The Work of Reconstruction: From Slave to Wage Labor in South Carolina, 1860–1870* (New York: Cambridge University Press, 1996), 5–11, 44.

20. Ibid., 56.

21. Ibid., 52–56, 62–63.

22. Stephen J. Ross, "Freed Soil, Freed Labor, Freed Men: John Eaton and the Davis Bend Experiment," *Journal of Southern History* 44 (May 1978), 213–232.

23. Ibid., 216.

24. Ibid., 216.

25. Eric Foner, *Reconstruction: America's Unfinished Revolution, 1863–1877* (New York: Harper & Row, 1988), 59.

26. Ross, "Freed Soil," 222.

27. Quoted in Richard Follett, "Legacies of Enslavement: Plantation Identities and the Problem of Freedom," in *Slavery's Ghost: The Problem of Freedom in the Age of Emancipation*, eds. Richard Follett, Eric Foner, and Walter Johnson (Baltimore: Johns Hopkins University Press, 2011), 57.

28. John C. Rodrigue, *Reconstruction in the Cane Fields: From Slavery to Free Labor in Louisiana's Sugar Parishes, 1862–1882* (Baton Rouge: University of Louisiana Press, 2001), 40.

29. Ibid., 41.

30. Ibid., 43.

31. David Brion Davis, *Inhuman Bondage: The Rise and Fall of Slavery in the New World* (New York: Oxford University Press, 2006), 327.

32. Foner, *Reconstruction*, 70.

33. Ibid., 71.

CHAPTER 2

PRESIDENTIAL RECONSTRUCTION: THE EMERGING CONFLICT

L
incoln's assassination in April 1865 created a power vacuum in Washington at a time when the nation desperately needed leadership on the unresolved issues surrounding Reconstruction. The congressional session had ended a month earlier, and the nation's legislators were not scheduled to return to the capital until the following December. This left the new president, Andrew Johnson of Tennessee, in a position to make critical, and at least for the foreseeable future, unchallengeable decisions about Reconstruction policy. Historians refer to this period as Presidential Reconstruction, two years in which the president seized the initiative and developed a framework for the readmission of southern states to the Union that imposed only the most basic conditions for their restoration to constitutional status. Although President Johnson's approach to Reconstruction was eventually repudiated by Congress, his control over the initial stages of the process created enormous obstacles for those who hoped to create an egalitarian, biracial democracy in the South. Responding to what they saw as an opportunity to thwart the designs of northern radicals and preserve key aspects of the old southern order, moreover, southern white leaders took advantage of Johnson's policies to reclaim power. Under Johnson's plan, they established provisional governments that strictly limited the rights and physical mobility of former slaves and elected scores of ex-Confederate leaders to political office. By 1867, presidential mismanagement and white southern

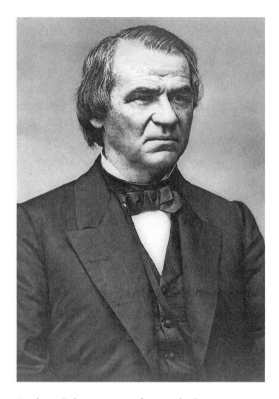

Andrew Johnson's conflict with Congress over
Reconstruction policies generated a political
and constitutional crisis. (Library of Congress)

intransigence generated outrage across the North and paved the way for a
more radical approach to Reconstruction designed by congressional
Republicans.

The nature of Presidential Reconstruction politics must be understood
in part as an expression of the personal and political character of Andrew
Johnson himself. Born into an extremely poor family in Raleigh, North
Carolina, in 1808, Johnson had no formal education and did not acquire
even basic literacy skills until he was nearly an adult. Losing his father at
a young age, Johnson was bound over as an apprentice in a tailor's shop
where he worked for five miserable years before fleeing along with his older
brother William. Still a teenager and not officially licensed to ply his trade,
he made his way to Greenville in eastern Tennessee where he set himself
up as a tailor, married the daughter of another local artisan, and started

a family. Johnson's success as a businessman allowed him to accumulate property, including as many as 10 slaves. His deepest ambition, however, was for political distinction, a goal that was generally reserved for men of wealth and education in the period before the Civil War.[1] But Johnson's arrival in Tennessee had coincided with the emergence of a more democratic politics exemplified by the rise of Andrew Jackson, a military hero turned cotton planter and slaveholder whose obscure origins were remarkably similar to Johnson's. Jackson's election to the presidency in 1828 and the making of the Democratic Party provided an avenue for men like Johnson to seek office and wield power on a level that would have been unthinkable a generation earlier. Elected to the state House of Representatives in 1835, Johnson began a remarkable career as a Democratic Party leader that resulted in his election as governor in 1853, elevation to the U.S. Senate in 1857, and eventually his election as vice president of the United States on the Republican ticket in 1864.

The combative political culture of antebellum Tennessee shaped the strikingly confrontational and aggressive political style that so marked Andrew Johnson's presidency. In a state where wealthy planters usually dominated the state government, Johnson emerged as an insurgent leader who successfully channeled the anger and disaffection of poorer whites in middle and east Tennessee against the slaveholding elite who controlled the western counties. Believing that the "stuck-up aristocrats" of the South were "not half as good as the man who earns his bread by the sweat of his own brow," Johnson saw himself as a tribune of the people, defending the interests of hardworking yeomen against the corrupt policies of pampered oligarchs.[2] Although he was viscerally opposed to both abolitionism and racial equality, Johnson was nevertheless deeply suspicious of the secession movement of 1860–61, believing that it constituted an unconstitutional seizure of power by the wealthy slaveholding interests of the South at the expense of poor whites. Calling secession a "political heresy" that amounted to making war upon the government, he insisted that there was no constitutional path for a state to leave the Union and warned that "he that is guilty of treason is entitled to a traitor's fate."[3]

When the state of Tennessee approved a referendum on secession in 1861, Johnson refused to give up his seat in the U.S. Senate, making him the only southern leader from a seceded state to remain in Congress. Returning to Tennessee in 1862 as military governor, moreover, he supported the Emancipation Proclamation as a means of destroying the rebellion and even participated in the recruitment of black troops for the Union army. While remaining a Democrat both in name and in political principle, Johnson earned the admiration of many Republicans who regarded him as a symbol of courageous southern Unionism. In choosing Johnson as his running mate in 1864, then, Lincoln was not only demonstrating his commitment to waging a bipartisan war but also his desire to build support for the Republican Party among loyal Unionists from the border states and the Upper South.

Johnson took office as president on the morning of April 15, 1865, having narrowly avoided assassination himself at the hands of George Atzerodt, one of John Wilkes Booth's less competent coconspirators. Congressional Republicans, who were at home in their constituencies, waited anxiously to know how the new president would act toward the defeated South, and the initial signs were that his earlier animus toward the planter elite would guide his policy. Echoing his own words at the time of secession, he told a delegation of Indiana citizens that treason was "a crime" and, like the crimes of rape and arson, "must be made odious" so that it would never occur again. In order to achieve that goal, Johnson told his visitors, traitors must not only be punished, but should also be "impoverished" and their "social power ... destroyed."[4] He had insisted that through their treasonous actions, southern planters had forfeited any claims they might have had to their confiscated land. "Their great plantations must be seized and divided into small farms," he had proclaimed, "and sold to honest industrious men."[5] Many radical Republicans were delighted by the tone of Johnson's remarks, going so far as to believe that God had chosen him to complete a process that the more moderate, charitable Lincoln was less suited to oversee. "I believe that the Almighty continued Mr. Lincoln in office as long as he was useful, and then substituted a better man to finish the work," wrote George Julian of Indiana.[6]

Such views were not only uncharitable, but they also betrayed a fundamental misinterpretation of the new president's views, for unlike the radicals, Johnson had no intention of altering the racial order in the South. Remarks like those made to the Indiana delegation were reflections of the president's desire to remake the white power structure of the South, diminishing the economic and political influence of the antebellum planter class and empowering the loyal white yeomanry, not a signal of

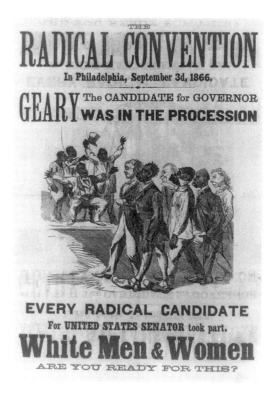

This poster ridiculing the idea of black suffrage in Pennsylvania indicates the depth of racism that existed in northern society during the Reconstruction period. (Library of Congress)

his intent to confer property or political power on former slaves. As historian Eric Foner has shown, Johnson gave voice to an odd, but widespread, view among poorer southern whites that enfranchised blacks would become the natural allies of the old planter class, thus perpetuating the powerlessness of land-poor whites. Johnson was quite willing to use emancipation as a weapon to "impoverish" the planter class, but he regarded any significant improvement in the social, economic, or political condition of freedpeople as inherently detrimental to the fortunes of his natural constituency among the yeoman class of the South.[7] Should southern states be subjected "to Negro domination," Johnson argued in 1867, "all order will be subverted, all industry cease, and the fertile lands of the South grow up into a wilderness."[8] While antebellum slaveholders had made similar arguments in defense of slavery itself, President Johnson wielded them in support of a highly curtailed conception of postwar black freedom.

The underlying political chasm between radical Republicans and Johnson became somewhat clearer on May 29, 1865, when the president issued two proclamations indicating his intention to seize control of Reconstruction policy and his larger approach to the issues. First, he offered general amnesty to most classes of ex-Confederates as long as they were willing to take an oath of future loyalty to the Union and to accept emancipation. To encourage participation by the mass of eligible white Southerners, the president offered oath takers the full restoration of their citizenship in the United States and the right to recover any property, except for slaves, that had been confiscated during the war. As in Lincoln's 1863 plan, high-ranking members of the Confederate government and military were ineligible for the amnesty, but Johnson also exempted any ex-rebels who owned $20 thousand or more worth of taxable property, a clear reference to the planter class he so powerfully disliked. These "excepted classes" could seek the restoration of their citizenship, but only through a presidential pardon, which the president promised to grant as long as it was compatible with the "peace and dignity of the United States."[9] Should wealthy Southerners refuse to acknowledge defeat and fail to accept their political subordination to the Union and its president, it was possible that confiscated land could be redistributed to freedpeople, poor whites, or some combination of both. But it was far more likely that Johnson intended to use the threat of long-term confiscation to compel the loyalty of the southern ruling class. The absence of any mention of the freedpeople from the proclamations suggests that their welfare was not very high on the president's priority list.

In addition to the amnesty provisions, the May Proclamations and subsequent policy statements offered a relatively rapid path to the South's "restoration," the term that Johnson favored over "reconstruction," to the Union. Unlike President Lincoln's plan, Johnson did not specify the numbers of citizens required to take an oath before the political reorganization of the state could occur. Instead he appointed civilian governors who were granted broad powers to oversee the writing of new state constitutions and the creation of provisional governments. Radical Republicans were pushing Johnson to include black voting rights in his list of requirements for southern state constitutions, but he rejected this option due to his racism and his Jacksonian states' rights principles. He insisted that eligibility to vote in the election of delegates to state constitutional conventions would remain consistent with prewar standards, meaning that blacks would be excluded. Senator Charles Sumner, a leading voice for the congressional radicals who had met with Johnson and received assurances that at least limited suffrage for the freedpeople would be included, confessed "immense disappointment" in the president's proclamation and condemned the "madness" of any plan that did not include voting rights for the loyal African Americans in the South.[10] But Johnson asserted that it was beyond the power of the federal government to establish suffrage qualifications, insisting that it had been a state prerogative since the very beginning of the American Republic.[11]

Having established a process by which new state governments could be created and having identified those who would be eligible to participate in them, Johnson went on to define his criteria for readmission. To meet with the president's approval, the new state constitutions would need to endorse the Thirteenth Amendment, repudiate the Confederate war debt, and formally disavow the legality of secession. These basic provisions were not even mandatory. Johnson offered them as suggestions because he assumed that Congress would refuse to seat the congressional delegations from ex-Confederate states that failed to meet them. This approach not only ignored the condition of former slaves, but the extraordinary leniency of its requirements suggests that Johnson's thinking about the South had undergone a dramatic reversal in just a few weeks after taking office. Although it is difficult to trace the development of the president's thought during this period, it seems likely to historians that his motives were mainly shaped by political considerations. Looking forward to the 1868 presidential election, Johnson recognized that he was unlikely to find much support from radical Republicans whose views on most issues diverged considerably from his own. Instead, he reasoned that a restrained policy on Reconstruction, one that returned power quickly to the states and preserved important aspects of the prewar social order, might win considerable support from Democrats and conservative Republicans.[12] The fact that large segments of the southern planter class would exercise power only if he personally granted them pardons suggested another way to build support among the leadership in ex-rebel states. Whatever his motives, Johnson was committed to a rapid Reconstruction process that would attach only the most basic conditions to the restoration of ex-Confederate states to the Union.

To defeated white Southerners, who had expected a much harsher policy from a man who had consistently threatened dire punishments for treason, the president's amnesty policy seemed almost too good to be true. Whitelaw Reid, an Ohio newspaper correspondent traveling in the South in the immediate aftermath of the war, claimed that most southern whites "longed for the blessings which any peace on any terms might be expected to bring in its train," and were even grudgingly prepared to accept black suffrage and extended military occupation. But after the May Proclamations, he observed a decided shift in attitudes, with ex-Confederates suddenly willing to "talk of their rights, and to argue constitutional points." Convinced that they were now on the verge of being restored to power, many white Southerners became much more aggressive in their attempts to limit the mobility and independence of former slaves. Reid was now told repeatedly that "the negro" was "saucy and rude; disposed to acts of violence; likely by his stupid presumptions, to start a war of races, which could only end in his extermination." Suddenly, the Freedmen's Bureau was also an object of overt white hostility, and the idea of legal or political equality for freedpeople was described as "so revolting a humiliation" as to be unthinkable.[13] To Reid, the aftermath of defeat had offered an opportunity for significant change that Johnson's lenient policies had squandered in the most irresponsible of ways.

During the summer of 1865, moreover, thousands of ex-Confederates exempted from Johnson's amnesty policy descended upon Washington in search of presidential pardons. Enjoying the spectacle of wealthy planters, or their wives and daughters, humbling themselves before a rough-hewn, plebeian president who had once received their contempt and derision, Johnson seemed unable to deny their requests. Although he had promised to be "liberal" in his willingness to issue pardons, the scale of his beneficence was truly staggering. Receiving some 15,000 requests for pardons between May 1865 and September 1867, Johnson granted 13,500 of them, issuing an average of one hundred per day at the height of the requests in September 1865.[14] The significance of these pardons was not lost on congressional Republicans and southern Unionists who understood that in reclaiming full citizenship by the authority of the president, the old elite in the South would now be free to vote, hold office, and recover any property that had been confiscated during the war. Despite his promises to make treason "odious," it now appeared to one Alabama Unionist that Johnson was willing to pardon "all of the worst & most bitter enemies of the government," thus returning them to power throughout the southern states.[15]

As Congress struggled to respond to the president's actions, events in the South were providing powerful evidence that Johnson's approach to Reconstruction was failing to produce results acceptable to the northern public. First, the provisional governments organized under the May Proclamations seemed unwilling to meet even the very lenient requirements that Johnson had suggested to them. Some states sought to pay down the Confederate war debt, others delayed ratification of the Thirteenth Amendment, and South Carolina merely repealed its 1860 ordinance of secession rather than repudiating the legality of the original act. Perhaps even more galling was that Johnson's indiscriminate use of the presidential pardon allowed large numbers of ex-Confederate leaders to run for office under the southern provisional governments; some of whom were elected to positions in the United States Congress. When Congress reconvened in December 1865, they were confronted with the distressing question of what to do with the "ten Confederate Generals, six Confederate cabinet officers, fifty-eight Confederate congressmen, and former Confederate vice-president Alexander Stephens," who wanted to take seats alongside their northern colleagues.[16] Beyond the humiliation of sharing power with men who months before had helped to lead a rebellion that destroyed the lives of hundreds of thousands of Union soldiers, Republicans in Congress could not help but wonder if the southern voting public could even be trusted to elect loyal men to public office.

In addition to the political resurgence of ex-Confederates, Presidential Reconstruction also set the stage for the passage of southern black codes, state laws that threatened to return African Americans to a condition close to slavery. In one sense, these codes represented the necessity that all southern states faced in defining the place of African Americans before the law. Since their status could no longer be defined by the category of chattel property, the provisional governments organized under Johnson's May Proclamations created a new legal framework recognizing the freed-people as persons before the law but also ensuring that their rights and privileges were distinct from those of whites. There was some variation in the ways that individual states approached the problem. The laws of South Carolina and Mississippi, for example, were openly discriminatory as their provisions applied only to blacks. Other southern states avoided direct reference to race, but the laws were applied exclusively to African Americans in practice. Because they contained recognition of blacks as legal persons, these laws sometimes concealed their discriminatory intent in high sounding language. In "An Act to Confer Civil Rights on Freedmen," the Mississippi legislature gave freedpeople the right to sue and be sued, to acquire personal property, and to testify against whites when an African American was party to the case. But the same law prohibited interracial marriage, made freedpeople's "desertion" of lawful employment a crime, and punished anyone who "enticed" a former slave to leave their employment before the expiration of the term of service. Blacks were also prohibited from carrying firearms, preaching without a license, making "seditious speeches," or engaging in "insulting gestures" toward whites.[17]

The most important purpose of the black codes, however, was to grant state and local officials the power to control black labor. Insisting that some form of coercion would be necessary to force former slaves to toil in the cotton fields, the planters wanted to limit the economic options of freedpeople in the chaotic postwar environment. Southern lawmakers responded to complaints that agricultural laborers were becoming insubordinate by passing a diverse series of measures. The black codes, for instance, required that all African Americans sign one-year employment contracts, which specified that wages were forfeit if employees left at any time before the year ended. While the wartime free labor experiments revealed that African Americans often wanted to exempt women and children from field work, the state black code in Texas included a provision that demanded the labor of the whole family when the head of household signed an annual contract. Fearing that freedom might lead former slaves to reject agricultural work entirely, South Carolina's code restricted freedpeople to occupational categories of farmer or servant, unless they paid an annual tax. Determined to exclude freedpeople from any form of independent landholding, Mississippi banned African Americans from renting or leasing land, except in urban areas, so that their labor would always be available for white planters. These codes were designed to guarantee that planters would have the labor supply they needed and to restrict the ability of former slaves to bargain over working conditions or compensation.[18]

The cheap source of agricultural labor that planters craved was augmented by vagrancy and apprenticeship laws that were also included in many black codes. Vagrancy laws stipulated that anyone who had not signed a labor contract by the second Monday in January would be designated as a vagrant and heavily fined, with those unable to pay the fine hired out to someone who would pay the fine for them. The terms of penal service for convicted vagrants varied from state to state, but in Florida, it could mean a year's uncompensated labor. Vagrancy laws were also stretched and modified to reinstate many of the social relations that had existed under slavery, as disrespect or "impudence" to an employer could easily lead to a vagrancy conviction in Florida. Like vagrancy laws, apprenticeship laws contained provisions that immediately reminded observers of the slave system. Although ostensibly developed to deal with a juvenile population dislocated and orphaned by the war, the arbitrary power assigned to the courts to apprentice children without the consent of their parents had an obvious parallel to the power of masters to separate families under slavery. Children in Mississippi, whose parents could not be found or who were deemed unable to care for them, were apprenticed to white masters with a preference given to the minor's former owner. The Freedmen's Bureau in Mississippi was confronted with numerous cases of distraught families seeking to reclaim children who had been apprenticed without the consent or even knowledge of their parents. To make the comparison with slavery even more apt, the black codes also gave masters the right to inflict "moderate corporeal chastisement" on apprentices who failed to work or obey to their masters' satisfaction.[19]

Given the obvious similarities between the black codes and slavery, a few southern politicians raised doubts about the wisdom of passing them at a time when Reconstruction was incomplete and when much of the South remained under military occupation. South Carolina state senator James Hemphill, for example, reminded his colleagues that the northern public still "hold[s] our fate in their hands," and warned that the black codes would be perceived by the "freedom shriekers" as "too much of a white man's law." He predicted that Congress would take up freedman's rights as its "special charge" and force white Southerners to see "the great

change that has taken place in the relations between the races."[20] Hemphill's prophecy was no doubt informed by a growing sense of outrage that
the black codes were producing in many areas of the North. The *Chicago
Tribune*, for example, could not find the words to describe the "baseness
of such efforts to smuggle slavery back into existence," and strongly
opposed the readmission of southern states whose provisional governments
had passed such laws. "To permit the State to come into the Union with
such a record," the *Tribune* insisted, "would be a mockery of freedom and
perfidy to the honor of the Government."[21] Horace Greeley, the reform-
minded editor of the *New York Tribune*, argued that the government possessed unprecedented power to nullify the black codes and to see that
justice was done to former slaves. "We have earned the right and power
to do it by fearful war," he wrote in June 1865. "If we let the opportunity
slip, then our Peace becomes a mere sheet of ink and parchment."[22]
To men like Horace Greeley, the passage of the black codes was clear evidence that President Johnson's policies threatened to undo the fruits of the
Union's terrible sacrifice and ultimate victory.

In December 1865, Congress came back into session amidst growing
unrest among Republicans over events in the South and anger over
Johnson's assumption of unilateral control over Reconstruction policy.
They began by rejecting the southern congressmen elected under the president's plan and went on to create a new congressional committee tasked
with investigating conditions in the South and reformulating the government's policy toward the region. The Joint Committee on Reconstruction
was made up of fifteen members, six from the Senate and nine from the
House, and it was led by William Pitt Fessenden, a moderate Republican
senator from Maine. Although it was dominated by Republicans, the committee should not be seen as a vehicle for the radical wing of the party.
Most of its members still wanted to work with President Johnson to
achieve a compromise position on key issues. Thaddeus Stevens of Pennsylvania was a strong and consistently radical member of the group, but
his arguments in support of black voting rights and land redistribution
never received the support of the majority of the committee's membership.
The moderates who controlled the Committee on Reconstruction represented districts with a large number of Democratic voters and, as a result,
were reluctant to endorse policies that were perceived as radical. As historian Michael Fitzgerald has argued, therefore, the committee initially

hoped to "fine-tune Presidential Reconstruction, not overturn it entirely."[23]

Between January and May 1866, the committee interviewed well over a hundred witnesses, including former slaves, Union army officers, southern Unionists, and provisional government officials, with a particular emphasis on the condition of freedpeople. The stories that emerged from the testimony were harrowing and suggested that the black codes were only one part of a larger campaign by the white South to keep blacks in their place. Rev. William Thornton, a black minister from Hampton, Virginia, was told by a local white landowner that "as soon as we can get these Yankees off the ground and move that [Freedmen's] Bureau, we will put you to rights; we will break up your church, and not one of you shall have a church here."[24] After a local black laborer unwittingly strayed briefly onto the property of an adjacent white farmer, Thornton recalled, the outraged farmer "went into the woods and deliberately shot him as he would shoot a bird." When the committee asked if there had been any legal action against the trigger-happy farmer, Thornton said that the man had been arrested and jailed briefly, "but they let him out last Sunday morning."[25] White observers confirmed the testimony of blacks and insisted that only continued military occupation could prevent wholesale violence against blacks and Unionist whites. Ezra Heinstadt, a Louisiana Unionist, told the committee that if the Union forces were withdrawn from his state, "Union men . . . would be driven from almost all the rural portions of the state . . . and the condition of the blacks would, to a certain extent, be worse than it was when slavery existed there."[26]

While Congress was taking testimony about the impact of Presidential Reconstruction, African Americans across the South were engaging in a large-scale political mobilization to meet the challenges of Reconstruction in general and the black codes in particular. Building on an antebellum northern tradition of black conventions, the postwar freedmen's conventions of 1865 and 1866 were led by literate blacks who had become free before the war and then returned to lead political movements in the very states where they had once been slaves.[27] But recently emancipated slaves were also present in sizable numbers at these gatherings, ensuring that issues of plantation labor and unfair employment contracts would receive at least some discussion. In the fall of 1865, *Chicago Tribune* correspondent Sidney Andrews attended two sessions of the North Carolina Freedmen's

Convention in Raleigh and wanted his readers to understand the gathering as a truly independent form of black political mobilization. It was "really a convention of colored men, not a colored man's convention engineered by white men," he said, and the delegates had been chosen by local political groups who took enormous risks to discuss contentious issues in the midst of a hostile white population. Some of the delegates who "were obliged to leave their homes in the night, are asking [for] safe-conduct papers from the military authorities, and will even then quietly return home in the night."[28]

As historian Steven Hahn has argued, freedmen's conventions produced documents that used the "tones of moderation and conciliation," but their very existence and the issues they addressed suggested a far more radical intent.[29] At a time when all but a small group of radical Republicans opposed African American voting rights, the convention in Virginia argued that "the elective franchise" was "our inalienable right as freemen, and which the Declaration of Independence guarantees to all free citizens of this Government."[30] Using the language of the American Revolution, the freedmen's conventions based their claim to equality in the traditional language of American republicanism, but they were also very clear that the black codes' denial of basic civil and political rights would be met by coordinated resistance if necessary. Since "we have among the white people of this State many who are our most inveterate enemies ... who despise us simply because we are black, and more especially, because we have been made free by the power of the United States Government," the Virginia convention insisted, political power was necessary as a means of self-defense. "[T]he time has come," they concluded, "when the colored people are to be felt in power in this government."[31] Such demands for suffrage and representation, of course, deeply disturbed southern whites who feared that black voting rights would overturn the traditional racial order and set the stage for African American "domination" of the South.

While African American leaders in the South were making the case for political rights in freedmen's conventions, northern black leaders attacked various forms of discrimination in their own region, ranging from segregated streetcars to restrictions on black testimony in court and the denial of voting rights. The use of black troops by the Union army during the Civil War had greatly enhanced claims that African American men had a right to suffrage. During the 1863 black convention in Kansas, for example, one delegate stated that "it will doubtless be discovered that it is necessary to make the black man a voter, as it was to make him a soldier. He was made a solider to RESTORE the Union. He will be made a voter to PRESERVE it."[32] Northern black leaders created a number of local, state, and national organizations to promote equality under the law, change state voter laws, and pressure businesses to desegregate. African American men could vote without restriction in only five New England states, and groups like the National Equal Rights League mounted challenges to the whites-only provisions in most state constitutions. Activists petitioned state legislatures and state constitutional conventions and regularly used black newspapers to make their case, but they confronted blatant racism. When Connecticut legislators were considering removing the whites-only clause in the state constitution, for example, Democratic legislators announced in their minority report that "This race, so inferior in the highest qualities of manhood to our own cannot in our view be benefited by the right of suffrage."[33] Efforts succeeded in three states, but most northern campaigns to enfranchise African American men between 1865 and 1869 failed.

As they fought for voting rights in northern states, African American communities built upon antebellum traditions of state and local organization to campaign for equal access to public accommodations. In Philadelphia, for example, activists used a variety of means to challenge laws that required separate seating and other forms of discrimination on the city's streetcars. Led by Octavius Catto of the Pennsylvania Equal Rights League, campaigners circulated petitions, lobbied the state legislature, held public meetings, and engaged in direct action against discriminatory practices. Catto had been born into a free black family in Charleston, South Carolina, but he emerged as a significant leader in Philadelphia during the Civil War, helping to recruit hundreds of black soldiers for the Union war effort. Like many northern black activists, Catto believed that African American service in the war entitled them to equality in the postwar nation. Although the streetcars in Philadelphia were officially desegregated in 1867, Catto's fearless advocacy of equality and voting rights made him a target for white supremacist hostility. Shot down in the street during a heated election campaign in 1871, Catto's murder demonstrates that the violent hostility to equal rights was hardly restricted exclusively to the South during Reconstruction.[34]

African American activist Octavius Catto led pro-
tests against racial discrimination in Philadelphia
before his murder in 1871. (Library of Congress)

In light of the difficulties involved in changing state laws, northern
black activists turned their attention to Washington, hoping that the
federal government would be more responsive. In February 1866, Frederick
Douglass led a delegation of black citizens to the White House where he
told the president that as Abraham Lincoln had "placed in our hands the
sword to assist in saving the nation," he now hoped that Johnson would
follow his predecessor by "placing in our hands the ballot with which to
save ourselves."[35] Johnson, who had never interacted with blacks on equal
terms, was clearly irritated by the request and delivered a stinging diatribe
in which he insisted that blacks had always looked down on poor whites
and would only use their political power to support the interests of the
old planter class. Johnson insisted that "the colored man appreciated the

slave owner more highly than he did the man who didn't own slaves," and he predicted that the enmity existing between the blacks and poor whites would precipitate a "war of races" should freedpeople get the vote. Remaining calm but resolute, Douglass attempted to show the president that blacks and poor whites shared economic interests and that a political alliance between the two might "raise up a political party" in the South that could advance their mutual welfare. But Johnson would not accept that line of argument, telling the black delegation that their economic interests would be better served by emigrating than by voting. "If [the freedman] cannot get employment in the South," the president said dismissively, "he has it in his power to go where he can get it."[36] Johnson was clearly infuriated by Douglass's assertiveness and after the delegation left the presidential office, his visceral racism bubbled to the surface. Turning to one of his secretaries the president blurted out his belief that Douglass was "just like any nigger, & and would sooner cut a white man's throat than not."[37]

The angry resistance of the president to their proposals convinced Douglass and other northern black leaders to turn to congressional Republicans, who listened more attentively to their case for political and civil rights. By the winter of 1865–1866, Congress began to act in response to the serious problems that had emerged in the South as a result of the president's policies. Moderate Republicans still believed that they could work with Johnson, and they formulated legislation they thought would meet with his approval. William Fessenden, the moderate Republican leader of the Joint Committee, told a family member that keeping the peace between the president and the radicals was "a most difficult undertaking," but he remained convinced that the moderate-conservative majority would "put things on a sound basis."[38]

Two pieces of legislation, each of which was sponsored by moderate Republican leader Lyman Trumbull of Illinois, were designed to protect the basic freedoms of former slaves and to invalidate the black codes. In early February 1866, Congress approved an extension of the Freedmen's Bureau that not only preserved the agency until such time as Congress chose to phase it out but also increased its power to protect freedpeople through a special court system run by bureau agents. Since these courts would lose their power upon a state's readmission to the Union, Trumbull also proposed a civil rights bill that would confer citizenship on African

Americans. This would enable them to challenge discriminatory laws passed by state governments, including the black codes that had denied freedpeople due process or equal protection of the laws. Although both measures represented important revisions of President Johnson's policies, neither included any provision for African American suffrage, an omission that fell well short of radical hopes for Reconstruction.

Moderate Republican leaders like Trumbull and Fessenden had been consulting regularly with Andrew Johnson during the debate over both the Freedmen's Bureau and Civil Rights Bills and, as a result, expected that he would sign them. It was, therefore, shocking to them when Johnson vetoed the extension of the Freedmen's Bureau. Explaining his action in a provocative message to Congress, the president claimed that the bill unduly expanded the power of the military over civilian affairs and violated the judicial system of the South by creating Freedmen's Bureau courts. In a rather startling argument given the context, Johnson went on to argue that the South should not be subjected to any federal legislation until all its representatives had been seated in Congress. He also made it very clear that he believed the executive branch had a far greater claim to direct the process of Reconstruction than Congress did, insisting that while members of Congress were elected from individual districts across the Union, "the President is chosen by the people of all the States." As far as he was concerned, there was neither any constitutional basis for further legislation like the Freedmen's Bureau, nor any need for it. "[I]n my own judgment, most of these States ... have already been fully restored," he insisted, "and are to be deemed as entitled to enjoy their constitutional rights as members of the Union." For Andrew Johnson, Reconstruction was nearly complete, and any further changes to the South would have to be approved by southern congressional delegations themselves.[39]

The sense of betrayal that Johnson's veto generated in the mainstream of the Republican Party is hard to overstate. Having resisted the demands for black suffrage made by the radicals in order to satisfy the president, Fessenden and Trumbull now found themselves rebuked by Johnson in the most public way possible. Each of them called on Congress to override his veto, pointing out the obvious inconsistencies between his actions as president and the principles he had espoused in the veto message. How could Johnson make demands on the provisional governments in the South while denying Congress's right to do the same thing? How could

Johnson use military tribunals to try southern civilians for offenses related to the rebellion and then castigate Congress for using such courts to protect the freedpeople against wanton violence? The president also seemed either oblivious or hostile to the larger goal, shared by all other members of his party, of building a Republican Party in the South. Handing power to white Democrats at the expense of southern Unionists and favoring the power of planters over the rights of former slaves, Johnson appeared to betray both the ideals and the interests of the political organization that had elevated him to power.[40]

While it was not clear that there were enough votes to pass the Freedmen's Bureau Bill over Johnson's veto, there was certainly enough support among Republicans to pass Senator Trumbull's Civil Rights Bill, which cleared both the House and the Senate by March 13, 1866. A landmark in the constitutional history of the United States, the bill that became the Civil Rights Act of 1866 invalidated nearly a century of law denying African Americans citizenship. Overturning the notorious *Dred Scott* case of 1857 in which the Supreme Court had ruled that blacks were not citizens by virtue of their race, the new law granted citizenship to anyone born within the jurisdiction of the United States. The act immediately conferred federal citizenship rights on African Americans, and it also empowered the national government to prohibit state violations of those rights. The latter provision was especially significant as it built on the language of the Thirteenth Amendment and prefigured similar provisions in the Fourteenth and Fifteenth Amendments. These enabling clauses gave Congress unprecedented powers to protect the rights of citizens against discriminatory state actions and constituted the legal foundation of much modern civil rights legislation. The most immediate effect of the Civil Rights Act of 1866, however, was to strike down the southern black codes that had singled out blacks for discriminatory treatment.

Though it might seem naïve in retrospect, congressional Republicans again expected the president to sign the Civil Rights Bill. Hoping to unite the party around centrist positions in advance of the fall midterm elections, Ohio's moderate Republican senator John Sherman believed that if Johnson were to veto the bill there would be an open break. "If the President vetoes the Civil Rights bill," a leading Ohio Republican warned Sherman, "I believe we shall be obliged to draw our swords for a fight and throw away the scabbard."[41] But veto it he did, and his message to

Congress was sweeping in its denunciation of moderate Reconstruction policy. Insisting that the Civil Rights Bill would "destroy our federative system of government and break down the barriers which preserve the rights of states," the president said that the "tendency of the bill must be to resuscitate the spirit of rebellion."[42] Johnson seemed unable to see beyond his conviction that any protection of the rights of freedpeople inherently undercut the position of whites. Despite the overwhelming evidence Congress had compiled of the violent campaigns against freedpeople, Johnson argued that the Civil Rights Bill was unnecessary and discriminatory against whites. As for making African Americans citizens of the United States, the president insisted that blacks, like others who were "strangers to and unfamiliar with our institutions and our laws," should undergo a "probationary period" during which they could prove that they had the "requisite qualifications" for citizenship. Echoing language that southern slaveholders had used before the war, he insisted that each state should be left free to enact legislation that concerned the "domestic condition of its people" and, if it was expedient, to "discriminate between the two races."[43]

In addition to its rejection of any federal legislative basis for racial justice, Andrew Johnson's veto of the Civil Rights Bill was a terrible political miscalculation. The president believed that the law was an expression of radical Republican sentiment, but it was in fact the work of conservative and moderate Republicans. While northern Democrats hailed Johnson's defense of white privilege, previously supportive Republican newspapers repudiated his course of action, and their sharp condemnations indicated that a shift was occurring within the Republican Party that had enormous consequences for the future. The *Philadelphia North American*, which had been friendly to Johnson until his vetoes of the two bills, now sounded quite radical in its tone. By insisting that the Republican Party "stultify itself and its whole past career and actions," the *North American* argued, the president "has managed to make the term radical synonymous with the entire mass of the dominant party."[44] Indeed, evidence for the growing radicalism and unity of Congress was immediately apparent as first the Senate and then the House overrode the veto of the Civil Rights Bill. Radicals now believed that the combination of Johnson's misguided leadership and events in the South had demonstrated that a conciliatory approach to Reconstruction was doomed to failure and that a broader

Reconstruction policy, implemented by congressional action, was necessary. Although radicals were still unable to control policy, the rupture between the president and the moderate wing of the party meant that radical voices would carry much more weight in the coming months and years.

Having passed the Civil Rights Act of 1866 over Johnson's veto, Republicans in Congress accelerated negotiations over a constitutional amendment that would replace Presidential Reconstruction with a more comprehensive plan of their own. At the end of April 1866, the Joint Committee on Reconstruction presented a draft of that amendment to Congress containing specific guidelines for the Reconstruction process. After several weeks of debate and modification, the proposed Fourteenth Amendment began by permanently removing race as a barrier to federal and state citizenship rights, essentially writing the language of the Civil Rights Act into the Constitution. Radicals had pushed for a federal guarantee of black voting rights, but the amendment instead punished states that disenfranchised blacks by reducing their representation in Congress in proportion to numbers of blacks barred from voting. In a complex set of provisions, the Fourteenth Amendment required that southern states repudiate the Confederate war debt and stripped the political rights of those who had broken oaths to uphold the U.S. Constitution by joining the Confederacy. To protect Union soldiers and their families, the amendment also guaranteed that the government would honor their pensions. The final section of the amendment gave Congress the power to enforce the provisions of the amendment by the enactment of appropriate legislation. Although it was very much a compromise between radicals and moderates, the Fourteenth Amendment passed the House and Senate by two-thirds majorities and was submitted to the states for approval in July 1866.

President Johnson was, not surprisingly, utterly opposed to the principles of the Fourteenth Amendment, and he repeated his earlier view that no congressional action of this kind should be undertaken prior to the restoration of the southern states. But during and immediately after the negotiations over the amendment, events in the South once again undercut the president's position and strengthened the hand of those who believed that conciliatory policies had failed. In early May 1866, a vicious race riot erupted in Memphis, Tennessee, in which the city's police force and firemen joined murderous white mobs as they targeted freedpeople over several days, killing at least 40 and committing several acts of rape and arson. Although federal troops were stationed nearby, the local commander did little to stop the mayhem, preferring to let the mobs disperse on their own. Instead, the violent white crowds attacked nearly all visible manifestations of black community building in the city, leaving the freedpeople's churches, businesses, and schools in charred ruins and littering the streets with the bodies of murdered black citizens. In the aftermath of the destruction, the city's most rabidly white supremacist newspaper defended the attacks as a necessary defense against an insurrectionary black population. The riots, wrote the editors of the *Avalanche*, showed that "the Southern man will not be ruled by the negro ... that it is best not to arouse the fury of the white man."[45]

In late July 1866, moreover, both black and white delegates attending a pro-equal rights constitutional convention in New Orleans were brutally assaulted by a mob that, as in Memphis, included members of the city's police force. Earlier that year, Louisiana's provisional state government, which had been organized under Johnson's May Proclamations and made up almost exclusively of former Confederates officers, had made a concerted effort to restore prewar conditions in the state. Among other measures, they had passed laws exempting former Confederates from the payment of back taxes, purged Louisiana Unionists from state offices, and passed a highly restrictive black code. In New Orleans itself, former Confederates gained control over the city government, resulting in the creation of a municipal police force of which two-thirds of the officers were Confederate veterans.[46] In order to counter these ominous trends, radicals in the state's Republican Party called for a constitutional convention that would meet at the Mechanics' Institute in New Orleans on July 30th to consider black suffrage and other important reforms. As the day approached, city officials declared the convention to be illegal and encouraged any local policemen who lacked weapons to purchase pistols from local gun shops. Fearful of these developments and aware of the terrible events in Memphis, at least 200 black Union veterans marched to the meeting hall in order to offer support and protection to the delegates. As in Memphis, the sight of uniformed blacks infuriated a growing crowd of white spectators who hurled "a volley of bricks" at both the veterans and the convention delegates who were trying to enter the hall.

On July 30, 1866, angry white mobs and armed city police officers killed thirty-seven blacks and three whites who were attending a pro-equal rights convention in New Orleans. (Library of Congress)

When the city police arrived, their officers gave orders to attack the marchers and within minutes several blacks had been shot to death on the street.[47]

Taking shelter from the bullets of the rioters, convention delegates fled inside their meeting hall only to find that the building was completely surrounded by the mob which proceeded to pour gunfire through the windows. Rioters waited until frightened delegates tried to escape and then mercilessly executed even those who made obvious signs of surrender. With no clear guidance from the president or the secretary of war over how to deal with the crisis, local military officials once again failed to intervene to prevent what one observer called "an absolute massacre by the police" of thirty-seven blacks and three whites.[48] In the aftermath of the riot, Johnson insisted that the delegates were mainly responsible for instigating the confrontation and he even went so far as to accuse his enemies in the Republican Party with planning it. Although General Philip Sheridan voiced no sympathy for the leaders of the New Orleans convention, labeling them "political agitators" and "bad men," he expressly criticized the actions of the police. In his report on the riot, Sheridan concluded that the police attacked African Americans "with fire-arms, clubs, and knives in a manner so unnecessary and atrocious as to compel me to say that it was murder."[49]

For many northerners, the horrific violence at Memphis and New Orleans clearly showed that it was President Johnson's policies, not congressional Republicans, which were stirring up the white South's "spirit of rebellion." As historian Hannah Rosen has argued, the atrocities committed by white Southerners in the spring and summer of 1866 pushed many Republicans "into supporting a broader vision of citizenship and its attendant rights and into backing what were then perceived as radical measures, including suffrage for former slaves."[50] As both the president and his critics prepared for the fall 1866 elections, it was clear that their relationship had reached a crisis point and that the Reconstruction of the nation was hanging in the balance. The *Chicago Tribune*, anticipating a visit from the president and fuming over the New Orleans riot, told its readers that Johnson would arrive in their city "with the blood of loyal men upon his garments."[51] For his part, the president told a crowd in Cleveland that the "traitors in the South" had already been "whipped," but now he was fighting "traitors in the North."[52] The Fourteenth Amendment was being debated in the states, and the American public would have a chance to weigh in for the first time since Lincoln's election in November 1864.

NOTES

1. Douglas R. Egerton, *The Wars of Reconstruction: The Brief, Violent History of America's Most Progressive Era* (New York: Bloomsbury Press, 2014), 57–8.

2. James M. McPherson and James K. Hogue, *Ordeal by Fire: The Civil War and Reconstruction* (New York: McGraw-Hill, 2010), 137.

3. A National Man, *Life and Times of Andrew Johnson: Seventeenth President of the United States* (New York: D. Appleton and Company, 1866), 131.

4. Andrew Johnson, Speech to Indiana Delegation, April 21, 1865, in *The Papers of Andrew Johnson*, vol. 7, ed. LeRoy P. Graf (Knoxville: University of Tennessee Press, 1986), 612.

5. Ibid.

6. Eric Foner, *Reconstruction: America's Unfinished Revolution* (New York: Harper & Row, 1988), 177–8.

7. Ibid., 181.

8. Andrew Johnson, 3rd Annual Message, December 3, 1867, in *The Papers of Andrew Johnson*, vol. 13, ed. Paul H. Bergeron (Knoxville: University of Tennessee Press, 1996), 289.

9. Andrew Johnson, "Proclamation of Amnesty and Reconstruction," May 29, 1865, in *The Papers of Andrew Johnson*, vol. 8: May–August 1865, ed. Paul H. Bergeron (Knoxville: University of Tennessee Press, 1989), 130.

10. Michael Les Benedict, *A Compromise of Principle: Congressional Republicans and Reconstruction, 1863–1869* (New York: W.W. Norton, 1974), 107.

11. Ibid., 108.

12. Michael Fellman, Lesley J. Gordon, Daniel E. Sutherland, *This Terrible War: The Civil War and its Aftermath* (New York: Longman, 2003), 302.

13. Whitelaw Reid, *After the War: A Southern Tour* (New York: Moore, Wilstach & Baldwin, 1866), 298.

14. Bradley R. Clampitt, " 'Not Intended to Dispossess Females': Southern Women and Civil War Amnesty," *Civil War History* 56 (December 2010), 325–349; McPherson, *Ordeal By Fire*, 545.

15. Margaret M. Storey, "The Crucible of Reconstruction: Unionists and the Struggle for Alabama's Postwar Home Front," in *The Great Task Remaining Before Us: Reconstruction as America's Continuing Civil War*, eds. Paul A. Cimbala & Randall M. Miller (New York: Fordham University Press, 2010), 75.

16. Fellman, *This Terrible War*, 303.

17. "An Act to Confer Civil Rights on Freedmen, and for other Purposes;" "An Act to Regulate the Relation of Master and Apprentice, as Relates to Freedmen, Free Negroes, and Mulattoes;" "An Act to Amend the Vagrant Law of the State;" & "An Act to Punish Certain Offences," *Laws of the State of Mississippi, Passed at a Regular Session of the Mississippi Legislature, Held in the City of Jackson, October, November, and December, 1865* (Jackson, 1866), 82–91, 165.

18. William C. Harris, "Formulation of the First Mississippi Plan: The Black Code of 1865," *The Journal of Mississippi History* 29 (September 1967), 181–201; Foner, *Reconstruction*, 199–200.

19. Barry A. Crouch, " 'All the Vile Passions': the Texas Black Code of 1866," *Southwestern Historical Quarterly* 97 (July 1993), 21–27; Donald G. Nieman, *To Set the Law in Motion: The Freedmen's Bureau and the Legal Rights of Blacks, 1865–1868* (Millwood, NY: KTO Press, 1979), 76; Joe M. Richardson, "Florida Black Codes," *The Florida Historical Quarterly* 47 (April 1969), 374–375.

20. Joel Williamson, *After Slavery: The Negro in South Carolina During Reconstruction, 1861–1877* (Chapel Hill: University of North Carolina Press, 1965), 76.

21. *Chicago Tribune*, December 24, 1865.

22. *New York Tribune,* June 23, 1865.

23. Michael W. Fitzgerald, *Splendid Failure: Postwar Reconstruction in the American South* (Chicago: Ivan R. Dee, 2007), 36.

24. Benjamin Burks Kendrick, *The Journal of the Joint Committee of Fifteen on Reconstruction* (New York: Columbia University Press, 1914), 270.

25. Ibid.

26. Ibid., 272.

27. Steven Hahn, *A Nation Under Our Feet: Black Political Struggles in the Rural South from Slavery to the Great Migration* (Cambridge: Harvard University Press, 2003), 121.

28. Sidney Andrews, *The South Since the War: Fourteen Weeks of Travel and Observation* (Boston: Ticknor and Fields, 1866), 124, 131.

29. Hahn, *A Nation Under Our Feet,* 120.

30. "Proceedings of the Convention of the Colored People of Virginia, August 1865," in *The Civil War and Reconstruction: A Documentary Collection,* ed. William E. Gienapp (New York: W.W. Norton, 2001), 329–330.

31. Ibid., 329, 330.

32. Hugh Davis, *"We Will Be Satisfied With Nothing Less": The African American Struggle for Equal Rights in the North during Reconstruction*(Ithaca: Cornell University Press, 2011), 16.

33. Ibid., 52.

34. Daniel R. Biddle and Murray Dubin, *Tasting Freedom: Octavius Catto and the Battle for Equality in Civil War America* (Philadelphia: Temple University Press, 2010), 429–30.

35. "Interview with a Colored Delegation respecting Suffrage," in *The Political History of the United States of America During the Period of Reconstruction, April 15, 1865–July 15, 1870,* ed. Edward McPherson (Washington: Philp & Solomons, 1871), 52.

36. Ibid., 54–55.

37. Annette Gordon-Reed, *Andrew Johnson* (New York: Henry Holt, 2011), 125–26.

38. Eric L. McKitrick, *Andrew Johnson and Reconstruction* (Chicago: University of Chicago Press, 1960), 280.

39. Ibid., 290.

40. Benedict, *A Compromise of Principle,* 156.

41. Benedict, *A Compromise of Principle,* 163.

42. Andrew Johnson, "Veto of Civil Rights Bill," March 27, 1866, in *The Papers of Andrew Johnson,* vol. 10, ed. Paul H. Bergeron (Knoxville: University of Tennessee Press, 1992), 319–320.

43. Ibid., 313, 314.

44. Benedict, *A Compromise of Principle*, 165.

45. Stephen V. Ash, *A Massacre in Memphis: The Race Riot that Shook the Nation One Year After the Civil War* (New York: Hill and Wang, 2013), 171.

46. James K. Hogue, *Uncivil War: Five New Orleans Street Battles and the Rise and Fall of Radical Reconstruction* (Baton Rouge: Louisiana State University Press, 2011), 34.

47. Ibid., 42.

48. McPherson & Hogue, *Ordeal by Fire*, 562.

49. James G. Hollandsworth, Jr., *An Absolute Massacre: The New Orleans Race Riot of July 30, 1866* (Baton Rouge: Louisiana State University Press, 2001), 144–145; Fitzgerald, *Splendid Failure*, 39; McKitrick, *Johnson and Reconstruction*, 426–427.

50. Hannah Rosen, *Terror in the Heart of Freedom: Citizenship, Sexual Violence, and the Meaning of Race in the Postemancipation South* (Chapel Hill: University of North Carolina Press, 2009), 27.

51. *Chicago Tribune*, August 27, 1866.

52. McKitrick, *Johnson and Reconstruction*, 433.

CHAPTER 3

TOWARD RADICAL RECONSTRUCTION

W ith so much at stake in the 1866 congressional elections, President Johnson spent several weeks in the late summer on an intensive speaking tour of critical battleground states. This "swing round the circle," as it was called, clearly exhausted him, and he was frequently interrupted by hecklers who taunted him into making embarrassing rejoinders. In Cleveland, when hecklers told him that he ought to "hang Jeff Davis," for example, an enraged Johnson asked them "why don't you hang Thad Stevens or Wendell Phillips?"[1] The notion that a Pennsylvania congressman and an antislavery activist from Massachusetts deserved the same treatment as the leader of the Confederate rebellion struck many people as bizarre and even raised questions about the president's fitness for office. The fact that Johnson was receiving much of his support from Democrats also exposed him to charges that he had thrown in his lot with a party that had opposed the Civil War and, though the charge was largely false, had sympathized with the rebellion. Indiana Republican Oliver Morton, a moderate who had recently broken with the president over his veto of the Civil Rights Act, described Johnson's Democratic support as "a common sewer . . . into which is emptied every element of treason, North and South and every element of inhumanity and barbarism which has dishonored the age."[2] Like Morton, many northern Republicans believed that the president had to be stopped lest he betray the sacrifices by which the nation had been preserved from the twin threats of slavery and rebellion.

Perhaps Johnson's most egregious act, as congressional Republicans saw it, was his deliberate attempt to prevent the ratification of the Fourteenth Amendment, the most comprehensive statement of what moderate Republicans wanted from Reconstruction. Having made it clear to southern states that immediate restoration to the Union would follow their ratification of the amendment, Republican leaders were shocked to find the president advising ex-rebel states to reject the measure.[3] It appeared that preventing any form of black citizenship, however limited that form might be, was more important to Johnson than his oft-stated goal of completing the Reconstruction process as quickly as possible. But believing as he did that the southern states had already been restored and that Congress was unjustly barring their representatives, Johnson acted on the principle that no additional terms could be imposed upon these states. He insisted that he was the chief magistrate of all 36 states, not simply of the 25 that had remained loyal to the Union during the Civil War. Johnson increasingly saw himself as the defender of states' rights constitutionalism against those who would use the crisis of the war to create a consolidated system of national supremacy. "He that is opposed to the restoration of the government . . . is as great a traitor as Jeff Davis," Johnson proclaimed in September 1866.[4] Who was a traitor and who was a patriot? It seemed that only the results of the election would decide.

Voters in fall of 1866 overwhelmingly chose the congressional Republicans over what they saw as a president who seemed bent on surrendering the peace to southern ex-Confederates. The Republicans won veto-proof majorities in both the House and Senate and took control of every northern state legislature and, perhaps most surprisingly, three of the border states. After large Republican victories in Ohio, Indiana, and Iowa, *Harper's Weekly* interpreted the election results as a "protest of the people" against Johnson's public criticisms of Congress as an "illegal body" and "against the fatal incompleteness of the conditions he proposed."[5]

But what was the position of Congress? Moderates and conservatives were fully committed to using the Fourteenth Amendment as the test for the readmission of the southern states, a position that was reinforced when Tennessee's senators and representatives were immediately seated after their state legislature approved the amendment. But other southern states were following the president's advice and rejected the amendment outright, a response that angered moderate Republicans. Such defiance played into the hands of radicals who believed that stronger measures, including explicit guarantees of political rights for freedpeople, were needed. Senator Charles Sumner argued that the Fourteenth Amendment was inadequate to meet the crisis in the South. "I would insist," he informed the Senate, "that every one of these States, before its

Senator Charles Sumner supported black suffrage and the civil rights of African Americans during his long political career. (Library of Congress)

Representatives were received in Congress, should confer impartial suffrage, without distinction of color."[6]

But as the political winds were shifting toward more radical policies in Washington, equally dramatic changes were occurring on the ground in the South. Indeed, the murky political debate in Washington in part reflected the social and economic ambiguities that had come with the end of slavery and the anxieties felt by white and black southerners over the meaning of Confederate defeat and emancipation. The war had certainly created new realities in the South, but the shape of those changes would need to be worked out in the daily interactions of those who had so recently been defined as master and slave. Over the last two decades, numerous historians have shown that it was the freedpeople themselves who initiated these new forms of social interaction by acting upon their own understanding of freedom and by seeking pragmatic alliances with northern and southern whites wherever possible. For African Americans, freedom entailed a rejection of all aspects of the slave system and the restraints it placed on their ability to shape their individual and collective destinies. As Eric Foner put it, "In some cases, this meant doing what was forbidden under slavery, in others, it meant openly practicing what had previously been forbidden and enjoyed only in secret."[7] In either case, the risks involved were significant as southern whites sought to negate black definitions of freedom through legislation such as the black codes and through extra-legal forms of violent repression.

One of the simplest ways that freedpeople asserted their freedom was by moving freely across the landscape of the postwar South. Under slavery, of course, legal prohibitions on black mobility had been enforced by slave patrols. These local enforcement groups existed in every southern state in order to recapture escaped slaves and reinforce plantation labor discipline by preventing unauthorized movement. For the enslaved, such restrictions prevented families who had been separated by the slave trade from visiting one another and condemned them to a life of endless toil on a single farm or plantation. Freedom, therefore, included the right to walk away from the place of enslavement to somewhere different, even if the destination itself was unknown to the traveler. A black preacher in northern Florida at the end of the war told members of his congregation that they would never feel really free until they were no longer within sight of the old plantation house. "You mus' all move – you mus' move clar away from de ole places what you knows, ter de new places what you don't know," he advised them. "Go whey you please – do what you please – furgit erbout de white folks," he insisted.[8]

Forgetting about white folks would be difficult in the postwar South, but even those who had lived on plantations with relatively less violence or brutality felt a deep need to enact their freedom in the form of a physical exodus. Former slaveholders, convinced of their own benevolence, were often shocked to the point of indignation that their most "pampered" servants took the first opportunity to walk away. Plantation mistress Grace Elmore of South Carolina, for example, felt herself highly "provoked" when the family's elderly nurse embraced emancipation and "took herself off" rather than continuing to care for Elmore's baby. "One cannot expect total sacrifice of self," she acknowledged in injured tones, "but certainly there should be some consideration of others." Thoroughly vexed,

Elmore vowed that if the old woman, who had given a lifetime of uncompensated service to her white owners, should ever need assistance in the future she would "not turn my heel to help her."[9] For white women like Elmore, emancipation meant the loss of customary power to compel the labor of black women, and they were placed in the unfamiliar position of performing the cooking and cleaning for themselves or hiring paid servants. Even when they did find domestics, white women then confronted the reality that black women servants could at anytime assert their freedom and leave if they did not like their situation.[10]

Of course the loyalty to planter families that white Southerners expected from freedpeople seemed particularly hypocritical to ex-slaves whose own families had been separated ruthlessly in the domestic slave trade before the war. Emancipation presented opportunities to reunite families separated in this way, and former slaves often used their newfound physical mobility to do just that. Although planters and slave traders attempted to conceal the destination of slaves sold in the domestic trade, slave communities had proved remarkably adept at passing on information concerning the whereabouts of those who had been sold. For years after the war, moreover, notices and requests for information about lost or separated family members appeared in black-owned newspapers such as the *Christian Recorder*. Lucinda Lowery, for example, a former slave living in Nashville, Tennessee, in 1865, offered a small reward for any information about the final destination of her daughter Caroline, who had been sold away three years earlier. Lowery knew the name of the slave trader who had bought her daughter, the city to which she had been taken, the name of the trading house where she had been held, and the fact that she had been sold a second time.[11] Although many freedpeople were never able to locate lost loved ones, dramatic stories of reunion did occur. Louis and Matilda Hughes, a black couple who had endured terrible suffering during their enslavement in northern Mississippi, left the South in the summer of 1865, hoping to find Matilda's mother, who had been sold away from her 10 years earlier. Acting on vague information that her mother was living in Cincinnati, Ohio, Matilda persuaded Louis to travel there on the chance that the rumors were true. Once they arrived in the city, the couple began stopping black residents in the street and giving a physical description of Matilda's mother. By an amazing stroke of luck, they met a man who gave them the precise address of the boarding house where she lived and the family was reunited.[12]

As they sought to undo the burdens that had been placed upon their families under slavery, many former slaves chose new names to signal their emancipation from white control. Although slaveholders had often insisted that slaves were part of their household, they denied their bondsmen the right to a surname and sometimes exercised the right to assign given names to slave children. As historian Joel Williamson had noted, planters often selected names like Pompey, Caesar, or Cato, "farcical" references to powerful men of the ancient world that reinforced the powerlessness of the people called by them.[13] After the war, however, black families not only took full control over the naming of their children but also adopted surnames that proclaimed their new status as families with emotional and legal relationships entitled to protection under the law. While some ex-slaves chose the surnames of their former owners, this was often done for the sake of convenience or expediency rather than from any lingering loyalty to white planter families. Since family names were required for any formal interaction with the Freedmen's Bureau or other government entities, black families who had been owned by the same master used his surname because it seemed "the easiest way to be identified."[14] Some former slaves chose last names that connected their bearers to famous Americans, including Washington or Lincoln, and those who chose names like Taylor based their decision on occupational categories. For those families who had passed on memories of their African ancestors, emancipation offered the chance to reassert their earliest familial identity in a formal way. Former Texas slave Martin Jackson said that "one of my grandfathers in Africa was called Jeaceo, and so I decided to be called Jackson."[15]

Newly reunited and bearing names of their own choosing, southern black families nevertheless faced enormous difficulties remaining together and staying healthy. The legacy of slavery and the vagrancy and apprenticeship laws imposed on freedpeople under the black codes represented serious threats to family security in the postwar years. Southern slave codes had not recognized the legal marriage between enslaved men and women, and any children that resulted from their relationships were the legal property of the masters. This historic disregard for the ties that existed among blacks under slavery carried over into the actions of the provisional governments organized under President Johnson's May Proclamations, resulting in egregious violations of basic human rights. Historian Leon Litwack has described the operation of apprenticeship laws as verging on "legalized kidnapping" in which state court judges had the power to apprentice a black child to a white "guardian" if he determined that it would be "better for the habits and comfort" of the child.[16]

These new apprenticeship laws posed special threats to the ability of freed-women to reconstruct their families after the war. As one woman lamented, not having a right to her children diminished the significance of freedom, because "It was on their account that we desired to be free." Impoverished after the war, freedwomen were deemed unable to care for their children and state courts would bind out their children, often to their former masters. Courts and planters alike stood by their decision to apprentice children, insisting that freedwomen were often not married when their children were born. One Virginia planter confidently informed a bureau agent that he had a right to two children who were "both illegitimate, neither of them having any recognized father."[17] The fact that antebellum slave codes had not recognized the validity of slave marriages and the ability of masters to separate husbands, wives, and children at will was simply ignored as southern states crafted policies that would maintain the power of white planters.

In addition to apprenticeship laws that made it difficult to reconstruct black families, freedwomen also faced physical violence and intimidation when they sought to reclaim their children. Determined to find better employment for herself and her family, Harriet Hill resolved to take her children and leave her former master at the end of 1865. While her former master had no problem with Hill taking her young children, he refused to relinquish his hold on her three older children, who ranged in ages from seventeen to twenty-two, asserting that they "belonged to him" as always. When Hill came to get her children she was threatened with "a rope around her neck."[18] On a daily basis, the Freedmen's Bureau received visits from women like Hill who would walk ten or twenty miles in the hopes that the bureau would help them get their children back. If the bureau would not help, freedwomen attempted to resolve the problem themselves and faced being whipped, clubbed, knocked down, or choked. The efforts of freedwomen to reconstruct their families led Brevet Brigadier General John Eaton to conclude that mothers "were known to put forth almost superhuman efforts to regain their children."[19]

Freedpeople attempted to resist such arbitrary disruption of their domestic ties by seeking the legalization of their marriages and the formal recognition of their parental rights through the Freedmen's Bureau, which drew up marriage contracts for ex-slaves and listed the names and ages of their children. Although the bureau's marriage policy may have been motivated in part by racist myths about black sexual promiscuity, many freedpeople saw formal marriage contracts as a repudiation of slavery and a defense against the hostile policies of southern provisional governments. At a November 1865 convention of South Carolina blacks, for example, delegates insisted that "the sanctity of our family relations" was a corner-stone of freedom. "In slavery we could not have *legalized* marriage," they argued, "*now* we can have it."[20]

Health was another major concern for freedpeople coming out of the Civil War, a problem that one historian has called the "largest biological crisis of the nineteenth century."[21] The mobilization of huge armies and the mass displacement of populations not only created unhygienic condi-tions in military camps and surrounding regions but also introduced patho-gens to populations with little previous exposure to them. Because of their refugee status and chronic lack of medical attention, freedpeople were especially vulnerable to diseases both during the war and after. Totally unprepared for the size and scope of the epidemics that swept through the army, the Union military's medical staff had little time or inclination to respond to the terrible conditions that former slaves faced. Enduring malnutrition and exposure, they were routinely confined to hastily con-structed "contraband camps," which one historian has likened to holding pens. In the midst of the fighting, moreover, Union military authorities had evaluated the health or illness of black refugees mainly in relation to their ability to labor for the northern cause. Historian Jim Downs has shown that black men who appeared well enough to work were con-scripted for labor with the army or in "free labor" colonies like Port Royal, South Carolina, while those deemed physically unfit were relegated to camps where freedom was sharply limited and where the lack of adequate food and shelter caused disease and death.[22]

The creation of a Medical Division of the Freedmen's Bureau was an attempt to respond to these conditions, but its ability to alleviate the physical plight of freedpeople was compromised by extreme underfunding and a belief that consistent medical care for former slaves would reinforce their supposed inclination toward chronic dependency. Medical officials generally refused medical care to those deemed healthy enough to work

During the Civil War, escaped slaves were often confined to temporary "contraband camps" like this one in South Carolina where they were subject to labor conscription and exposed to unhealthy living conditions. (Library of Congress)

while consigning the elderly, orphans, and the permanently disabled to poorly funded asylums or almshouses. During periodic outbreaks of smallpox, moreover, such officials were also hampered by the widely held notion that African Americans were inherently more susceptible to the disease and that its prevalence among them might even result in their ultimate extinction. Despite growing knowledge about the environmental causes of disease among medical scientists, the government failed to respond effectively to the outbreak among blacks because they attributed it to "biological differences among the races."[23] White activists with abolitionist backgrounds often acted as advocates for sick and suffering freedpeople, but they were unable to dislodge the basic assumptions about race and labor that guided federal policy. Thus, in addition to the burdens placed on freedpeople by hostile state governments in the South and by a white population determined to curtail their economic and political activity, they also fought the ever-present, and perhaps even more intractable, specter of illness and disease.

A Freedmen's Bureau agent stands between two armed men and attempts to end the conflict between them. (Library of Congress)

Given the obstacles they faced, freedpeople understood that economic independence, either through fair wages or through the acquisition of land, was a critical element in making freedom a reality. Wartime free labor experiments had undermined racist myths of black indolence, and the confiscation of abandoned rebel lands in the South had opened the possibility that a class of black landowners might result from the conflict. For former slaves, landholding was extremely attractive because it would allow them to live and work on their own terms, not those dictated by whites seeking to preserve as much of the old slave labor system as possible, and to use their skills as farmers to good effect. Freedmen who called for land redistribution in the South, moreover, were aware of the lingering doubts about their capacity for hard work and they repeatedly assured white reformers and Freedmen's Bureau officials that personal property ownership was a surefire method to erase the dependencies of the old system. South Carolina black leader Richard Cain insisted that "the possession of lands and homesteads is one of the best means by which a people is made industrious, honest, and advantageous." He claimed that the system of contract labor, which had emerged under Union occupation in parts of the Deep South, would fail to spur black productivity and initiative because it so closely resembled the slave system. "As long as people are working on shares and contracts, and at the end of the year are in debt, so long will they and the country suffer," Cain argued. "But give them a chance to buy land, and they will become steady, industrious men."[24] During the early stages of Presidential Reconstruction, there was every reason to believe that at least some percentage of the southern black population would realize Cain's dream. In the Sherman Reserve along the Florida, Georgia, and South Carolina coasts, 40,000 freedpeople were living on 400,000 acres of confiscated land, and ex-slaves in other occupied areas of the South were calling upon the Freedmen's Bureau to sell abandoned lands at cheap prices.

But President Johnson's actions quickly undermined the economic aspirations of the freedpeople, especially their ambition to obtain title to confiscated land. In his May 1865 proclamations, the president ordered the return of confiscated land to its original owners, giving the Freedmen's Bureau the distasteful task of informing freedpeople that they would have to sign labor contracts with the white owners or be forcibly evicted from land they had once hoped to call their own. The leader of the Freedmen's Bureau, General O. O. Howard, was sympathetic to the plight of ex-slaves, and while he carried out the president's instructions to inform the freedpeople in the South Carolina Sea Islands of the new policy, he delayed its implementation on technical grounds for as long as possible. A similar dynamic occurred in the Sherman Reserve, where Rufus Saxton, a Union army general with an abolitionist background, ignored the claims of returning white landowners as long as possible in order to give Congress the time to challenge the president's policy. Saxton was disgusted by the prospect that the freedpeople, many of whom had served in the Union army, would be evicted in favor of ex-Confederates. He noted that ex-slaves "and their ancestors [had] passed two hundred years of unremitting toil" on the land and he could scarcely bring himself to believe that the government intended to "drive out these loyal men who have been firm and loyal" in the "darkest days" of the rebellion.[25]

The strategy of delay employed by Howard and Saxton nearly worked. The new Freedmen's Bureau legislation that was passed by Congress in early 1866 contained language confirming the legality of Sherman's field order and guaranteeing the freedpeople's right to stay on the land for several more years. But Johnson vetoed the Freedmen's Bureau Bill in the winter of 1866, and while Congress passed a new bill over his veto a few months later, the revised legislation was stripped of its earlier land-title guarantees. The result was the forcible eviction of freedpeople from the land and its immediate return to the original white owners, men who had only a year earlier been fighting in the Confederate army or serving in its counsels of war. On Edisto Island, South Carolina, where former slaves had been working the land independently for nearly four years, angry freedpeople petitioned President Johnson, asking him to remember that while white landowners had been leading secessionists, blacks had always been "true to this Union." Writing with a poignant sense of irony, they wondered why their "rights as a free people and good citizens of these United States" were less important than "those who were found in rebellion against this good and just government?"[26] Johnson was issuing thousands of pardons to former Confederates who appealed to him for the restoration of their citizenship and property, but freedpeople found that he had no interest in their plight. While the Republican Congress did offer cheap land to ex-slaves in the Homestead Act of 1866, the poor implementation of that measure was yet another consequence of Presidential Reconstruction.

With the hopes of land confiscation fading under Presidential Reconstruction, freedpeople sought to gain economic leverage through the ownership of their own labor power. In this effort, the Freedmen's Bureau was an important, if flawed, ally. As historian James Schmidt has noted, the bureau's role as a mediator in the new economic relationships emerging between the black laboring class and white landowners represented "an unprecedented intervention into social relations in general, and the labor market in particular," a role that would not be replicated by any U.S. government agency until well into the twentieth century.[27] But at the same time, bureau agents were products of a nineteenth-century middle-class culture that was deeply imbued with the free market values of self-help, efficiency, and productivity. Many entertained negative stereotypes about the work ethic of "others," a category which included immigrants, poor whites, and African Americans. Despite the wartime free labor experiments, therefore, the bureau's more than 500 agents struggled to balance their mandate to protect freedpeople from economic exploitation with their fears that bureau intervention would somehow reinforce habits of dependency they perceived among ex-slaves.[28] Given the intense demand for labor in the South following the war, this deep-seated ambivalence sometimes led bureau agents to neglect the interests of the freedpeople in favor of the landowners.

During the first two years of Reconstruction, for example, the bureau encouraged and oversaw the drafting and signing of labor contracts between ex-slaves and white employers, a process that generally pleased planters who were desperate for workers. Sharing far more in common culturally with southern whites than with blacks, some agents acted with unvarnished paternalism toward freedpeople and instructed them to lower their expectations for freedom. Bureau agent Charles Soule, for example, reprimanded the freedpeople of Orangeburg, South Carolina, for "talking too much; waiting too much; asking too much." He wanted them to understand that "all your working time belongs to the man who hires you . . . therefore you must not leave work without his leave, not even to nurse a child, or go and visit a wife or husband."[29] While Soule's policies restricted the physical mobility of freedpeople and encouraged obedience to the labor demands of landowners, other agents were less friendly to the planters and intervened in cases where whites sought to reimpose slave labor conditions. In Louisiana, for example, Agent John Brough was angered by the fact that many planters were "not disposed to settle upon fair terms" with the freedmen and adjudicated several disputes in favor of black workers.[30] Some bureau agents in the sugar parishes of Louisiana even confiscated harvests and arrested planters for failing to negotiate in good faith. But once contracts were agreed upon and signed by both parties, bureau officials generally upheld them, even if freedpeople insisted they were unfair. Trusting that the sanctity of contract was a foundation of free labor societies, they were determined to hold both parties to the agreement despite the frequently unequal nature of the original settlement.

Historians have been rightly critical of the Freedmen's Bureau's partiality toward planters in the process of negotiating contracts, but it is important not to discount more positive aspects of the agency's legacy. As historian Randall Miller has argued, the simple presence of the bureau in the South "altered the assumptions and calculus of local power and race relations" and at the very least signaled to whites that the system of slavery had ended.[31] In addition to its role in mediating labor relations, moreover, the bureau also oversaw the building, staffing, and administration of freedmen's schools, institutions that were essential to improving the economic condition and political empowerment of former slaves. By 1870, there were more than 4,300 such schools in the South with some 250,000 African American men, women, and children in attendance. Though not all were run directly by the Freedmen's Bureau, the agency nevertheless provided a critical impetus for their creation.[32]

The teachers who staffed these Freedmen's Bureau schools were often recruited by missionary organizations such as the American Missionary Association, and they approached their students with the same mixture of idealism and paternalism that Freedmen's Bureau agents displayed. But local southern whites, who understood that it would be more difficult to control an educated black population, regarded teachers at freedmen's schools with intense hostility. Deeply disturbed by the level of social equality with which some northern white teachers interacted with their students, one white southern observer complained that they "went in among the negroes, ate and slept with them, paraded the streets arm-in-arm with them."[33] It was the black teachers, however, whose situation was the most precarious, because in addition to the condescension they often received from white colleagues, they were correctly regarded by southern whites as potential leaders who would help freedpeople to negotiate fairer labor contracts and to organize politically. Threatened and sometimes killed by angry local whites, black teachers regularly called on the Freedmen's Bureau to protect their schools from the ever-present threat of arson.

While the Freedmen's Bureau was an important resource for African Americans seeking to realize their economic and educational aspirations, the southern black church provided critical spiritual and temporal resources for freedpeople as well. Under slavery, African American Christians had practiced their faith in both open and covert ways, often sitting in segregated galleries of white-led churches on Sabbath mornings while participating in secret religious gatherings on Sunday evenings. In those latter meetings, slave preachers had often expressed the Christian message in a highly liberationist language, with Moses and Jesus as prophets of freedom and the exodus story of the Bible as the central motif of scripture. After the 1831 rebellion in Virginia, an uprising led by black preacher Nat Turner, fearful southern whites attempted to suppress unauthorized religious meetings among slaves, but the distinctive theology of the slave church, and its physically and musically expressive styles of worship, survived in the secret "hush harbor" churches that still met on the edges of many southern plantations. At the same time, a more formal black church was emerging among free African Americans in the North, with an educated and politically active clergy at the helm of denominations such as the Philadelphia-based African Methodist Episcopal (AME) Church. Black regiments in the Civil War were often served by chaplains from these northern churches, men who accompanied soldiers into the South and then sometimes remained there to build new institutions among freedpeople. With the end of the war, therefore, came the opportunity for the covert slave church to take overt, institutional form and for northern black clergymen to extend their religious and political activism into the Reconstruction South.[34]

During Reconstruction, the black church served multiple purposes: as a symbol of the black community's geographical rootedness, as a meeting place where political and economic issues could be discussed openly without the presence of whites, and as a cultural center for the preservation and nurture of the community's spiritual values. Deserting the churches they had been compelled to attend along with their masters, African Americans overwhelmingly chose to support their own religious institutions, with Methodists flocking to the AME and the AME Zion churches and black Baptists choosing a multiplicity of options within that large, decentralized tradition.[35] For many of the former slaves who joined such churches, the political and spiritual meaning of the Civil War and its aftermath were inseparable. The destruction that had come upon the South, they believed, was a judgment of God upon the terrible system of slavery, and they looked to Reconstruction as the fulfillment of a process that began with the war and emancipation. Rev. Richard Cain, an AME pastor who would later be elected to represent South Carolina in the U.S. House of Representatives, viewed the wrecked remains of Charleston's mansions as "a monument of God's indignation and evidence of His righteous judgments."[36] Cain believed, as did other black ministers, that the founding of independent black churches and the political mobilization of the freedpeople were both critical steps toward the creation of a new, more righteous society that would receive God's blessings. Cain was just one among more than 240 black ministers who filled public offices during the Reconstruction years.[37]

But like freedmen's schools and their teachers, black churches (which often doubled as schools) and their ministers became increasing targets of white violence as Presidential Reconstruction unraveled in 1866. Republican leaders in Congress sometimes received letters like the one Thaddeus Stevens opened from a freedman in Arkansas reporting that a recently finished AME church where he lived had been burned down and that 24 black men, women, and children had been lynched nearby.[38] During the May 1866 race riot in Memphis, Tennessee, moreover, black schools and churches were key targets of mob violence, and the northern press focused on the destruction of these institutions as evidence of the need for more stringent Reconstruction legislation. Just a few days before the events in Memphis, *Harper's Weekly* reported on the burning of two black churches in Petersburg, Virginia. The magazine condemned the "wanton destruction of churches for no other reason than that they are frequented by colored people," and noted that while parts of one church had been saved from the flames, "the school room was entirely destroyed." Having heard that "a good feeling" had existed between the races in Petersburg, *Harper's* editors wondered what might be happening in places where blacks were the "objects of intense and unrelenting hatred?"[39] As news from Memphis came in, that question seemed to answer itself.

As former slaves asserted their own expansive understanding of freedom in the face of mounting white hostility, the political conflict between President Johnson and congressional Republicans reached a crisis point. The stunning Republican victories in the fall elections of 1866 had emboldened the president's critics to pass legislation weakening his influence over Reconstruction and proposing alternative policies to be administered by Congress. Although moderates like Fessenden and Trumbull were still in the majority, they no longer had any illusions about working with Johnson. His vetoes of the Freedmen's Bureau and Civil Rights Bills as well as his overt role in obstructing the ratification of the Fourteenth Amendment in the South convinced them that he would likely undermine other Congressional Reconstruction policies. The result was the passage of legislation that curtailed presidential power in unprecedented ways. In order to ensure that the impending expiration of the congressional session would not leave Johnson in control as it had in the spring of 1865, for example, they called for a special session that would begin right after the scheduled adjournment on March 4th. The huge and more radical

Republican majority elected in November 1866 thus convened a full nine months before the traditional date, taking their seats immediately upon the close of the previous session.

Once the 39th Congress had ensured that the transition to the new Congress would be uninterrupted, it then passed a series of important and controversial legislative acts to control the president. First, over Johnson's irate veto, Congress passed the Tenure of Office Act, a law that required explicit senatorial consent to the removal of any official who had previously been appointed by the president and then confirmed by the Senate. Although it was unclear whether the law prevented Johnson from removing officials appointed by President Lincoln, Congress was intent on using it to protect the position of Secretary of War Edwin Stanton, now a key ally of House and Senate leaders. Republicans also hoped to prevent the president from obstructing their plans for Reconstruction by curtailing his power as commander in chief. In a clause added to the Army Appropriations Act of 1867, Congress insisted that the president's directives to military commanders be communicated first to the general in chief, Ulysses S. Grant, before they were passed onto field officers. Congress also restricted the president's ability to remove Grant. Like Stanton, Grant had become disgusted with Johnson and congressional Republicans regarded him as reliable in the event that riots like those in Memphis and New Orleans were repeated elsewhere in the South. With these actions, Congress demonstrated its intention to chart "a bold and independent course with regard to the President."[40]

Having severely limited the president's options, Congress turned its attention to the far more complex and difficult task of designing a substantive alternative to his Reconstruction policies. Given the structural weakness that opposition Democrats faced as long as southern representatives were barred from Congress, the main challenge to achieving a new plan was the ongoing differences among Republicans. President Johnson described all Republicans who opposed his policies as "radicals," but his designation obscured significant variations within the party over key issues. On questions such as black suffrage, the disenfranchisement of ex-Confederate whites, the redistribution of confiscated land, the extent and duration of military rule in the South, and even the constitutional basis for Reconstruction policies, there was substantive disagreement among Republicans. But as historian Michael Les Benedict has noted, Johnson's

tendency to call his all opponents by the same name was mirrored in contemporary press accounts, and for much of the twentieth century it led historians to overstate the amount of unity in the Republican Party during
Reconstruction.[41] Among Republican leaders at the time, however, the
differences were very clear and required delicate negotiations over policies
where high-stakes issues were being decided. The opposition Democrats
also appreciated the serious divisions within the majority party and,
despite their inability to control events, sought to exploit their opponents'
internal factionalism wherever possible. Thus, the image of a united
radical Republican program for Reconstruction is inaccurate and should
be replaced by an understanding that Congressional Reconstruction legislation, including such "radical" measures as the Fifteenth Amendment,
was always the product of political compromise hammered out amidst
rapidly shifting intraparty alliances.

At one end of the Republican Party spectrum were congressmen like
Thaddeus Stevens of Pennsylvania and George Julian of Ohio who consistently championed laws that would effect a thoroughgoing transformation
of Southern society. With stronger ties to the prewar abolitionist movement, these men believed that the twin evils of slavery and rebellion had
corrupted Southern society to such an extent that the political restoration
of southern states should be delayed until both had been thoroughly rooted
out.[42] Some radicals argued that the act of rebellion against the United
States had reduced ex-Confederate states to territorial status, meaning that
they could be administered directly by Congress, the military, and a federally appointed governor until their institutions had been thoroughly
regenerated. To effect such far-reaching change, moreover, radicals argued
that most former rebels should be disenfranchised and the political process
placed in the hands of loyal southerners, by which they meant freedmen
and white southern Unionists. A coalition of this kind would not only
ensure loyalty, they insisted, but might also pave the way for land reform,
publicly financed schools, and the improvement of infrastructure. In the
absence of such changes on the state level, most radicals were willing to
use federal legislation to ensure the development of both a biracial democracy and a free labor economy in the South. The events of 1865–1866,
radicals believed, proved conclusively that rebellious white southern
Democrats intended to reimpose slavery, elect disloyal men to federal
office, and re-create the brutal, lawless culture that radicals insisted had

Congressman Thaddeus Stevens was a leader among radical Republicans who sought expanded federal powers in order to effect far-reaching changes in the South. (Library of Congress)

caused the war. What "rebellious districts" of the South needed, insisted George Julian, "was not an easy and speedy return to the places they had lost by their treasonable conspiracy," but rather a lengthy probationary period during which they would "prove their fitness for civil government." To more conservative leaders who insisted that republican forms of government were all that were necessary for readmission, Julian argued that "forms are worthless in the hands of an ignorant mob."[43]

While more moderate Republicans shared at least some views in common with men like Julian, fewer of them had been abolitionists before the war and they generally viewed issues such as black suffrage pragmatically, not idealistically. At the core of their differences with radicals was a "constitutional conservatism" that rejected the territorialization of the South as too drastic a departure from traditional American political culture. While the defeated rebel states remained "in the grasp of war," they had not lost their identity under the Constitution. Rather than impose political or social change upon the South from Washington, moreover, moderates believed that change must come from within the South itself, as the product of state governments controlled by loyal voters. In the Fourteenth Amendment, they had stopped short of a federal mandate for black suffrage and, despite the terrible events of 1866, they still shrank from such a bold assertion of national power over the states. The moderates were also worried about the financial costs of a long-term military occupation of the South, which would likely rise substantially if the radicals' far-reaching goals were sanctioned. During congressional debate over the Military Reconstruction Acts, however, moderates came to accept that African American suffrage, conferred by revised state constitutions and protected by reorganized state governments, might in fact offer practical solutions to the problems of Reconstruction. Black suffrage was presented as both a political necessity—without black voters white Unionists could not organize loyal governments—and a principled act in support of political equality. As so many of the freedmen's conventions had argued, moderates came to believe that enfranchised freedpeople might use the vote to defend themselves, their property, and their freedom without the presence of the government or the Union army.[44]

Negotiations among Republicans resulted in the passage of the Military Reconstruction Acts in 1867, legislation that demanded a complete reorganization of southern states. State governments established under Johnson's plan were denied legal status and, with the exception of Tennessee, all ex-Confederate states were placed under military rule. Now divided into five districts to be supervised by military officials, southern states were told that restoration to the Union would depend upon the adoption of new state constitutions that ratified the Fourteenth Amendment and enfranchised black men. The first law was passed on March 2, 1867, and it contained language that prohibited ex-Confederate leaders from participating in constitutional conventions and explicitly authorized black men to do so. When southern whites made it clear that they would choose to "remain in limbo under military rule" rather than comply with the provisions of the new law, a supplementary act placed implementation in the hands of military officials.[45] The commanding general of each district was instructed to register explicitly loyal voters without respect to race, thus bypassing uncooperative local whites and setting the stage for state conventions that could undertake significant reforms. In July, yet another law increased the power of the military governors over existing state governments, giving them the authority to "suspend or remove from office" officials of any "so-called State" that obstructed the implementation of the law, as well as the power to appoint more cooperative replacements.[46]

In the Military Reconstruction Acts, Congress assumed greater power to remake state governments and dictate the terms for readmission to the Union. President Johnson, who opposed the specifics of the plan and the congressional assertion of power, vetoed all three bills. In what was now a familiar pattern to all involved, Congress easily overrode each veto. Johnson argued that the Military Reconstruction Act assigned too much power to the commanding officers of the military districts, turning them into absolute monarchs. He also maintained that Congress had violated the Constitution and state sovereignty when it tried "to change the entire structure and character of State Governments" by mandating suffrage.[47] Congressman James Blaine acknowledged that the Military Reconstruction Act "was the most vigorous and determined action ever taken by Congress in time of peace," but argued that white southern resistance to Congressional Reconstruction made it necessary.[48] Suffrage had only become a condition for readmission after white Southerners rejected more moderate options, including the Fourteenth Amendment. Blaine argued that the victorious Union and not the defeated Confederacy should decide the terms of Reconstruction and any settlement depended upon there being a population of loyal men. To those who suggested that uneducated black men were not qualified to vote, Blaine responded that "a poor man, an ignorant man, and a black man, who was thoroughly loyal, was a safer and a better voter than a rich man, an educated man, and a white man, who, in his heart, was disloyal to the Union."[49]

African Americans were elated by the abrupt turn in Reconstruction policy that the Military Reconstruction Acts signified. William Beverley Nash, a former slave who was soon to run as a delegate to the South Carolina state constitutional convention, felt "that the clock of civilization has been put forward by a hundred years."[50] Blacks throughout the South began to organize in advance of the constitutional conventions where they would now play a critical role. In Mobile, Alabama, for example, a freedmen's convention declared that since their "political oppressors" intended to use "unfair and foul means" to prevent them from organizing, they would henceforth regard themselves as "part of the Republican Party of the United States and the State of Alabama."[51] Black churches went into high gear mobilizing their congregations to participate, and one minister confessed that as soon as "politics got in our midst ... our revival or religious work for a while began to wane."[52] Political rallies among the freedpeople seemed to be going on everywhere in the South, a testament not only to the courage of former slaves but also to the strength of the nascent institutions they had built and protected in the immediate postwar period.

Ex-Confederate southern whites, by contrast, were horrified by the new laws and found it difficult to see anything but disaster resulting from them. Upon hearing of the passage of the Reconstruction Acts, South Carolina planter William Richardson described himself as the most "miserable & wretched" man in all the world. He predicted that southern states would be "subjugated to the negroes completely & all our offices will be filled by them," and that blacks would "divide our lands" amongst themselves.[53] In the face of what looked to them like a revolutionary shift in social and political norms, planters experienced an unfamiliar sense of powerlessness and confusion. Cooperation with the new biracial governments to be organized under military rule seemed inconsistent with the principles of honor and white supremacy that were so deeply entrenched in their culture. Yet withdrawal from political life would mean surrendering entirely to the will of a political system that seemed bent on destroying the society for which they had sacrificed during the war. One white Southerner insisted that to be "debased and degraded below the negro is very hard," but it was equally impossible to "join a party and say Hurra for those who has put me Politically below a negro."[54] Though it would take time to emerge, such men would eventually develop a strategy of counterrevolutionary political violence that would prove a grave threat to the entire project of Reconstruction.

NOTES

1. Andrew Johnson, speech in Cleveland, September 3, 1866, in *The Papers of Andrew Johnson*, vol. 11, ed. Paul H. Bergeron (Knoxville: University of Tennessee Press, 1994), 176.

2. Oliver P. Morton, speech at Masonic Hall, June 20, 1866, in William Dudley Foulke, *Life of Oliver P. Morton: Including His Important Speeches*, volume 1 (Indianapolis: Bowen-Merrill, 1899), 475.

3. On the break over the 14th Amendment, see Robert Sawrey, "Give Him the Hot End of the Poker": Ohio Republicans Reject Johnson's Leadership on Reconstruction," *Civil War History* 33 (June 1987), 155–172.

4. Andrew Johnson, speech in Cleveland, September 3, 1866, in *The Papers of Andrew Johnson*, vol. 11, 177.

5. "Congress," *Harper's Weekly*, November 17, 1866, 722; *Harper's Weekly*, October 27, 1866, 674; James M. McPherson and James K. Hogue, *Ordeal by Fire: The Civil War and Reconstruction* (New York: McGraw-Hill, 2010), 563.

6. Hans Trefousse, *The Radical Republicans: Lincoln's Vanguard for Racial Justice* (New York: Knopf, 1969), 350.

7. Eric Foner, *Forever Free: The Story of Emancipation and Reconstruction* (New York: Vintage, 2005), 82.

8. Leon F. Litwack, *Been in the Storm So Long: The Aftermath of Slavery* (New York: Vintage, 1979), 296-7.

9. Ibid., 302.

10. Thavolia Glymph, *Out of the House of Bondage: The Transformation of the Plantation Household* (New York: Cambridge University Press, 2008), 146–163.

11. John David Smith, *Black Voices from Reconstruction, 1865–1877* (Gainesville: University Press of Florida, 1997), 51.

12. Stephen V. Ash, *A Year in the South: 1865* (New York: Harper Collins, 2002), 141–142.

13. Joel Williamson, *After Slavery: The Negro in South Carolina during Reconstruction, 1861–1877* (Chapel Hill: University of North Carolina Press, 1965), 310.

14. Litwack, *Been in the Storm*, 250.

15. Ibid.

16. Ibid., 237.

17. Mary J. Farmer-Kaiser, *Freedwomen and the Freedmen's Bureau: Race, Gender, and Public Policy in the Age of Emancipation* (New York: Fordham University Press, 2010), 103.

18. Georgia Freedwoman to the Freedmen's Bureau Acting Assistant Commissioner for Georgia, February 5, 1866, in *Freedom: A Documentary History of Emancipation, 1861–1867*, series 3, vol. 2, *Land and Labor, 1866–1867*, eds. Rene Hayden, Anthony E. Kaye, et al. (Chapel Hill: University of North Carolina Press, 2013), 576–577.

19. Farmer-Kaiser, *Freedwomen and the Freedman's Bureau*, 96.

20. Amy Dru Stanley, *From Bondage to Contract: Wage Labor, Marriage, and the Market in the Age of Slave Emancipation* (New York: Cambridge University Press, 1998), 39–40; Nancy Cott, *Public Vows: a History of Marriage and the Nation* (Cambridge: Harvard University Press, 2000), 86.

21. Jim Downs, *Sick From Freedom: African American Illness and Suffering during the Civil War and Reconstruction* (New York: Oxford University Press, 2012), 168.

22. Ibid., 7–17.

23. Ibid., 103.

24. Smith, *Black Voices from Reconstruction*, 82.

25. William S. McFeely, *Yankee Stepfather: General O.O. Howard and the Freedmen* (New Haven: Yale University Press, 1968), 127.

26. Foner, *Forever Free*, 77–78.

27. James D. Schmidt, " 'A Full Fledged Government of Men': Freedmen's Bureau Labor Policy in South Carolina, 1865-1868," in *The Freedmen's Bureau and Reconstruction: Reconsiderations*, eds. Paul A. Cimbala and Randall M. Miller (New York: Fordham University Press, 1999), 250.

28. Randall M. Miller, "Introduction: The Freedmen's Bureau and Reconstruction: An Overview," in *The Freedmen's Bureau*, xix.

29. Charles Soule to the Freed People of Orangeburg District, [June 1865], in *Freedom: A Documentary History of Emancipation, 1861–1867* series 3, volume 1: *Land and Labor, 1865*, eds. Steven Hahn et al. (Chapel Hill: University of North Carolina Press, 2008), 220.

30. John C. Rodrigue, "The Freedmen's Bureau and Wage Labor in the Louisiana Sugar Region," in *The Freedmen's Bureau*, 202.

31. Miller, "Introduction," *The Freedmen's Bureau*, x.

32. Ibid., xxxviii.

33. Litwack, *Been in the Storm*, 491.

34. For information on the black church, see Daniel W. Stowell, *Rebuilding Zion: The Religious Reconstruction of the South, 1863–1877* (New York: Oxford University Press, 1998), 80–99; Michael Battle, *The Black Church in America: African American Christian Spirituality* (Malden, MA: Blackwell Publishing, 2006), 43–65.

35. Stowell, *Rebuilding Zion*, 74–79.

36. Litwack, *Been in the Storm*, 456.

37. Foner, *Forever Free*, 87.

38. Douglas R. Egerton, *The Wars of Reconstruction* (New York: Bloomsbury Press, 2014), 144.

39. *Harper's Weekly*, May 19, 1866, 317–318.

40. Brooks D. Simpson, *The Reconstruction Presidents* (Lawrence: University Press of Kansas, 1998), 112–113.

41. Michael Les Benedict, *A Compromise of Principle: Congressional Republicans and Reconstruction, 1863-1869* (New York: W.W. Norton, 1974), 23.

42. Trefousse, *Radical Republicans*, 4–5.

43. Harold M. Hyman, ed. *The Radical Republicans and Reconstruction, 1861–1870* (New York: Bobbs-Merrill Company, 1967), 365.

44. Xi Wang, *The Trial of Democracy: Black Suffrage & Northern Republicans, 1860–1910* (Athens: University of Georgia Press, 1997), 39.

45. McPherson and Hogue, *Ordeal by Fire*, 567.

46. "Supplement to the Reconstruction Act," July 19, 1867, in Hyman, 404.

47. Andrew Johnson, veto of the First Military Reconstruction Act, March 2, 1867, in *The Papers of Andrew Johnson*, vol. 12, ed. Paul H. Bergeron (Knoxville: University of Tennessee Press, 1995), 91.

48. James G. Blaine, *Twenty Years of Congress*, vol. 2 (Norwich, CT: The Henry Bill Publishing Co., 1886), 262.

49. Ibid., 264.

50. Williamson, *After Slavery*, 337.

51. Smith, *Black Voices*, 91.

52. Foner, *Reconstruction*, 282.

53. James L. Roark, *Masters Without Slaves: Southern Planters in the Civil War and Reconstruction* (New York: W.W. Norton, 1977), 186.

54. Ibid., 189.

CHAPTER 4

CONGRESSIONAL RECONSTRUCTION AT HIGH TIDE

T he defeat of Presidential Reconstruction and the advent of more radical policies toward the South were made possible in part by the northern public's outrage at ex-Confederates' political intransigence and their unwillingness to accept free labor practices. As historian Heather Cox Richardson has suggested, many Northerners believed that there was a clear connection between the resurgence of the prewar elite in the South and the continued stagnation of the region's economy. They read press accounts suggesting that prosperity reigned in areas where amicable relations existed between black workers and white landowners, while white-initiated racial violence had left other areas stagnant and unproductive. The eagerness of former slaves to acquire education, their enthusiasm to purchase land, and their general aspiration to improve themselves struck many northern whites as quintessential traits of free workers. By contrast, southern whites seemed primarily interested in thwarting these legitimate desires through wanton violence and property destruction. Although antebellum whites in both sections had often blamed the work ethic of enslaved African Americans for what they saw as southern economic backwardness, it now looked as if blacks were more than happy to work efficiently as free laborers if only the white South could accept that slavery was dead. And so despite their discomfort with the expansion of government power that accompanied the Reconstruction Acts of 1867, majorities in the North came to accept that voting rights for freedpeople, protected by the military, was the only means to ensure their freedom and the economic rejuvenation of the South.[1]

Most Northerners were eager for eventual reconciliation with southern whites, but they wanted it on terms that were consistent with their understanding of Union victory in the war. When crop failures in the spring of 1867 left many Southerners, both black and white, on the brink of starvation, for example, churches and charitable organizations across the North went into high gear to provide relief to the suffering.[2] Republican Senator Henry Wilson of Massachusetts hoped that the time had come when "the passions, prejudices, and bitter memories," of the war could be put aside in pursuit of national reunion.[3] But at the same time, the Republican press insisted that lasting reconciliation would never be successful if it handed over power to those guilty of causing the war. *Harper's Weekly* rejected as "the very ecstasy of folly" the idea that the war had been a "silken joust of arms" in which the victor would simply "bow gracefully to the defeated knight and invite him to dinner that all may be serene." Any attempt to achieve a lasting reconstruction of the nation by allowing the "late rebels to resume control of the various States that attempted secession" would be, they argued, "incalculably disastrous."[4]

For hundreds of thousands of veterans of the Union army, moreover, men whose suffering and dedication had ensured the success of their nation's cause, it was especially important to create a lasting and just peace that acknowledged both the guilt of secessionists and the wrong of slavery. As they organized the Grand Army of the Republic (GAR), the largest veterans association in the North, former soldiers often took pains to insist that the war had been "a conflict between right and wrong – between truth and error."[5] Though most of these men had gone to war only to preserve the Union, the experience of waging war in the South convinced at least some that the destruction of slavery, and with it the power of slaveholders, was the only way to save their nation. Since slavery was "the sole cause of the rebellion," declared a soldier from the Midwest, failure to stamp it out completely would "give but a breathing spell for a renewed struggle."[6] Recent studies have shown that many GAR units across the North were integrated and allowed black and white soldiers to generate a shared memory of their "won cause" that preserved an emancipationist view of the conflict. Though it is impossible to know how most Union soldiers voted in congressional or presidential elections, it seems likely that sizeable numbers of them would have regarded any policy that surrendered the lessons learned in the war as a betrayal of their shared sacrifice.[7]

At the same time, however, there were also clear contradictions within northern political culture that would eventually weaken support for Reconstruction. Perhaps the most significant was the ambivalence with which northern voters approached the question of black suffrage. While many Northerners came to support equal suffrage for African American men in the South, only five northern states had themselves granted blacks the vote and there was little reason to suspect that this would change dramatically after the war. In part, this reflected the nature of partisan politics in the North, where Democrats remained a potent force on the state level. Correctly assuming that the enfranchisement of blacks would benefit the Republicans, they used blatant racism to erode support for expanded suffrage. In 1865, for example, Connecticut Republicans who attempted to amend the state constitution to enfranchise African Americans were met by a furious Democratic opposition describing blacks as a "degraded element" and condemning the amendment as "an outrage that could only be conceived by fanatics."[8] The Democratic *Hartford Times* insisted that "Negroes have shown as yet no capacity to compete with the white race in the march of civilization." Although Republicans continued to back it, popular support for the amendment wilted under the Democratic assault and it failed to pass in a referendum held in October 1865. Six other states, including Wisconsin, Minnesota, Kansas, Ohio, New York, and the Nebraska territory, rejected black suffrage. While most Republicans supported equal voting rights, the Democrats had been able to defeat the measures by drawing enough conservative Republicans into antisuffrage coalitions.[9]

A similar ambivalence existed in northern political culture with respect to the legal and economic issues surrounding more radical Reconstruction policies. The image of former slaves as independent farmers was common in the North, but widespread belief in limited government and the sanctity of property rights meant that there was also great reluctance to embrace land confiscation as a means toward that end. In March 1867, when Thaddeus Stevens introduced legislation calling for widespread land redistribution in the South, the response in many parts of the North was negative, with some opponents accusing Stevens of inciting a class war in the South that might eventually engulf the entire nation. Although African Americans and their radical allies in the North believed that generations of uncompensated labor entitled former slaves to "forty acres and a mule," the dominant free labor ideology insisted that government intervention on such a large scale would violate the rights of white landowners and erode the nascent work ethic of the freedpeople. "The only class we know that takes other people's property because they want it," argued the editor of the *New York Tribune*, "is largely represented in Sing Sing [prison]."[10] The increasing labor unrest in postwar northern cities fueled concerns of property owners that wealth confiscations in the South might become precedents for working-class political movements in the North. The *New York Times*, a moderate Republican paper, feared that land confiscation would produce a more general "war on property."[11] Insisting that black suffrage alone guaranteed that the economic opportunities of former slaves would be protected by law, then, the northern public generally opposed land redistribution as a radical and ultimately illegal social experiment.[12] These attitudes suggested that radical policies would face an increasingly skeptical and divided northern public.

In the short term, however, the implementation of the Reconstruction Acts of 1867 was reshaping the political realities in the South and generating the conditions for a full-scale constitutional crisis in Washington. Beginning in the fall of 1867, states in the five military districts began the process of electing delegates to constitutional conventions, which, if they followed the requirements set down by Congress, paved the way for their readmission to the Union. A dramatic but complex new reality took shape, as African American men entered the southern political landscape for the first time. Blacks constituted a majority of the whole population only in South Carolina and Mississippi, but with a segment of the white population disqualified due to loyalty requirements, they comprised a slim majority of the qualified voters in all southern states. Their numerical advantage, however, did not ensure the ratification of new state constitutions. Since existing law stipulated that constitutions must be approved by a majority of registered voters, white Democrats could block their ratification by registering to vote and then staying home on election day. In early 1868, a proposed constitution in Alabama was defeated by this strategy of "abstention." Congress responded with a fourth Reconstruction Act, passed in March 1868, requiring only a majority of those who actually voted to ratify the constitutions. Even so, ex-Confederates had shown a high degree of unity and cleverness in resisting a Reconstruction process that depended upon state action.

Yet despite the opposition of white Democrats, the state constitutional conventions were remarkable gatherings and they produced landmark documents in the political history of the South. Louisiana's convention, for example, met in the same New Orleans building where black delegates had been shot to death by a white mob a year earlier. The dominant group at the Louisiana convention was a coalition of freedpeople and northern-born white Republicans, with African Americans making up just over 50 percent of the total number of delegates. Meeting for more than three months, the convention endorsed full equality before the law for all citizens, irrespective of race, and extended voting rights to all adult males who had resided in the state for at least a year. High-ranking ex-Confederates, or those ex-rebels who were obstructing the Reconstruction process, were disenfranchised. South Carolina's convention, which met in Charleston for the first time in January 1868, was an equally powerful statement of Reconstruction's potential to alter what had been the South's most proslavery state. In addition to guaranteeing legal equality and universal manhood suffrage, the majority African American convention joined Louisiana in endorsing an integrated public school system and in protecting the poor against the seizure of their property for debt.[13] Protections for debtors not only benefitted those African Americans who had managed to acquire modest property holdings but also poor southern whites who were struggling to survive economically. Although a few of the conventions discussed modest efforts to make cheap land available to former slaves, none of the conventions seriously debated the sort of property redistribution advocated by Thaddeus Stevens.

But the most important achievement of the southern constitutional conventions of 1867–1868 was the creation of political systems in which African Americans could participate as voters and as office holders at every level. That freedpeople were more than ready to assume such a role is powerfully demonstrated in the rise of the Union League movement. These were originally secret political associations affiliated with the Republican Party and often promoted by the Freedmen's Bureau, which had emerged during the darkest days of Presidential Reconstruction. Angered by the black codes and the exploitative labor practices of the planters, blacks had flocked to clandestine meetings with northern white Republicans and southern Unionists where they discussed the rights of citizenship, formulated strategies to resist Democratic Party resurgence, and considered the possibility of armed resistance should ex-rebels adopt violent tactics.

If an earlier generation of historians condemned the leagues for manipulating ignorant ex-slaves for political gain, recent works have shown conclusively that African Americans used these organizations to address their own concerns about the coercive practices that were being used on plantations in the rural South. It was hardly difficult for league organizers to convince African Americans that the Democratic Party was hostile to their interests, and the movement provided freedpeople with essential information about registering to vote and about candidates who were likely to support the welfare of rural blacks. Southern planters clearly believed that Union League membership made their workers harder to control. Attempting to explain why his laborers suddenly did not work "as well as they did before," one Alabama landowner simply pointed to the fact that "they all belong to the union league."[14]

If the political education provided by the Union Leagues helped to prepare and mobilize the mass of the southern black population, the emergence of a strong cadre of black leaders was also essential for the partisan struggles that would occur under Congressional Reconstruction. As historian John Hope Franklin has shown, the diversity of their backgrounds makes it nearly impossible to create a composite portrait of African American leaders during Reconstruction. But on the whole they were experienced, literate men who understood that a moment of extraordinary promise was at hand. In Charleston, South Carolina, for example, only a small number of black political leaders were listed as illiterate, and several of the city's key leaders were men who had received some form of higher education. Free blacks like Francis Cardozo, Richard Cain, and Martin Delaney, for example, had either received formal college degrees or had at least a year of college instruction. Cardozo, who had been born in Charleston to a Jewish father and a free black mother, went on to study for the ministry in Edinburgh, Glasgow, and London. Martin Delaney had studied to become a physician at Harvard Medical School and, despite being forced to leave because of the racial hostility of white students, went on to practice medicine in the Midwest. During the Civil War, he had become a commissioned officer in the Union army, eventually reaching the rank of major.[15]

Former slaves were also represented in South Carolina's political leadership class, with Robert Smalls as perhaps the state's most famous African American leader. Held as a slave in Charleston during the war, Smalls had daringly sailed a Confederate transport vessel, the *Planter*, past

A former slave whose daring escape from
Confederate Charleston, South Carolina, made
him a celebrity in the North, Robert Smalls was
elected to Congress during Reconstruction.
(Library of Congress)

Confederate harbor defenses where he turned it over to the Union forces
blockading the city. Becoming an instant hero to many Northerners,
Smalls worked diligently to acquire the literacy skills he had been denied
as a slave and returned to lead his native state during Reconstruction.
During the constitutional convention in 1868, he introduced language
making free education open to and compulsory for all of the state's citizens.
Although the backgrounds of men like Robert Smalls and Francis Cardozo
were remarkably different, they both possessed a deep sense of the value of
education to former slaves.[16]

Black political leaders did not agree on everything, however, and as
they worked toward creating a new South, the differences over strategy
and tactics sometimes caused fissures that southern white Democrats

were able to exploit. Among the most serious was the question of re-enfranchising ex-Confederates who had been disqualified from voting under the Fourteenth Amendment and the Military Reconstruction Acts. While many white radicals in the South were committed to long-term disenfranchisement of former rebels, some African American leaders feared that such policies would deepen racial antagonisms and dilute the universal suffrage ideals upon which blacks based their claims to political power. Former slave Beverly Nash, another South Carolina leader, gave voice to these feelings when he imagined a time when "you would see the white man and the black man standing with their arms locked together, as the type of friendship and union which we desire."[17] Whether the time had come to act on such hopes was a question that black and white Republican leaders in the South would continue to debate in the face of increasing violence by white Democrats.

As men like Nash and Smalls prepared to run for office, serious legal challenges to the reorganization of southern politics emerged. In 1867, in fact, there was reason to believe that the U.S. Supreme Court might invalidate congressional legislation on Reconstruction because a year earlier the justices had issued two decisions that had angered radicals in Congress. In *Ex parte Milligan*, the court had undermined the legitimacy of military law in the South by insisting that military tribunals could not be used to try private citizens as long as civil courts were open. In *Cummings v. Missouri*, moreover, the court had ruled that public officials could not be required by state governments to take loyalty oaths as a condition for holding office. Democrats were delighted by these developments with the *New York World* advising radical Republicans "to give due weight to the fact that the Supreme Court is an insurmountable barrier in their unconstitutional designs."[18] Perceiving the court as a potential opponent, congressional Republicans tried various means to restrict judicial power, including an unsuccessful measure requiring a two-thirds vote of Supreme Court justices in decisions that struck down acts of Congress.

While congressional Republicans sought mechanisms to protect legislation from judicial interference, Democrats hoped that the court would rule on the constitutionality of the Military Reconstruction Acts. In a series of cases that came before the Supreme Court in 1867, southern states sought injunctions against the enforcement of the laws. Because of the specifics of each case, the suits were dismissed and the evenly divided Supreme Court chose neither to invalidate nor to sustain the Military Reconstruction Acts. Although it would later intervene more directly to limit federal enforcement of the Fourteenth Amendment and other guarantees of black rights, the 1867 court insisted "the matters involved, and presented for adjudication, are political and not judicial, and, therefore, not the subject of judicial cognizance."[19]

Opponents of Reconstruction found President Johnson a far more reliable ally than the Supreme Court, as he seemed perpetually willing to risk a dramatic showdown with Congress over political matters. Almost as soon as the Military Reconstruction Acts were passed, the president sought to limit their effect and soon drew the ire of congressional radicals who had already raised the possibility of impeaching him in January 1867. A key point of contention was the president's insistence that military commanders in the five southern districts had no right to remove civil officials from office with the exception of those who had been officially disenfranchised by the Fourteenth Amendment. When General Philip Sheridan of the Louisiana and Texas district removed the officials responsible for the New Orleans massacre of 1866, for example, Johnson censured him and secured a ruling from Attorney General Henry Stanbery declaring their removal illegal. Johnson also clashed with General Daniel Sickles who had issued orders to establish a racially inclusive jury system in South Carolina. Against the wishes of both Secretary of War Edwin Stanton and General in Chief Ulysses S. Grant, the president fired both Sickles and Sheridan and installed more conservative commanders in their place.[20]

In addition to causing a resurgence of violence in the Deep South, Johnson's actions prompted a clash between the president and Secretary Stanton, a man whom congressional Republicans had relied on to moderate executive obstructionism. By the terms of the recently passed Tenure of Office Act, Johnson could not fire Stanton outright, but he took advantage of a congressional adjournment to suspend the secretary and appoint an interim candidate in his place. In choosing Ulysses S. Grant as the new head of the War Department, however, Johnson installed someone who was deeply uncomfortable with the confrontational path the president had chosen.

The fall elections of 1867 seemed to bolster Andrew Johnson's position. Several northern black suffrage amendments had gone down to defeat, and the Democrats had taken power in the key states of Ohio and New York.

But as he had done a year earlier, Johnson misread the political tea leaves and overplayed his hand. When Congress reconvened at the beginning of December 1867, the president sent a message to the Senate informing them of his reasons for suspending Secretary of War Stanton and formally appointing Grant. When the Senate rejected his request, Johnson instructed Grant to block Stanton's return until such time as the Supreme Court could rule on the constitutionality of the Tenure of Office Act. After Grant refused to be complicit in the president's schemes, Johnson attempted to discredit the popular Union general by leaking information to the press and suggesting that Grant was conspiring with Stanton. In early 1868, the confrontation with Congress intensified as Johnson defied the Senate, removed Stanton from office, and appointed General Lorenzo Thomas as secretary of war. Around the same time, the president continued his obstructionist behavior and removed two more pro-Reconstruction military commanders and appointed successors whose actions hindered the ratification of new state constitutions in Alabama and Georgia.[21]

By this point, Republican moderates had come to believe that the president was out of control and could not be trusted to uphold the law, either in Washington or in the South. The redoubtable old radical Thaddeus Stevens, resolute yet weakened by illness, implored the House of Representatives to impeach the president. Using his characteristic hyperbole, Stevens proclaimed that Johnson was "guilty of as atrocious attempts to usurp liberty and destroy the happiness of this nation, as were ever perpetrated by the most detestable tyrant whoever oppressed his fellow men."[22] On March 2–3, 1868, the House gratified Stevens's wishes and passed 11 articles of impeachment against Johnson, insisting that by his actions, the president had brought the highest office of the land into "contempt, ridicule, and disgrace, to the great scandal of all good citizens."[23] The specific charges of the indictment focused on the president's violation of the Tenure of Office Act, with eight of the eleven articles detailing the many ways in which he had attempted to circumvent or violate the law in his effort to replace Secretary of War Stanton. The remaining articles accused Johnson of bringing Congress into disrepute and of undermining specific legislative acts. Whatever its legal merits, the language of the indictment seemed inadequate as an expression of the deep divisions between Johnson and his enemies. Far from demonstrating

Andrew Johnson's trial before the United States Senate began on March 4, 1868, and lasted eleven weeks before the prosecution fell just one vote short of a conviction. (Library of Congress)

Johnson's role as "the most detestable tyrant," the articles of impeachment were, in the words of one historian, "painfully narrow and obscurely legalistic" and accused him "of misapplying a personnel statute."[24]

The decision to impeach President Johnson remains one of the most controversial acts in American political history, and historians have often been extremely critical of what they regard as a politically motivated assault on the office of the presidency. The fact that impeachment centered on Johnson's alleged violation of the Tenure of Office Act, a law that was declared unconstitutional in the twentieth century, has added to the view that the attempt to remove him from office was illegitimate.[25] What were the "high crimes and misdemeanors" that Johnson was supposed to have committed, scholars have asked, beyond his violation of a constitutionally questionable statute passed by his political detractors? But as Annette Gordon-Reed has observed, the United States Constitution provides very few options for dealing with a president who is periodically incompetent and consistently unwilling to carry out executive functions consistent with the spirit of the law. No president can be forced to resign, and unlike a parliamentary system such as that of Great Britain, it is impossible to alter the executive branch of government through a vote of "no confidence" in the leader. Yet the House vote on impeachment in March 1868 was strikingly similar to the removal of parliamentary executives in that it was a straight, party-line vote by a majority in the legislature calling for a removal of its own titular leader. And some contemporary legal scholars had promoted what was known as a "broad view" of impeachment, one suggesting that even if no "high crime" had been committed, a president could be removed for "acts of misfeasance and malfeasance that damaged the office."[26]

It is also important to note that the decision to impeach Johnson was not simply the decision of radical Republicans. The adoption of articles of impeachment in March 1868 came after a series of earlier votes in which radical Republicans had unsuccessfully sought to bring the president to trial. In January 1867, moderate Republicans on the House Judiciary Committee had declined to recommend impeachment, and a second attempt in December 1867 failed as well, indicating that moderates were reluctant to pursue a potentially divisive policy in the lead-up to a presidential election. There was also concern that should Johnson actually be removed from office, radical senator Benjamin Wade of Ohio, as president pro tempore of the Senate, would become the chief executive of the United States. Conservative Republicans loathed Wade so much that many of them were willing to put up with Johnson in order to avoid putting the Ohio senator in power. One Washington newspaper predicted that "if impeachment fails, be sure of one fact – dislike for Mr. Wade has done it."[27] In addition to his radical positions on the South, Wade's support for high tariffs, inflationary monetary policy, and women's suffrage threatened to divide the Republican Party at a time when unity was absolutely essential. Despite their concerns about any and all of these issues, moderate House Republicans were horrified enough by the conduct of the president that they temporarily put aside their differences with radicals and voted for impeachment.

President Johnson's trial before the Senate began on March 4, 1868, and it lasted for more than two months with Chief Justice Salmon P. Chase presiding. From the beginning, Johnson's defense team, which included a former Supreme Court justice, conducted itself with great effectiveness. Although Johnson had threatened to appear before the Senate in person should proceedings move against him, his lawyers were able to prevent what would certainly have been a highly detrimental personal clash between the president and his detractors. In general, they argued that the indictment against the president was politically motivated and based upon a flagrantly unconstitutional law, the Tenure of Office Act, which threatened to destroy the constitutional principle of separation of powers. William Evarts, the conservative Republican lawyer who defended the president, insisted that Johnson's motives in removing Secretary Stanton were not criminal, but rather stemmed from his desire to produce a constitutional challenge to what he regarded as an intolerably bad law. The defense also created significant doubts as to whether the Tenure of Office Act even applied in the case of Secretary of War Stanton since he had been appointed by Abraham Lincoln rather than Andrew Johnson.[28] Although radicals in the Senate continued to support removal, moderate support began to waver as the trial went on. Concern over a Wade presidency and the terrible damage it might inflict on the party in the fall elections of 1868 led many moderates to seek a solution short of removing the president from office. Thus when Iowa Republican senator James Grimes received personal assurances from Johnson that an acquittal would not mean renewed obstruction of the Military Reconstruction Acts, enough moderate Republicans defected to ensure that the final pro-removal tally, 35:19, was just a single vote short of the two-thirds required for conviction.[29]

Johnson's narrow escape from the ignominy of removal did not restore his political fortunes. Although his continued cultivation of southern conservatives extended to pardoning ex-Confederate President Jefferson Davis in December 1868, he ceased the disruptive policy of removing officials sympathetic to the Reconstruction Acts. Thus Congress was now able to ignore the president and turn its full attention to the reorganization of the ten southern states still under military occupation, a project moderates hoped to complete before the fall elections took place. Just a few weeks after the Senate's acquittal of Johnson, in fact, seven ex-Confederate states had complied with the terms of the Military Reconstruction Acts, including the ratification of the Fourteenth Amendment, and were ready to re-enter the Union. These states, which included Alabama, Arkansas, Florida, Georgia, Louisiana, North Carolina, and South Carolina, were subsequently readmitted to the Union by congressional action. Although the radicals were able to attach language to the readmission bills prohibiting these states from any future attempts to disenfranchise African Americans, historians have noted that radicals had failed to achieve much of what they had wanted from Congressional Reconstruction. If there was to be any property redistribution, guarantees for universal education, or extended disenfranchisement of ex-rebels, those goals would have to be achieved by the new state governments rather than by federal action.[30] Most importantly, the emergence of a biracial democracy in the South would hinge on the willingness of the federal government to enforce established rights against attacks by resurgent white Democrats in the South.

Enforcement, of course, would depend largely on the man who would occupy the White House during the next four years, and moderate Republicans were nearly united in their belief that Ulysses S. Grant should be the next president. Without a clear candidate of their own, radicals were largely willing to support Grant, and his open support for the Military Reconstruction Acts meant that he faced no serious opposition at the convention in Chicago. The only point of contention occurred over the party platform, which radicals hoped would endorse a constitutional amendment guaranteeing the political rights of African Americans. Opposition to black suffrage was still strong in the North, however, and since the Democrats were likely to engage in their traditional politics of race baiting in the upcoming election, moderates blocked any language committing their party to such an amendment. But renewed attacks on black political power in the South during the fall of 1868 suggested that some form of national suffrage guarantee might be necessary to ensure the success of Reconstruction. In Georgia, for example, a coalition of white Republicans and conservative southern Democrats formed an alliance to expel the black legislators who had recently been elected under that state's new constitution, claiming that blacks were disqualified for office under the new state constitution.[31] Congress would eventually rescind Georgia's readmission to the Union until it reversed its policy toward black officeholders, but similar attacks on freedpeople's political rights were happening all over the South. Although Grant was running for president under the ambiguous slogan "Let Us Have Peace," there seemed little peace for those who were struggling to create a biracial democracy in the ex-Confederate states.

Grant's victory over New York Democrat Thomas Seymour in the 1868 presidential election provided further impetus toward a suffrage amendment. According to Congressman James Blaine, many Republicans were "heartily ashamed" that the party had been so inconsistent—the Military Reconstruction Acts imposed black suffrage on southern states, but northern states were "free to decide the question for themselves."[32] As a result, black men remained disenfranchised in half of the northern states and all of the border states in 1868. In this mixed environment of pragmatism and principle, then, debate on the suffrage amendment began as soon as Congress reconvened in December. Almost immediately disagreement centered on whether the states or the federal government had the authority to determine qualifications for voting. Radicals favored an affirmative guarantee that all men over 21 would have the right to vote—a proposal that would enlarge the power of the federal government. Moderates, on the other hand, insisted that the authority to set qualifications should remain with the states, but they were willing to place some restrictions on what states could do. There was consensus that race could not be used to restrict voting, but some insisted that other obstacles such as literacy, nativity, or property qualifications should not be permitted either. In addition to these concerns, some members of Congress, responding to the situation unfolding in Georgia, argued that race could not be used to disqualify a person from voting or office holding.[33]

In the final version that passed on February 26, 1869, the Fifteenth Amendment reflected the compromise position of moderate Republicans. It asserted that the citizens of the United States could not be denied the right to vote, either by federal or state governments, on the basis of "race, color, or previous condition of servitude." Historian Xi Wang has argued that the amendment recognized "the principle of political equality between black and white male Americans," without directly conferring suffrage on anyone.[34] Many of the radicals were disappointed by the fact that it did not guarantee suffrage for African Americans, but only prevented states from explicitly using race to disenfranchise them. They were well aware that other devices, such as literacy tests, grandfather clauses, and poll taxes, could be used to deny freedpeople the vote. But as one prominent historian has argued, Republicans believed that broader guarantees would "jeopardize the prospects of ratification in the North" where many states wanted the right to erect barriers to the voting rights of immigrants and the poor.[35] Republicans in California, for example, were unwilling to accept the Fifteenth Amendment if it meant that Chinese immigrants would have the vote.

This print commemorates the Fifteenth Amendment. It contains the text of the amendment and two columns equating the advancement of science and education with the extension of voting rights for former slaves. The print includes scenes of a black teacher with young students as well as images of industrious black laborers. African American political leaders Frederick Douglass (bottom left) and Hiram Revels (bottom right) are included while the top portion focuses on white benefactors: Abraham Lincoln (center), President U.S. Grant and Vice President Schuyler Colfax (top left) and John Brown and Hugh Lenox Bond (top right). Schneider & Fuchs, 1870. (Library of Congress)

But radicals in the North were also split because of another weakness of the Fifteenth Amendment, its failure to include any language guaranteeing women's suffrage. Prior to the Civil War, an organized women's rights movement, closely associated with radical abolitionism, had emerged in the North, holding its first convention at Seneca Falls, New York, in 1848. Some of the movement's key leaders, women such as Elizabeth Cady Stanton, Susan B. Anthony, and Lucy Stone, had become staunch supporters of the Republican Party during the war and played an important role in lobbying Congress and President Lincoln to move more quickly on emancipation and black rights. At the same time, women across the North had bolstered the Union war effort in crucial ways, working in federal arsenals and other war-related industrial production, tending farms in the absence of men, and serving as nurses and relief workers in organizations such as the United States Sanitary Commission, the Christian Commission, and the Women's Central Relief Association. For many of those activists who had advocated full citizenship and political equality before the war, the overwhelming patriotism women had shown during their nation's greatest crisis provided an even more powerful argument for removing gender as a barrier to suffrage.

The end of slavery and the subsequent national debate over the political future of freedpeople further encouraged women's suffrage activists to make a strong stand in favor of full citizenship for women. They were shocked, therefore, to find that section two of the Fourteenth Amendment, which was designed to encourage the enfranchisement of African Americans, punished states for denying voting rights only to "male inhabitants," thereby injecting gendered language into the Constitution for the first time. Elizabeth Cady Stanton, who was angered by the fact that fellow abolitionist Wendell Phillips was supporting the amendment because it opened the possibility of black suffrage, demanded to know if Phillips believed that "the African race is composed entirely of males?"[36]

Convinced that they needed a movement of their own, women's rights campaigners met in New York City in May 1866 to create the American Equal Rights Association, an organization committed to overturning legal and political discrimination based on race and gender at all levels of government. As the struggle for black rights intensified, however, radical Republicans increasingly proved unwilling to work for both causes simultaneously, insisting that the ongoing violence against blacks in the South required more immediate attention than women's rights. Frederick Douglass, who had supported gender equality throughout his long career as an abolitionist, now declined to pursue women's rights and freedmen's rights together, insisting that "the cause of the negro is more pressing" than that of women.[37]

In 1869, this tension came to a head during the debate over the Fifteenth Amendment which, while banning disenfranchisement on the basis of race, said nothing about gender. In effect, the women's rights movement was forced to choose between two extremely unpalatable

options. They could support an amendment that provided a thin guarantee
of voting rights for black men while effectively denying any such rights to
white or black women, or they could oppose the amendment despite decades of work by women's rights activists on behalf of emancipation and racial
equality. The divergent answers that suffrage activists gave to this question
resulted in a bitter split in the American Equal Rights Association, with
Elizabeth Cady Stanton and Susan B. Anthony opposing the ratification of
the Fifteenth Amendment and other activists led by Lucy Stone and Julia
Ward Howe favoring it. During the summer and fall of 1869, these divisions
resulted in the creation of two rival suffrage organizations, the National
Woman Suffrage Association led by Stanton and Anthony and the
American Woman Suffrage Association led by Stone and Howe. Yet even
amidst their ongoing factionalism, the activism of both groups ensured that
gender equality would remain a vital aspect of American culture.

Although it was unlikely that the opposition of the National Woman
Suffrage Association alone would prevent the ratification of the Fifteenth
Amendment, the repeated defeat of black suffrage amendments in
northern states in the years following the Civil War meant that ratification
was not guaranteed. Ratification occurred easily in those northern states
where the Republican Party was firmly in control, but the process was contentious in states where the Democratic Party was strong. In Ohio, for
example, where Democrats held a majority in the state legislature at the
time the Fifteenth Amendment passed the U.S. Congress, the amendment
was initially defeated. After Republicans eked out a tiny majority in the
fall 1869 elections, a second vote was held and the amendment passed by
the slimmest of margins.[38] In New York, the situation was reversed.
Republicans in Albany managed a successful ratification vote in 1869,
but resurgent Democrats held a second vote rescinding ratification in early
1870. In the West, Democrats successfully played on fears that the
Fifteenth Amendment would enfranchise Chinese immigrants, and
the amendment only passed in Nevada. As a result, the final passage of
the amendment required southern support and all of the ex-Confederate
states, except Tennessee, ratified the Fifteenth Amendment within
one year. Those southern states already readmitted to the Union
had implemented black suffrage under the Military Reconstruction Acts
and thus ratification did not significantly alter the political landscape.
Texas, Virginia, Mississippi, and Georgia, however, had not yet been

Elected president in 1868, Ulysses S. Grant
supported Congressional Reconstruction and
worked for the ratification of the Fifteenth
Amendment. (Library of Congress)

readmitted to the Union, and Congress mandated the ratification of the
Fifteenth Amendment as a condition for the readmission of those states.[39]

When U.S. Secretary of State Hamilton Fish certified that the Fifteenth
Amendment had been ratified on March 30, 1870, the high tide of
Congressional Reconstruction had been reached. For Congressman James
Garfield, the amendment conferred "upon the African Race the care of
its own destiny. It places their fortunes in their own hands."[40] Increasingly,
Republicans voiced the opinion that since formal political equality had
been achieved, the authority of Congress over the political reorganization
of the South should be at an end.

Whatever the limits of this view, the major decisions of Reconstruction
would now occur in the southern states themselves, where an alliance

between African Americans and white Republicans had come to power under the new state constitutions. But white southern Democrats, some of whom were disenfranchised by section three of the Fourteenth Amendment or by the terms of new state constitutions, remained a powerful force in the region, and they had arrived at two overlapping approaches to dealing with a new order they refused to accept as permanent. The first strategy among those who were free to participate in southern politics was to seek political office in the Reconstruction state governments and then work to destroy them from within. In Georgia, for example, this approach had nearly succeeded in completely unraveling the gains made under Reconstruction, with the total expulsion of African American officeholders averted only by the direct intervention of Congress to rescind the state's readmission to the Union. The second strategy was to use organized violence to prevent the new Republican-led governments in the southern states from functioning effectively and to terrorize the black population away from the voting booth. This approach was spearheaded by secret, but heavily armed, white supremacist organizations that were often made up of ex-Confederate soldiers and their officers. Although they went by many names in different parts of the South, the best known of them was an organization founded in Pulaski, Tennessee, called the Ku Klux Klan.

As historian George Rable has shown, the Ku Klux Klan "had an overriding purpose—the destruction of the Republican Party in the South."[41] While the preservation of a white-dominated society was a commitment shared by all who joined the Klan or similar white supremacist organizations, that goal was understood in the postwar period as achievable only by demolishing the biracial political alliance made possible by Congressional Reconstruction. Between 1866 and 1868, such organizations emerged in nearly every southern state, and they mobilized violent resistance to the machinery of Reconstruction. This included attempts to prevent the election of delegates to state constitutional conventions, efforts to scuttle the ratification of the constitutions themselves, and campaigns to disrupt the election of the new governments created under those documents. In order to avoid arrest and prosecution by military authorities, Klansmen concealed their identities beneath hoods that covered all but the eyes, nose, and mouth, and they often appeared at the homes of politically active African Americans in the dead of night. Committing murders, inflicting brutal beatings, burning homes, and destroying livestock, violent white supremacists attempted to convince blacks and some white Republicans that the personal costs of political participation were too high. One Klan sympathizer in South Carolina said that the organization would "teach the misguided African to stand in the subordinate position nature intended."[42] The Klan was not formally supported by the state governments as antebellum slave patrollers had been, but the two groups were similar in their intention to suppress the black population socially, economically, and politically. Insisting that emancipated blacks were a threat to the social order, white supremacists were determined to use any means necessary to restore it.

As southern states were readmitted to the Union, the most immediate threat to black freedom and Republican rule was the possibility that white southern Democrats would form an effective, coordinated alliance with these organized white supremacist vigilantes. Signs that such an alliance was in the offing appeared throughout the South in 1868, with Democratic newspapers printing notices from anonymous Klansmen threatening violence against those who supported Republican positions on the state and local level.[43] But under military occupation, most white Democratic Party leaders in the South kept a public distance from violent militias, even when they approved of them privately. After all, it was egregious acts of violence against blacks and white Republicans that had discredited Presidential Reconstruction and handed over control of the postwar settlement to moderate and radical Republicans in Congress. But shrewd white Democrats like Mississippi's Lucius Quintus Lamar came to understand that ongoing racial violence against blacks might itself become an argument against Reconstruction. If the violence went on long enough, Lamar told a political friend, Congress would have to conclude that Reconstruction itself, not the racist lawlessness of southern whites, was the problem. "I have not given you as distinct an idea of my plan as I thought of giving," Lamar wrote with judicious circumspection, "but you can probably glimpse it."[44]

Yet even as the long-term success of Congressional Reconstruction hung in the balance in the South, a difficult and important road had been traveled since 1866. Congress had defeated President Johnson's disastrous policies and built a constitutional foundation around which a new southern political culture had emerged. All of the ex-Confederate states had been restored to the Union by 1870, and African American suffrage had become, at least in formal, legal terms, a national standard. White Southerners viewed Congressional Reconstruction as revolutionary, but it hardly satisfied radicals. It had consisted mainly in the enactment of four Military Reconstruction Acts, the passage and ratification of the Fourteenth and Fifteenth Amendments, and the unsuccessful attempt to remove Andrew Johnson from office. Radical Republicans in Washington had been important participants and sometimes leading figures in the congressional program, but their proposals for the Fifteenth Amendment had been rejected, they had failed to convict Andrew Johnson in the Senate, and they had been forced to abandon land confiscation entirely. If the South was to be transformed in the way that radicals like Thaddeus Stevens and Charles Sumner had envisioned, that transformation would have to come through the actions of black and white Southerners themselves.

NOTES

1. Heather Cox Richardson, *The Death of Reconstruction: Race, Labor, and Politics in the Post-Civil War North, 1865–1901* (Cambridge: Harvard University Press, 2001), 34, 41.

2. Ibid., 26.

3. David Blight, *Race and Reunion: The Civil War in American Memory* (Cambridge: Harvard University Press, 2001), 50–51.

4. *Harper's Weekly*, February 22, 1868, 115.

5. Caroline E. Janney, *Remembering the Civil War: Reunion and the Limits of Reconciliation* (Chapel Hill: University of North Carolina Press, 2013), 110.

6. Chandra Manning, *What This Cruel War Was Over: Soldiers, Slavery, and the Civil War* (New York: Vintage, 2007), 152.

7. Barbara A. Gannon, *The Won Cause: Comradeship in the Grand Army of the Republic* (Chapel Hill, University of North Carolina Press, 2011), 145–146.

8. This quote and the *Hartford Times* quote are both in Lex Renda, " 'A White Man's State in New England': Race, Party and Suffrage in Civil War Connecticut," in *An Uncommon Time: The Civil War and the Northern Front*, eds. Paul A. Cimbala and Randall M. Miller (New York: Fordham University Press, 2002), 262.

9. Eric Foner, *Reconstruction: America's Unfinished Revolution, 1863–1877* (New York: Harper & Row, 1988), 223.

10. James M. McPherson and James K. Hogue, *Ordeal By Fire: The Civil War and Reconstruction* (New York: McGraw-Hill, 2010), 549.

11. Foner, *Reconstruction*, 309.

12. Richardson, *Death of Reconstruction*, 47.

13. Richard L. Hume and Jerry B. Gough, *Blacks, Carpetbaggers, and Scalawags: the Constitutional Conventions of Radical Reconstruction* (Baton Rouge: Louisiana State University Press, 2008), 172.

14. Michael W. Fitzgerald, *The Union League Movement in the Deep South: Politics and Agricultural Change during Reconstruction* (Baton Rouge: Louisiana State University Press, 2002), 148.

15. John Hope Franklin, *Reconstruction After the Civil War* (Chicago: University of Chicago Press, 2013), 88–89; William Hine, "Black Politicians in Reconstruction Charleston, South Carolina: A Collective Study, *Journal of Southern History* 49 (November 1983), 561.

16. Philip Dray, *Capitol Men: the Epic Story of Reconstruction through the Lives of the First Black Congressmen* (New York: Houghton Mifflin, 2008), 47.

17. Franklin, *Reconstruction*, 90; Michael W. Fitzgerald, *Splendid Failure: Postwar Reconstruction in the American South* (Chicago: Ivan R. Dee, 2007), 80–83.

18. Stanley I. Kutler, *Judicial Power and Reconstruction Politics* (Chicago: University of Chicago Press, 1968), 34; Hans Trefousse, *The Radical Republicans: Lincoln's Vanguard for Racial Justice* (New York: Knopf, 1969), 374.

19. Lawrence Goldstone, *Inherently Unequal: The Betrayal of Equal Rights by the Supreme Court, 1865-1903* (New York: Walker & Company, 2011), 54; Stanley I. Kutler, "Ex Parte McCardle: Judicial Impotency? The Supreme Court and Reconstruction Reconsidered," *American Historical Review* 72 (April 1967), 838; Kutler, *Judicial Power*, 96–113.

20. James G. Hollandsworth, Jr., *An Absolute Massacre: The New Orleans Race Riot of July 30, 1866* (Baton Rouge: Louisiana State University Press, 2001), 153.

21. Brooks Simpson, *The Reconstruction Presidents* (Lawrence: University Press of Kansas, 1998), 121–123.

22. David O. Stewart, *Impeached: The Trial of President Andrew Johnson and the Fight for Lincoln's Legacy* (New York: Simon & Schuster, 2009), 151.

23. The Articles of Impeachment, 1868 in *The Political History of the United States of America During the Period of Reconstruction, from April 15, 1865 to July 15, 1870*, ed. Edward McPherson (Washington: Philp & Solomons, 1871), 266–270.

24. Stewart, *Impeached*, 156.

25. In 1887, Congress repealed the Tenure of Office Act and in 1926, it was ruled unconstitutional by the U.S. Supreme Court in *Myers v. US*.

26. Annette Gordon-Reed, *Andrew Johnson* (New York: Henry Holt, 2011), 132.

27. Michael Les Benedict, *A Compromise of Principle: Congressional Republicans and Reconstruction, 1863–1869* (New York: W.W. Norton, 1974), 300.

28. Stewart, *Impeached*, 212–18; David Herbert Donald, Jean Harvey Baker, and Michael F. Holt, *The Civil War and Reconstruction* (New York: W.W. Norton, 2001), 572–573.

29. Simpson, *Reconstruction Presidents*, 126–127.

30. Benedict, *A Compromise of Principle*, 324.

31. Franklin, *Reconstruction*, 131.

32. James G. Blaine, *Twenty Years of Congress: From Lincoln to Garfield*, vol. 2 (Norwich, CT: The Henry Bill Publishing Company, 1886), 412.

33. Xi Wang, *The Trial of Democracy: Black Suffrage & Northern Republicans, 1860–1910* (Athens: University of Georgia Press, 1997), 42–43.

34. Ibid., 46.

35. Foner, *Reconstruction*, 446–447.

36. Ellen Carol DuBois, *Feminism and Suffrage: the Emergence of an Independent Women's Movement in America, 1848–1869* (Ithaca: Cornell University Press, 1979), 60.

37. Ibid., 167.

38. Kevin F. Kern and Gregory S. Wilson, *Ohio: A History of the Buckeye State* (Malden, MA: Wiley Blackwell, 2014), 244.

39. LaWanda and John H. Cox, "Negro Suffrage and Republican Politics: The Problem of Motivation in Reconstruction Historiography,"*Journal of Southern History*, 33 (August 1967), 318–319; Wang, 49–50.

40. Simpson, *Reconstruction Presidents*, 144.

41. George Rable, *But There Was No Peace: The Role of Violence in the Politics of Reconstruction* (Athens: University of Georgia Press, 2007), 95.

42. Joel Williamson, *After Slavery: The Negro in South Carolina during Reconstruction, 1861–1877* (Chapel Hill: University of North Carolina Press, 1965), 264.

43. Fitzgerald, *Splendid Failure*, 66.

44. Nicholas Lemann, *Redemption: The Last Battle of the Civil War* (New York: Farrar Straus and Giroux, 2006), 97.

CHAPTER 5

RECONSTRUCTION IN THE STATES

A mong the most radical results of Reconstruction was the rise of black voters and officeholders in the South. Because of the requirements for readmission laid down in the Military Reconstruction Acts and the subsequent ratification of the Fifteenth Amendment, reorganized southern states formally recognized blacks as citizens and conferred political rights on adult black men. Blacks overwhelmingly supported the Republican Party, not because it perfectly represented their interests, but rather because they associated the party of Abraham Lincoln with emancipation and black citizenship. The result was the creation of Republican majorities in all 11 of the ex-Confederate states and the election and appointment of African Americans to positions of leadership and power. But since blacks constituted the majority of the population in only Mississippi and South Carolina, they could not govern without making alliances with white Republicans, either native-born southern men who saw the need for change or northerners who had resettled in the South following the war. With the disfranchisement of a portion of the white population due to federal and state proscriptions, these alliances were able to control politics into the 1870s. These coalitions were often mired by corruption and internal factionalism, but they brought about remarkable results as well. Public education, infrastructure improvements, and integrated public facilities were just some of the most positive results of southern Reconstruction.

But the foes of Reconstruction state governments in the South were well organized, and their powerful opposition rhetoric created a negative mythology about Republican rule that has remained part of the American culture ever since. White southern Democrats, who were horrified at the possibility of African American political power, regarded Republican governments as a reversal of the natural racial hierarchy that they believed placed whites over blacks. Thus, even when the facts showed that whites remained a majority, Democrats consistently described the Reconstruction state legislatures as instruments of "Negro domination," or as President Andrew Johnson put it, the "Africanization" of the South. Since they believed that blacks were inherently incapable of using political power responsibly, white Democrats insisted that African Americans were either vile agents of corruption and misrule, or the willing dupes of corrupt white Republicans who exploited their ignorance and credulity for their own gain. Unsure whether to describe blacks as the clownish puppets of whites or savage revolutionaries seeking to prey upon white southern women, Democrats used both images to suggest that Reconstruction had subjugated white civilization to the forces of barbarism. This image of black politics in the Reconstruction South was memorialized in D. W. Griffith's 1915 film *The Birth of a Nation*, which was based on a novel called *The Clansman* (1905) written by Thomas Dixon, who grew up in Reconstruction North Carolina. In language that summarized white Southerners' deepest fears, Dixon described life under the Reconstruction governments as a "Negro reign of terror," and celebrated the Ku Klux Klan as liberating the South from the "chains of Negro rule" and the "black abyss of animalism."[1]

This image of Reconstruction is inaccurate, not only in its racist assumptions but also in its basic description of how power was distributed in state governments throughout the South. As John Hope Franklin has shown, "Blacks were not in control of the state governments at any time anywhere in the South," and they struggled to obtain the highest offices that were available in Republican-controlled administrations.[2] Although Mississippi blacks were the clear majority in both population and registered voters, for example, they were never able to achieve power commensurate with their numbers. They constituted 40 of the 115 members of the first Mississippi legislature that met after the adoption of the new state constitution, and they hardly monopolized local offices even in the river counties where blacks outnumbered whites by huge majorities. Blacks in South Carolina held 55 percent of the seats in the state legislature in 1868, but even there the governorship continued to be filled by white Republicans.[3] Outside Mississippi and South Carolina, moreover, the underrepresentation of blacks was a significant problem throughout Reconstruction. In the state of Texas, for example, only 19 African

Americans served as legislators in the entire period before the return of Democratic rule and in North Carolina the number was just 30.[4]

Though black "domination" was a racially charged myth, African Americans did become increasingly assertive over time and ultimately wielded a level of political power that would have been unthinkable before the Civil War in either the North or South. Over 800 African Americans served in state legislatures and an even larger number held county and municipal offices. In Louisiana, the site of some of the period's most vicious antiblack riots, 87 black legislators served in the state House of Representatives during Reconstruction and P. B. S Pinchback became the first African American to serve as governor when the sitting executive was suspended from office in late 1872. Blacks served as lieutenant governor in three states, treasurer in two, secretary of state in three, and secretary of education in four, while others sat on state supreme courts or acted as attorneys general.[5] In addition, 16 African Americans served in either the United States Senate or the House of Representatives in the period between 1865 and 1877, a sight that pleased radicals and horrified conservatives in the North and South.

Hiram Revels, elected as a U.S. Senator from Mississippi in January 1870, took the seat that had been vacated 10 years earlier when Jefferson Davis resigned it in order to become President of the Confederacy. Born to a free black family in North Carolina, Revels had attended college briefly before taking up a career as a minister and serving as chaplain to a black regiment from Maryland during the Civil War. White Southerners attempted to prevent him from being seated, denying that he was a citizen of the United States and conjuring up false accusations about a criminal past, but radicals like Charles Sumner leapt to his defense and he was sworn in on February 25, 1870. One of his first acts was to demand congressional action against Georgia for its recent expulsion of all black delegates from the state legislature. Uncomfortable with the extensive number of offices held by African Americans at all levels of politics, one northern journalist referred to the political transformation as "the spectacle of a society suddenly turned bottomside up."[6]

A second aspect of opposition mythology was that of the "carpetbagger," a term that white southern Democrats used to demonize northerners who settled in the postwar South and who became officeholders in

Republican-controlled state governments. The carpetbag itself was a cheap nineteenth-century carrying case, and critics argued that northern-born Republicans were generally men of slender means whose meager belongings could fit inside such a small container before they managed to enrich themselves by pillaging and defrauding the defeated South. According to this view, the carpetbagger professed sympathy for African American rights but was really a malevolent charlatan who manipulated ignorant blacks solely for the purpose of obtaining wealth and power. The origins of the myth can be found at the beginning of Congressional Reconstruction, when some southern conservatives attempted to woo black voters away from the Republican Party and its radical policies. In 1868, for example, Virginia conservative W. M. Elliot warned blacks in the state that northern carpetbaggers were using them "as the mere instruments by which to acquire office."[7] But the image became a regional trope, encompassing everything that white Southerners detested about both the North and the effects of Congressional Reconstruction. Albion Tourgée, an Ohio-born Union army veteran who served as a judge in Reconstruction North Carolina, wrote that southern whites viewed carpetbaggers as the "incarnation of Northern hate, envy, spleen, greed, hypocrisy, and all uncleanness."[8]

Like the myth of "Negro domination," the image of the unprincipled carpetbagger was generated in part by the sense of loss and helplessness that many white southern Democrats felt under Reconstruction and in part as a tactic to discredit their political enemies. Historian Richard Current has argued that while carpetbaggers certainly did not come "close to candidacy for sainthood," they were neither as numerous nor as venal as their critics alleged. Coming from far more affluent backgrounds than the southern stereotypes suggested, most had served as officers in the Union army and therefore possessed much higher levels of skill and education than was acknowledged by Democratic propaganda. Neither did they all come to the South with the intention of manipulating inexperienced African American voters. Many had arrived in the region during the war or during Presidential Reconstruction when any form of black suffrage seemed highly unlikely. In addition, many of them were involved in reform activities including free labor experiments, the education of freedmen, and missionary work well before engaging in politics.[9]

Their initial foray into politics came during the constitutional conventions held in the South in 1867–1868, and they did play something of an

Condemned as a "carpetbagger" by white southern Democrats, Adelbert Ames of Maine was a former Union general who was twice elected as the Republican governor of Mississippi during Reconstruction. (Library of Congress)

outsized role in the reorganization of new state governments under Congressional Reconstruction. According to one historian, some 17 percent of the delegates to these state constitutional conventions were "recent arrivals" from the North, and they often represented districts with high percentages of freedpeople. But evidence also suggests that carpetbaggers like Adelbert Ames of Maine, who served two terms as governor of Mississippi, sincerely believed in legal and political equality for African Americans. There is little doubt that some carpetbaggers were guilty of corruption, but they were no more prone to venality than white Democrats. If carpetbaggers were often "young men in a hurry," eager to invest and make profit in the postwar American economy, they were no different than their contemporaries in every other region of the country.

At the same time, many brought needed capital and managerial expertise to a devastated South lacking both for revival.[10]

Given their relatively small numbers, which never exceeded a few thousand in the Reconstruction South, carpetbaggers achieved political office by cultivating the support of African Americans and a growing number of white southern Republicans. Democrats referred to this latter group as "scalawags," meaning that they were traitorous men who were willing to turn their backs on their region and their race to curry favor with northern Republicans. Scalawags presented southern Democrats with a serious problem because they demonstrated that significant division existed within the white South over the region's future, and their persistent support for the Republican Party threatened to create a permanent partisan alternative to the Democrats. It was essential, therefore, to discredit the moral legitimacy of southern-born Republicanism, and as such the creation of the scalawag mythology was at least as important as notions of carpetbag corruption and Negro domination. Scalawags, then, were often caricatured as scoundrels, thieves, and swindlers. Southern writer Thomas Dixon described a scalawag as a "Judas Iscariot who sold his people for thirty pieces of silver, which he got for licking the feet of his conqueror and fawning on his Negro allies."[11] Like the carpetbaggers, they were understood to be poor and uneducated and therefore driven more by impulses and passions than reason. They were the "mean, lousy and filthy kind that are not fit for butchers or dogs," wrote South Carolina Democrat Wade Hampton.[12]

Despite the hyperbolic language used by men like Hampton, scalawags are not easily categorized. In general, southern white Republicans were dissenters, either critics of the pre-Civil War planter aristocracy, opponents of secession, victims of repressive wartime policies, or some combination of all of these.[13] Some were former members of the antebellum Whig party, but historians have found that they were more likely to come from upcountry or mountainous regions of the South rather than from plantation districts.[14] Perhaps because of their sense of alienation from the political economy that had supported slavery and cotton production, many scalawags had an interest in the economic transformation of the South that the Republican Party was promising. At the same time, their harsh experiences as Unionists in the Confederate South meant that some scalawags nursed serious grievances against the dominant planter class and

Among the most powerful images of Reconstruction was that of the evil northern carpetbagger intent on exploiting the defeated South. Historians have shown that these images were largely politically motivated myths that were designed to discredit Republican-controlled state governments in the region. (Library of Congress)

they were horrified by Andrew Johnson's willingness to return power to those who had caused secession and tyrannized over dissenters. Eager to keep the old Democratic Party leadership out of politics as long as possible, scalawags generally supported long-term disenfranchisement of ex-rebels and endorsed black suffrage as a practical means of reshaping the political landscape of the South. Among the most famous scalawags was ex-Confederate General James Longstreet, who, though he fails to fit the social profile of most southern-born white Republicans, nevertheless played an important role in Louisiana's Reconstruction government. In May 1869, he accepted a patronage position as customs surveyor of New Orleans from President Grant, a decision that led some former comrades to regard him as a "leper" and led later southern historians to view critically his military leadership in the Confederate army.[15]

The governments created by this alliance of black and white Republicans in the South have been the subject of intense scrutiny by historians. In the early twentieth century, scholars such as William Dunning and John Burgess condemned them as illegitimate, incompetent, and utterly corrupt, constituting a "mere travesty of civilized government." Starting from the premise that black suffrage was "the blunder-crime of the century," they interpreted the problems of Republican rule in the South as evidence of blacks' incapacity to use political power responsibly.[16] What these historians were either unable or unwilling to acknowledge was that the portraits of Republican misrule in the South were often deliberately exaggerated by those who brought them down through campaigns of violence and terrorism. For those who were determined to reestablish white rule in the South, it was essential to stigmatize Reconstruction governments so that "any means were deemed acceptable" to destroy them.[17] The rhetoric of the so-called redemption movements that swept Republicans from power in the South and returned political control to white-supremacist Democrats in the mid-to-late 1870s thus became the basis of historical interpretation for the first half of the twentieth century. In 1947, for example, historian E. Merton Coulter described the African American delegates to the South Carolina legislature derisively as men "of all shades, from the lightest mulattoes to the darkest negroids, fresh from the kitchen and the field." In response, pioneering black historian John Hope Franklin called for greater objectivity in evaluating the Reconstruction governments and insisted that simply citing the "celebrations attending 'redemption'" did not constitute reliable evidence.[18]

Following Franklin's lead, subsequent historians have provided a more balanced account of Reconstruction state governments. Recent assessments acknowledge both their real successes and serious failures. Historian Steven Hahn, for example, has argued that "the body politic of the South" was reconstructed by the new state governments that emerged. Former slaves were enfranchised and mobilized to participate in the political system as equals, with over 90 percent of the eligible black men registered to vote in every ex-Confederate state except Mississippi. Black voters and black legislators seriously challenged the traditional power of former slaveholders and advocated for "potentially far-reaching legislation in the areas of civil rights, labor relations and landownership."[19] As state governments set about repealing black codes, creating an equitable tax structure, and reforming law enforcement, however, the limits of black political power were also exposed. In most state legislatures, African Americans simply did not hold enough seats to set the agenda, and it was more often white Republicans who made policy.

As a group, southern Republicans were committed to the modernization of the South, improving their states' transportation infrastructures, creating public schools, and reforming the legal and judicial systems. They also sought investment capital to diversify and develop economies that had been damaged in the war and stunted by cotton monoculture. Like northern states before the war, Reconstruction governments issued bonds, incorporated businesses, and purchased stock in construction companies to finance building projects, which, they insisted, would benefit whites and blacks alike. Among the most important element in this area was the building of railroads, a critical aspect of economic development in which the pre-Civil War South had lagged badly behind the North both in terms of track miles and the coordination of lines. Because of the enormous capital outlay necessary for rail construction, southern state governments often heavily subsidized railroad companies, which in turn created many opportunities for graft. But the result was nevertheless a huge increase in the number of railroad miles in the region. Between 1868 and 1871, the states covered by the Reconstruction Acts saw a 31 percent increase in mileage, from 8,400 miles to 11,000. Even the "redemption" governments of the post-Reconstruction period celebrated the successful record of railroad construction achieved by their otherwise-hated predecessors.[20]

Public education was another key accomplishment of Reconstruction governments. In part a response to the enormous desire for literacy and general knowledge among freedpeople, public schools were a crucial reform that Republicans believed would benefit the entire community. In South Carolina, for example, black leaders Francis Cardozo and Robert Smalls had succeeded in making mandatory, state-financed education a part of the state constitution, and their activism led to the creation of more than 3,000 schools.[21] Given the near absence of free schooling in the antebellum

South, moreover, nearly every state in the region saw dramatic increases in the numbers of children receiving basic education during Reconstruction.

Higher education was also encouraged by Reconstruction governments, with several states providing funds for the creation or expansion of public colleges. In Mississippi, for example, the state legislature created Alcorn University, a state-funded institution for black students that was governed by an African American board of trustees and led by former Mississippi Senator Hiram Revels. In South Carolina and Arkansas, the Republican legislatures instructed existing state colleges to admit black students, although only the University of South Carolina made special efforts to recruit black students and to provide them with the financial and academic resources necessary to succeed. Although they were not directly funded by state governments, historically black colleges such as Fisk, Howard, and Atlanta University were also founded during this period in order to educate teachers for the South's new public school system. Most southern schools remained segregated during this period, but the efforts of Reconstruction governments succeeded in doubling the literacy rates of the black population in just over a decade.[22]

Although largely unsuccessful in creating an integrated public school system, African American Republicans in the South were determined to use the law to establish equal access to many other public facilities and accommodations. Perhaps the most pronounced efforts of this kind were in South Carolina, where state legislators banned any form of public or private discrimination on the basis of race and imposed heavy fines on violators. Other states and municipalities enacted antidiscrimination laws, often resulting from the direct action of African Americans who were willing to risk life and limb for equal access. In New Orleans, Louisiana, for example, where railroad companies, streetcars, and steamboats routinely relegated black customers to separate and inferior facilities, activists such as P. B. S. Pinchback and William Nichols routinely entered "whites only" cars and refused to leave when whites protested. In cases where blacks were physically removed, they used their newfound access to state and federal courts to challenge such behavior and transportation companies often dropped their discriminatory policies rather than be forced to pay court-ordered damages. These undertakings were not the direct result of southern Republican legislatures, but they drew upon the citizenship and empowerment of black Southerners that such governments represented.[23]

Hiram Revels was the first African American to serve in the United States Senate. (Library of Congress)

At the same time, however, Republican governments in the South were also prone to intense internal factionalism, a condition that ultimately weakened their hold on power. The factionalism was in part the result of the different constituencies that made up the Republican Party in the South. Divisions existed between black and white Republicans, carpetbaggers and scalawags, and even within the black community itself. The latter problem was especially serious in South Carolina where issues of prewar status (free or slave), biracial ancestry, education levels, and geography created "different political sensibilities" among blacks.[24] Freeborn blacks in South Carolina, for instance, were more willing than freedmen to support a relaxation of the laws that disenfranchised white Southerners.[25] The competition for government patronage, a problem that beset

American politics as a whole in this period, also pitted one group against another. As historian Lawrence Powell has suggested, Republicans came to power at a time when economic conditions in the South were extremely poor, and government jobs such as registrars, sheriffs, and tax collectors provided steady income for those who possessed the necessary political connections. Politically active blacks, who were often refused private employment by suspicious white Southerners, were especially dependent on patronage appointments.[26] These divisions sapped the ability of the Republican Party to remain united in the face of Democratic opposition.

Competition for lucrative patronage appointments was also an important source of corruption in the southern governments. Large-scale graft usually occurred as states awarded construction contracts to railroad companies or other ventures involved in economic development projects. Seeking a direct loan of $2 million in state bonds from the Alabama legislature, for example, an official of the Alabama and Chattanooga Railroad engaged in the wholesale bribery of state legislators. In the face of a ballooning state debt, moreover, Alabama's Republican governor William H. Smith concealed the fact that he had illegally endorsed bonds well beyond the state-mandated limit.[27] Given their commitment to rapid modernization, Republican governments in the South routinely spent more than they could afford, and while some of the debt was addressed through taxation, governments also issued state-backed securities whose value was based on inaccurate pictures of government finances. As in Alabama, South Carolina officials in 1868 covertly issued bonds in violation of statutory limits and then sold them on the open market to buyers who were assured of the state's fiscal health. Unlike Alabama, where a sizable number of state legislators had to be bribed to secure the bond issue, South Carolina governor Robert Scott, a carpetbagger from Ohio, simply signed the illegal bonds surreptitiously and then a small coterie of investors and corrupt officials profited from the artificial increase in the price of the securities. A similar scandal under Scott's successor, Franklin Moses, left the state with a financial burden for ordinary taxpayers and a record of corruption that white Democrats exploited with great effect.[28]

But as many historians have pointed out, the corruption of Reconstruction-era state governments was hardly unique in a post-Civil War America where fraud, graft, and bribery were all too common aspects of national politics. Ulysses S. Grant's presidency, for example, was marred by repeated scandals resulting from the same combination of economic adventurism and political fraud that beset Reconstruction governments in the South. In the Credit Mobilier affair of 1872–1873, for example, officials of the Credit Mobilier construction company vastly overcharged the United States government for its work on the Union Pacific Railroad and then bribed congressional Republicans with cheap shares in the company in order to prevent an investigation. A second scandal involved attempts by rapacious financiers Jay Gould and Jim Fisk to influence President Grant's monetary policies in order to seize control of the gold market. While Republican scandals grabbed national headlines, Democrats were hardly immune to the temptation of fraud. In New York City, the Tammany Hall Democratic machine run by "Boss" William Marcy Tweed was a morass of corrupt practices in which public works projects were sold to those who paid the highest bribes. Members of the "Tweed Ring" extended public services like sewage and running water into areas of the city where they personally owned property, thus driving up its value. It should also be noted that the southern Democrats' use of terrorism to bring down Reconstruction governments belied their rhetoric of respect for law and public order.

While earlier generations of historians sometimes painted distorted images of Reconstruction politics in the South, an exclusive focus on political development can also produce an inaccurate picture of ordinary experience in this period. After all, the overwhelming majority of white and black Southerners never participated in a constitutional convention, ran for office, or made a political speech. Instead, most rural Southerners spent their time trying to survive in an agricultural economy still shattered by war and altered by the realities of emancipation. Former slaves had not been the beneficiaries of land redistribution as radicals had hoped earlier in Reconstruction, but Congressional Reconstruction had at least invalidated the coercive black codes that had threatened to practically re-enslave them. In the 1870s, therefore, rural blacks sought to build new relationships with the land that rejected the conditions of slavery while falling short of the full economic independence they had sought at the beginning of the period. As this process unfolded, however, the experiences of rural African American men and women were not always the same. Emancipation resulted in voting rights for black men and affirmed their right to own property and to exercise legal personhood, but the status and place of black women in society and at home was far from clear. As they adjusted to the new economic realities that northerners called the free labor system, then, black families needed to sort out the implications of freedom for their work patterns and for their most important domestic relationships.

Nothing was more important to freedpeople during Reconstruction than economic security, a condition that would ensure the personal autonomy and independence from former owners that defined freedom for many former slaves. Although some 15,000 freedpeople migrated to Kansas at the end of Reconstruction, a group that has sometimes been called the "Exodusters," the vast majority of freedpeople hoped to achieve their economic goals in the South, which meant that their economic opportunities would depend in part on the region's overall commercial health.[29] And as historian James McPherson has shown, economic conditions in the years immediately following the Civil War seemed to offer incentives for blacks and whites to find common ground. Demand for cotton on the international market remained fairly high between 1865 and 1868, a fact that made white planters even more determined to prevent any form of land confiscation during Reconstruction. But since they could find no viable alternative to using black labor to produce the valuable crop, planters were also under significant pressure to arrive at some accommodation with former slaves. This was especially true after the black codes had been invalidated by the Fourteenth Amendment and the Military Reconstruction Acts. African Americans, moreover, were consistently assertive in negotiating higher compensation for their labor, either in the form of higher wages or a greater share of the cotton crop.[30]

But the southern economic recovery was hindered by numerous factors. Because of the disruption to cotton production during the war, for example, many planters lacked "heirloom seeds," which had been developed over decades of cultivation to ensure vigorous, high-quality plants. At the same time, drought and armyworm infestation ensured that the postwar cotton yields would not reach their prewar levels until Reconstruction was nearly over. By that time, moreover, international conditions had changed, and British consumers of raw cotton had begun to seek new supplies in their colonial possessions in India and Egypt. Cotton prices dropped to historic lows as a result, and the South's chronic lack of investment capital and technological innovation prevented the region from increasing production enough to ensure profits, especially for small- and medium-sized growers.[31]

Although agricultural diversification might have provided an answer to some of the economic problems of the region, black and white southern farmers became increasingly mired in a cycle of debt that tied them inescapably to cotton production alone. Northern merchants who were interested in purchasing cotton supplied credit in the form of loans, food, clothing, and agricultural implements, but they placed liens on the forthcoming crop as collateral. Poor annual yields, which were frequent during these years, meant greater indebtedness and increased dependency on the one crop that could easily be exchanged for cash or credit. "The South found itself in a depression," writes historian Steven Hahn of the postwar economy. "[P]etty producers, white and black, landed and landless . . . found themselves increasingly mired in a position tantamount to debt peonage."[32]

Although poor whites sometimes started out with land at the beginning of Reconstruction, such was not the case for most African Americans, who found their economic options narrowed by white racism on the one hand and cycles of debt and poverty on the other. Since payment of wages became increasingly difficult in a region with very little circulating cash, blacks entered into a variety of land-use relationships with white planters, the most common of which were sharecropping and the crop lien system. Determined to forsake the old gang labor arrangements that had been the hallmark of slavery, landless rural blacks engaged in these new arrangements in part because they usually allowed black families to live and work together on separate plots of ground that were rented from planters on an annual basis. In sharecropping, for example, blacks agreed to contracts, which stipulated the percentage of the yearly cotton crop that would be split between black workers and white landowners. In cases where blacks already possessed seeds, tools, and other farming necessities, they usually retained half of the cotton at the end of the year, but only one-third if the landowners supplied materials. The crop lien system was different in that tenant families did not have to share the crop directly but rather received direct loans to purchase the equipment and provisions needed to cultivate some part of the planter's property. With all of their property held as collateral (under a mortgage lien) until after the initial loan was paid off with interest, tenants in this system were to meet their obligations by selling all of their cotton for cash or credit at the end of the year. Although these systems have rightly become notorious for the ways in which they trapped generations of African American families in serf-like conditions, many freedpeople of the Reconstruction era had believed that they would be temporary arrangements, hoping to emerge as independent property owners.[33]

As a general rule, however, no amount of hard work or devotion to improvement could overcome the structural unfairness of these systems. Because they were under great pressure to devote as much of their land as possible to the cultivation of the cash-producing cotton crop, families that lived and worked under the sharecropping or crop lien systems were forced to buy necessary provisions on credit from local stores. Credit was generally expensive throughout the South after the war, and the region's poorest people were victims of a chain of commercial exploitation that began with northern banks that charged high rates to southern borrowers and who in turn charged consumers high rates for their goods and services. Beleaguered tenants also found that high tax rates, imposed by Reconstruction state governments in order to expand the infrastructure, placed them under even greater financial pressure. Thus in years when cotton prices were especially low or when yields were affected by weather conditions or pests, tenants were often unable to pay even the interest on their mortgage liens, and sharecroppers were unable to pay their own debts after the final division of the cotton crop.

For those trapped at the bottom of this system, anything less than a bumper crop could mean eviction from the land. More often it simply meant that tenants began the next year already in debt, desperately hoping that prices would go up and that yields would improve enough to allow them to pay what they owed. But contracts were often designed to prevent sharecroppers from achieving any long-term freedom from debt. They typically contained detailed descriptions of the maintenance work required during the course of year, and landlords deducted portions of the tenants' share for anything they believed had deviated from the original agreement. In addition, since tenants rarely owned cotton gins, they were forced to pay a fee for ginning that was set by landowners, further reducing their proceeds from the crop. Former slaves who worked assiduously to achieve economic independence through sharecropping experienced tremendous disillusionment when the system produced dependency instead.

As one former slave put it, "we soon found out that freedom could make folks proud, but it didn't make 'em rich."[34]

For black women, the new economic realities that came with emancipation had significant implications for their roles within the family. Under slavery, black women had faced special circumstances as they worked long hours in fields or plantation houses and played critical roles in the maintenance of their families. After Matilda Hughes gave birth to twins, for example, her northern Mississippi owners refused to lighten her duties so that she could nurse her babies and care for them when they were sick. Indeed, it was Matilda's maternal dignity and intense devotion to her children that seem to have infuriated her mistress. As her husband Louis looked on, then, the babies grew weaker and eventually died from the lack of sustained attention. "My heart was sore and heavy, for I could see that my wife was almost run to death with work," he wrote later. "So the little things, instead of thriving and developing, as was their right, dwindled toward the inevitable end."[35] While affluent white American families adhered to a "separate spheres" ideology in which men worked for wages outside the home and women and children were assigned a purely "domestic" role, the families of enslaved African Americans were subjected to a work regimen that was enforced across the lines of gender and age. These were issues that African Americans would address as they reclaimed full control of their family lives during Reconstruction.

Following emancipation, work remained central to the lives of black women, and freedwomen hoped to exert more control over the nature of the work they performed and to identify their priorities without interference from whites. Believing that they should define free labor for themselves, freedwomen in the lowcountry of South Carolina, for instance, became increasingly assertive, unwilling to work under former overseers and refusing to follow every order they were given by planters.[36] Freedwomen who defied their employers, however, risked severe punishment. When Hagar Barnwell was ordered by Clark Sanders, her former master, to work in the kitchen, she defiantly refused, emphasizing that "she had contracted to work in the field." After his threats did not convince Barnwell to do his cooking, Sanders "tied her up by the thumbs" with her feet nearly suspended off the ground for an hour.[37] Countless women like Hagar Barnwell understood freedom to mean the right to reject work patterns that had been established under slavery, but they confronted postwar employers who expected that the number of hours, the conditions, and the form of discipline would remain the same as during slavery.

In response to challenges to employers' power, one planter concluded that "The women have got rather lazy. . . . They wish to stay in the house, or in the garden all the time."[38] White Southerners routinely asserted that black women after the Civil War withdrew from agricultural work so that they could "play the lady," and employers were irritated by this development. It deprived them of cheap labor in the fields and in the plantation houses during a period when labor shortages affected the region as a whole. Some Freedmen's Bureau agents concurred with white planters, deploring the new "evil of female loaferism" and suggesting that formerly industrious black women "now have aspirations to be like white ladies and, instead of using the hoe, pass the days in dawdling over their trivial housework and gossiping among their neighbors."[39]

Historians, however, do not accept this nineteenth-century assessment for two main reasons. First, it is clear that contemporary accounts have significantly exaggerated the extent to which freedwomen withdrew from agricultural work. In her study of lowcountry South Carolina, for example, historian Leslie Schwalm concluded that between 1866 and 1868, women signed about half of the contracts to work in the rice fields, roughly the same percentage of women working in the fields as had done so under slavery. The difference, however, was the length of their workday. In most of the contracts, freedwomen refused to work a full day, preferring instead to contract as part-time workers. Scholars agree that women did not withdraw from field work, but instead they claimed their status as free laborers to determine the number of hours and days they would be under contract.[40]

Second, historians reject the idea that this alteration in their work patterns is evidence that freedwomen were lazy or sought an escape from hard work. As Jacqueline Jones has argued, "freedwomen perceived freedom to mean not a release from back-breaking labor, but rather the opportunity to labor on behalf their own families and kin within the protected spheres of household and community."[41] By the end of the war, the plantation infrastructure lay in ruins in large areas of the former Confederacy and food shortages were rampant. Families often lacked basic necessities like bedding and cookware. Given these postwar realities, freedwomen chose to devote their labor to caring for their family instead of heeding the demands of white Southerners. Although it was not paid by wages or supervised by whites, black women's household labor had enormous economic value to their families, as it included the planting and maintenance of provision gardens, the raising of livestock, and the production of food items that sustained the family during lean times. Given slaveholders' constant intrusions into the domestic lives of enslaved women before the Civil War and the pressing needs of their family after the war, it is hardly surprising to find freedwomen choosing whenever possible to labor in a newly autonomous domestic context.

The economic conditions faced by rural black families were important concerns for the Reconstruction state governments created after 1867. But with railroad and infrastructure development as their main responses to the region's economic stagnation, too little attention was given to the specific problems that beset those mired in escalating debt peonage. Policies that were designed to help the debt-strapped rural poor included caps on the interest rates that merchants could charge their customers, limitations on the kinds of property that could be seized for debt, and laws giving agricultural workers initial liens on the cotton they grew that protected their shares from seizure by their employer's creditors.[42] But the only state to directly address the problems that came with black landlessness was South Carolina, which created a special land commission devoted to placing poor rural families of both races on homesteads of their own. The commission was authorized by the state constitution to purchase available land with state funds and to make it available at low prices and on favorable credit terms to family farmers. Although its efforts were constantly marred by incompetent and corrupt leadership, the commission still managed to purchase 168 plantations totaling 93,000 acres of land. At least 2,000 African American families became property owners as a result of these efforts. South Carolina also attempted to use a progressive tax policy to reduce the size of landholdings in the state, thereby transferring property from the very rich to the very poor. Large landowners paid an ever increasing tax bill during the 1870s and forfeited land for nonpayment, but small holders were exempted from tax seizures. By the end of the century, these efforts resulted in a threefold increase in the number of black property owners in South Carolina.[43]

Although South Carolina's efforts to address the deepest needs of the rural poor met with some success, they were not typical of other southern

states under Republican control. "Given the importance of the land question," writes one historian, "it is remarkable how few concrete actions the
Republican governments took."[44] It is difficult to assess the significance of
this failure in the larger history of the Reconstruction, but the fact that the
basic needs of the rural poor of both races were neglected by state governments suggests a crucial missed opportunity. Indeed, the rise of populism in
the South during the 1890s indicates that there was a rural constituency
for economic justice that Reconstruction governments might have cultivated through more effective land reform and debt relief policies. Economic weakness likely exacerbated the hostility of poor whites toward
former slaves, and thus more effective land and debt policies might have
moderated the racial conflict of the period. At the same time, however, a
more aggressive commitment to wealth redistribution in the South clearly
conflicted with the free labor principles that enjoyed such widespread
acceptance in nineteenth-century America. With its emphasis on self-
help, economic individualism, property rights, and the merits of hard
work, the dominant ideology precluded sustained government intervention in the economy. South Carolina, which went further than most states
in addressing poverty and indebtedness, received increasing criticism from
its former allies in the North who now decried its experiment in "socialism." In an 1874 article, for example, the New York-based journal
The Nation enthusiastically supported a growing white "tax payers" movement in South Carolina, which was protesting the state's progressive economic policies. "Farms are sold to pay taxes; the old, rich plantations are
broken up," the editors complained. "[I]t is this machinery which makes
socialism in America the dangerous, deadly poison it is." But if free labor
ideas militated against a stronger response to economic inequality, the
ideology of white supremacy was equally powerful. "The rich Congo thief
[is] on top," wrote the disgusted editors of The Nation, "and the degraded
Anglo-Saxon [is] at the bottom."[45]

Articles like that in the Nation indicated an emerging northern reaction
against Reconstruction during the mid-1870s that would, along with rising
white violence against blacks in the South, destroy the Republican Party
in the region. But the eventual downfall of these governments should
not obscure their significance in political history of South and of the larger
United States. The alliance between former slaves and so-called "carpetbaggers" and "scalawags" represented an unprecedented experiment in

This Currier and Ives image contains likenesses of seven black politicians elected to the 41st and 42nd Congress of the United States. (Library of Congress)

biracial political cooperation that amazed both its warmest supporters and most violent detractors. The sight of black politicians in state capitols around the South and in the halls of the United States Congress was a stunning reminder to contemporaries that both the Civil War and Congressional Reconstruction had created opportunities for a revolutionary transformation of the United States. If white and black leaders sometimes squandered these opportunities through political myopia and personal self-interest, that was hardly surprising in a postwar American culture that had shrugged off so much of its prewar idealism. And yet in a nation that had only a decade earlier declared that African Americans had no rights "a white man was bound to respect," black men and women in the Reconstruction era said otherwise and courageously launched a political movement for liberty and civil rights that would outlive all of its opponents.[46]

NOTES

1. Thomas Dixon, *The Clansman: An Historical Romance of the Ku Klux Klan* (New York: A Wessels Company, 1907), 362, 371.

2. John Hope Franklin, *Reconstruction after the Civil War* (Chicago: University of Chicago Press, 2013), 132.

3. Ibid., 133, 132.

4. Eric Foner, *Reconstruction: America's Unfinished Revolution* (New York: Harper & Row, 1988), 355.

5. Philip Dray, *Capitol Men: the Epic Story of Reconstruction through the Lives of the First Black Congressmen* (New York: Houghton Mifflin, 2008), 380.

6. Steven Hahn, *A Nation Under Our Feet: Black Political Struggles in the Rural South from Slavery to the Great Migration* (Cambridge: Harvard University Press, 2003), 218; Dray, *Capitol Men*, 73.

7. W.M. Elliot, "The Negro Throwing off his Fetters," *Richmond Whig*, April 14, 1868, in *The Reconstruction Era: Primary Documents on Events from 1865 to 1877*, ed. Donna L. Dickerson (Westport, CT: Greenwood Press, 2003), 212.

8. Albion Tourgée, *A Fool's Errand By One of the Fools* (New York: Fords, Howard & Hulbert, 1879), 161.

9. Richard Nelson Current, *Those Terrible Carpetbaggers: A Reinterpretation* (New York: Oxford University Press, 1988), 422–425, quote on 425; James M. McPherson and James K. Hogue, *Ordeal by Fire: The Civil War and Reconstruction* (New York: McGraw-Hill, 2010), 605.

10. Michael W. Fitzgerald, *Splendid Failure: Postwar Reconstruction in the American South* (Chicago: Ivan R. Dee, 2007), 78.

11. James Alex Baggett, *The Scalawags: Southern Dissenters in the Civil War and Reconstruction* (Baton Rouge: Louisiana State University Press, 2003), 2.

12. McPherson and Hogue, *Ordeal by Fire*, 604.

13. Baggett, *Scalawags*, 260–261.

14. Allen W. Trelease, "Who were the Scalawags?" *Journal of Southern History* 29 (November 1963), 466.

15. Jeffry D. Wert, *General James Longstreet: The Confederacy's Most Controversial Soldier* (New York: Simon & Schuster, 1994), 413.

16. John Burgess quoted in Adam Fairclough, "Was the Grant of Black Suffrage a Political Error? Reconsidering the Views of John W. Burgess, William A. Dunning, and Eric Foner on Congressional Reconstruction," *The Journal of the Historical Society* 12 (June 2012), 165.

17. Ibid., 166.

18. John Hope Franklin, "Whither Reconstruction Historiography?" *Journal of Negro Education* 17 (Autumn 1948), 461, E. Merton Coulter quoted p. 451.

19. Hahn, *A Nation Under Our Feet*, 198, 203, 259, 260.

20. McPherson and Hogue, *Ordeal by Fire*, 608; Fitzgerald, *Splendid Failure*, 104.

21. Dray, *Capitol Men*, 48.

22. Foner, *Reconstruction*, 368; Fitzgerald, *Splendid Failure*, 152–153.

23. Douglas R. Egerton, *The Wars of Reconstruction* (New York: Bloomsbury Press, 2014), 274–5.

24. Hahn, *A Nation Under Our Feet*, 261.

25. Thomas Holt, *Black over White: Negro Political Leadership in South Carolina during Reconstruction* (Urbana: University of Illinois Press, 1977), 59–61.

26. Lawrence N. Powell, "The Politics of Livelihood: Carpetbaggers in the Deep South," in *Region, Race, and Reconstruction: Essays in Honor of C. Vann Woodward*, eds. J. Morgan Kousser and James M. McPherson (New York: Oxford University Press, 1982), 315–347.

27. Sarah Woolfolk Wiggins, *The Scalawag in Alabama Politics, 1865-1881* (Tuscaloosa: University of Alabama Press, 1977), 43–44.

28. Joel Williamson, *After Slavery: The Negro in South Carolina during Reconstruction, 1861–1877* (Chapel Hill: University of North Carolina Press, 1965), 283–284.

29. John David Smith, *Black Voices from Reconstruction, 1865–1877* (Gainesville: University Press of Florida, 1997), 85.

30. McPherson and Hogue, *Ordeal by Fire*, 628–629.

31. Heather Cox Richardson, "A Marshall Plan for the South? The Failure of Republican and Democratic Ideology during Reconstruction,"*Civil War History* 51 (December 2005), 380.

32. Steven Hahn, *The Roots of Southern Populism: Yeoman Farmers and the Transformation of the Georgia Upcountry, 1850–1890* (New York: Oxford University Press, 1983), 186.

33. Foner, *Reconstruction*, 173–174; Williamson, *After Slavery*, 170–171; Leon Litwack, *Been in the Storm So Long: The Aftermath of Slavery* (New York: Vintage, 1979), 448.

34. Litwack, *Been in the Storm*, 449.

35. Louis Hughes, *Thirty Years a Slave: From Bondage to Freedom* (Milwaukee: South Side Printing Company, 1897), 96.

36. Leslie A. Schwalm, *A Hard Fight for We: Women's Transition from Slavery to Freedom in South Carolina* (Urbana: University of Illinois Press, 1997), 173–175.

37. Freedmen's Bureau Agent at Combahee Ferry, South Carolina to South Carolina Freedmen's Bureau Assistant Commissioner, October 10, 1865, in *Freedom: A Documentary History of Emancipation, 1861–1867*, series 3, volume 1, *Land and Labor, 1865*, ed. Steven Hahn et al. (Chapel Hill: University of North Carolina Press, 2008), 561; Schwalm, 178.

38. Schwalm, 205.

39. Jacqueline Jones, *Labor of Love, Labor of Sorrow: Black Women, Work and the Family, From Slavery to the Present* (New York: Vintage, 1985), 59; Eric Foner,

Forever Free: The Story of Emancipation and Reconstruction (New York: Vintage, 2005), 86; Schwalm, 205.

40. Schwalm, 206–207; Noralee Frankel, *Freedom's Women: Black Women and Families in Civil War Era Mississippi* (Bloomington: Indiana University Press, 1999), 74–76; Hahn, *A Nation Under Our Feet*, 171; Robert L. Ransom and Richard Sutch, *One Kind of Freedom: The Economic Consequences of Emancipation* (New York: Cambridge University Press, 1977), 232–236.

41. Jones, *Labor of Love, Labor of Sorrow*, 78.

42. Foner, *Reconstruction*, 373.

43. Dray, *Capitol Men*, 369–370; Williamson, *After Slavery*, 147–148; Hahn, *A Nation Under Our Feet*, 260.

44. Foner, *Reconstruction*, 375.

45. "Socialism in South Carolina," *The Nation*, April 16, 1874, 248.

46. In 1857, the Supreme Court ruled in *Dred Scott v. Sandford* that blacks were not citizens of the United States. Chief Justice Taney wrote that Scott was not a citizen because blacks (both free and slave) "had for more than a century before been regarded as beings of an inferior order … so far inferior, that they had no rights which the white man was bound to respect." Overturning the Dred Scott decision, the Fourteenth Amendment defined that "all persons born or naturalized in the United States" were citizens.

CHAPTER 6

The Defeat of Reconstruction

A mong the most important forces driving Reconstruction had been the northern public's unwillingness to accept the results of President Andrew Johnson's lenient policies. Race riots in Memphis and New Orleans, in which white police officers had colluded with mobs in massacring African Americans, had led many in the North to vote for Republicans in the 1866 congressional elections. But by the mid-1870s, northern support for Reconstruction was waning, and the surge of racist violence that toppled Republican state governments in the South failed to generate the same levels of outrage. In the fall of 1875, for example, when northern-born governor Adelbert Ames of Mississippi requested federal aid to protect the state's Republican voters against terror and assassination, he received a message from U.S. Attorney General Edwards Pierrepont informing him that President Grant would not intervene directly to stop the violence. "The whole public are tired out with these annual autumnal outbreaks in the South," Grant had insisted rather irritably, "and the great majority are ready now to condemn any interference on the part of the Government."[1] For Governor Ames, the consequences of the president's lackluster response ensured the violent suppression of black voters by armed white terrorists and with it the final defeat of Reconstruction in Mississippi. Yet if most historians have been critical of Grant's response, they have nevertheless generally agreed with his assessment of public attitudes at the time. Thus to understand the retreat from Reconstruction in the face of southern lawlessness, it is essential to explore the evolution of northern sentiment in relation to the postwar South.

Northern Democrats, of course, had opposed Reconstruction from the outset and their persistent and determined antagonism to it had played a significant role in moderating Republican policies at every stage.

Having used white supremacy as a major political weapon since the 1830s, Democratic leaders in the North during Reconstruction were adept at exploiting racial fears in their campaign against congressional policies, especially black suffrage. In the 1868 presidential campaign, Democrats ran under the slogan "This is a White Man's Country" and vice presidential candidate Francis Blair made speeches insisting that "the 'white race is the only race in the world that has shown itself capable' of self-government."[2] The Democratic Party platform insisted that the Military Reconstruction Acts were unconstitutional, and it called for the abolition of "all political instrumentalities designed to secure negro supremacy."[3] Democrats were massively outnumbered prior to the readmission of ex-Confederate states, but their ferocious criticism of Reconstruction began to undermine Republican power. In a series of sweeping victories in the fall of 1874, they gained a 60-vote majority in the House of Representatives and made significant gains in historically Republican areas in the Northeast and Middle West. In Mississippi, Governor Adelbert Ames was horrified by these events and feared that "the old rebel spirit" would soon "roam over the land, thirsty for revenge." He concluded gloomily that "the war is not yet over."[4]

Northern opponents of Reconstruction made inroads not simply because of racism, but also because they linked broader economic concerns to the public's increasing desire to see the military occupation of the South come to an end. Democrats routinely emphasized the growing cost of Reconstruction in order to capitalize on a widespread aversion to taxation. New York Democrat Horatio Seymour claimed in 1868 that maintaining a military presence in the former Confederacy cost $150 million a year, a price tag that did not include the money the federal government paid in pensions to veterans. This strategy gained support, even among Republicans, when concerns about taxes were linked to accusations of political corruption. In May 1871, the *New York Tribune* ran a story that blamed government corruption in South Carolina on the "incompetent" African Americans who were running the state. This story might not have been especially noteworthy had it appeared in the Democratic press, but the *Tribune* was a Republican paper with a history of supporting black equality. It now framed its criticism of Reconstruction in economic language, focusing on tax policies that "robbed" hardworking property owners to fund extravagant government programs. Historian Heather Cox Richardson has suggested that northern Republicans were increasingly anxious about labor unrest and perceived the actions of the South Carolina government as fostering class antagonism.[5]

By the early 1870s, the divisions that had existed within the Republican Party since the end of the war were becoming acute and the power of radicals was rapidly ebbing away in favor of a far more conservative party leadership. By the 1872 presidential election, many of the most experienced and influential radical Republicans had died or retired from political life, and a new generation of leaders, with fewer connections to the party's historic antislavery roots, was taking power. In addition to these generational shifts, a growing minority within the party had become disaffected from both the Grant administration and from the Republican leadership in southern states. More than a few of these critics were disappointed office seekers, but others were firm believers in a "laissez-faire" philosophy, which held that intervention by the government in the social and economic sphere would reward idleness and create both inefficiency and rampant corruption. The scandals that beset both the Grant administration and the Republican governments in the South seemed to confirm this view, and the "reformers" within the party began to argue that it had been a terrible mistake to seek a rapid transformation of the South. E. L. Godkin of the *Nation* insisted that a "scientific" view of society required a cautious approach to change, and he blamed radicals for what he believed was naïve social engineering. "The wise radical is content to wait," Godkin wrote, "and slowly to build up when the work of pulling down is properly over."[6]

Aware that they would not be able to prevent President Grant's renomination in 1872, these Liberal Republicans, as they called themselves, met at a separate convention in Cincinnati, Ohio, where they nominated *New York Tribune* editor Horace Greeley for president and diplomat Charles Francis Adams as his running mate. During the campaign, the Liberal Republicans attacked Grant as a tyrant and decried Reconstruction for disfranchising white Southerners. Senator Carl Schurz of Missouri, for example, now believed that black voters were too "ignorant and inexperienced" to lead the South and that it had been a mistake to disenfranchise men of "intelligence" and "personal integrity" simply because of their participation in the rebellion.[7] While men like Greeley and Schurz remained loyal to the basic principles of the Fourteenth and Fifteenth Amendments, they nevertheless promoted amnesty for all southern whites and the

abandonment of military intervention in southern politics. Favoring reconciliation, Schurz criticized Grant for failing to understand that the war
was over and that it was now time for former enemies to "clasp hands over
the bloody chasm of war."[8]

Some Liberal Republicans believed that a program of amnesty for
ex-Confederates would stem the tide of white terrorism that was sweeping
across the South, while others simply sought an alliance with southern
Democrats in pursuit of free trade and civil service reform. Northern
Democrats were willing to endorse Greeley if it meant the rebirth of the
southern wing of their party, and they stood little chance of winning the
election on their own. Seeing that northern Democrats and Liberal
Republicans were united under a common platform and candidate, opponents of black political power began to mount a major political offensive
against equal rights. Old-line Democrats like the former presidential candidate Horatio Seymour detested Greeley but saw the campaign as an opportunity to defeat Reconstruction. "I can see my way clear to vote for him,"
Seymour told fellow Democrat Samuel Tilden, "as he can be made of use
in driving negroes out of office."[9]

Fortunately for those who supported African American political rights
in the South, Greeley proved to be an incompetent candidate whose
attempts to curry favor with southern whites bordered on the absurd.
As historian William Gillette has shown, Greeley seemed unable to
develop any sort of disciplined message and regularly "reopen[ed] volatile
political questions" that a more "politically astute" candidate would have
avoided. During a speech in September 1872, he castigated Union army
veterans for refusing to reconcile fully with their former enemies and went
so far as to suggest that he would have accepted the secession of the South
had it been achieved democratically. Just a few days later, Greeley even
appeared to disavow his earlier abolitionist views and suggested that black
voters were "ignorant, deceived and misguided."[10] President Grant, by
contrast, remained largely silent during the campaign and looked statesmanlike in comparison to the blundering and periodically offensive
Greeley. The result was a resounding defeat for the Liberal-Democratic
coalition. Greeley received 43.8 percent of the popular vote, less than
Seymour's Democratic total in 1868. Yet despite their poor showing at
the polls, conservative opponents of Reconstruction, both Republicans
and Democrats, had championed the idea of a final "reconciliation" with

the South as a solution to the problems the nation faced, and this idea would prove politically irresistible in the years ahead.

The 1872 presidential campaign was conducted during a period of resurgent white violence in the South and a growing debate in Washington over how to deal with it. Although the Ku Klux Klan and similar organizations had failed to prevent the election of President Grant in 1868, their widespread campaigns of terror became a permanent part of southern political life in the Reconstruction years. Because of its secrecy and its decentralized, interstate structure, moreover, the Klan presented state and federal law enforcement officials with intractable problems. Southern state governments generally lacked the financial resources to wage a sustained battle against Klan violence, and even modest attempts to curtail violence caused greater resentment among the larger white population. When Klan suspects were brought to trial by state officials, it was nearly impossible to find witnesses willing to testify against them or jurors willing to convict on the evidence. In York Country, South Carolina, for example, nearly 80 percent of adult white men were members of the Klan and during a 10-month period in 1870–1871, they murdered 11 blacks and committed at least 600 nonlethal forms of assault or abuse. Although the state government activated the county militia to suppress this campaign of lawlessness, the troops were nearly all African Americans, whose armed presence in the county incited the local Klan to further acts of violence. As a fierce showdown approached at Yorkville, pitting black militiamen against swelling numbers of Klansmen, Republican governor Robert Scott ordered the black militiamen to withdraw from the town and to give up their weapons. The governor hoped that disbanding the militia would appease angry whites, but the most immediate effect of his action was to leave blacks vulnerable to subsequent attacks.[11] The only way for disarmed blacks to avoid the wrath of the Klan in York County, it seemed, was to promise to vote for the Democratic ticket.

With similar campaigns of terror being waged in other parts of the South, congressional Republicans held an investigation into Klan violence and crafted enforcement legislation designed to protect black voting rights. In the spring of 1870, a joint congressional committee was formed for the purpose of gathering testimony about Klan activity. At locations across the South, African American witnesses provided chilling accounts of night raiders who murdered, whipped, and threatened them into

In April 1871, President Grant signed the Ku Klux Act, an enforcement measure designed to suppress white supremacist violence through federal police action. (Library of Congress)

abandoning Republican political activity. Charles Hendricks, for example, who had been appointed as a local election official in Georgia, testified that he had been attacked by the Klan at his home in Gwinnett County. When Klansmen declared their intention to lynch and shoot him, Hendricks attempted to flee. As he ran toward the nearby woods, he was shot in the upper thigh and later the bullet had to be removed surgically. As the committee pressed Hendricks further on his political activity, it became clear that he had also been attacked during a previous election when a local landowner had knocked him down with a stick as he waited to vote. Later that same day, as Hendricks walked home from the polling place, a notorious local Klansman waylaid him on the road and cut his clothes with a knife as a warning to take no further part in politics. Like many other black witnesses who appeared before the select committee, Hendricks recognized that it was his work on behalf of the Georgia Republican Party that made him the target of violence. "I took an active part in trying to teach the colored people of that district what to do," he testified, "and they just concluded that I should not live there."[12]

With evidence of a violent and often highly coordinated campaign to suppress the black vote, Congress concluded that subduing the Klan would require enforcement legislation that increased federal power in areas traditionally reserved for the states. In 1870–1871, a series of statutes, each of which was based on the enforcement sections of the Fourteenth and Fifteenth Amendments, were passed by party-line votes and signed into law by President Grant. The first of them, the Enforcement Act of May 31, 1870, made any form of race-based voter intimidation a federal crime and gave federal district courts jurisdiction over cases arising under the new law. Two subsequent enforcement acts gave federal marshals the authority to supervise congressional elections and the power to arrest without warrant those who they suspected of bribery, fraud, or voter intimidation. But as the select committee's evidence of white supremacist violence piled up, Congress became determined to target the Klan and similar organizations in a more direct way. In the Enforcement Act of April 1871, a law that became known as the Ku Klux Act, Congress authorized the president to take extraordinary measures to suppress violent white supremacists. These included the suspension of the writ of habeas corpus, the imposition of temporary military rule in areas where civil officials were unable to deal with Klan threats, and the barring of Klansmen from sitting on federal juries. But as historian Allen Trelease has pointed out, the Ku Klux Act rejected the use of military tribunals to try suspected Klan activists. Instead, these cases would be heard in federal courts that, in states like South Carolina, remained extremely vulnerable to threats and intimidation.[13]

With the 1872 election approaching, President Grant was careful in making use of his new anti-Klan powers. Much of the Republican base remained committed to enforcing the laws, but the president was under increasing criticism from Democrats and Liberal Republicans for protecting corrupt Reconstruction regimes and imposing "bayonet government" on the South. Yet as reports of massacres and the assassination of black politicians poured into Washington, Grant determined to move in a decisive way against the Klan. His most dramatic act was to suspend the writ of habeas corpus in nine counties of South Carolina, including York, and to dispatch federal military units into the region so that arrests could be made and trials commenced. Many Klansmen fled rather than face justice, but federal authorities made as many as 600 arrests, and it appeared to military officials that the Klan's organizational coherence was being destroyed. "The rank and file were bewildered, demoralized," wrote Major Lewis Merrill of the 7th United States Cavalry. In order to get advice from their "chiefs and counsellors," ordinary Klansmen had to "go to them in jail or follow their flight," and so most recognized that "the game was up, that the organization was broken."[14]

If the military execution of the Ku Klux Act at least temporarily disrupted the systematic nature of white violence, the trials of individual Klansmen in South Carolina demonstrated that there was a serious weakness at the heart of the federal enforcement program. U.S. Attorney Daniel T. Corbin had hoped that the Klan trials would establish broad national authority to guarantee the rights established under the Fourteenth and Fifteenth Amendments. But skillful defense lawyers, including prominent national Democratic leaders like Henry Stanbery and Reverdy Johnson, used the cases to challenge the constitutionality of the enforcement acts. They insisted that the broad scope of the laws usurped state jurisdiction over individual acts of lawlessness and therefore violated the most basic principles of state sovereignty. Even more ominous for the future was the fact that Democrats were not alone in doubting the propriety and constitutionality of the Ku Klux Act. Supporters of the law like Ohio Republican James Garfield worried that in passing the law his party was "working on the very verge of the Constitution."[15] A Michigan congressman agreed with Garfield that the Klan Act was "extraordinary legislation" but insisted that the Klan would only be stopped by "strong and vigorous laws ... promptly executed by a firm hand, armed, when need be, with military power."[16] The internal Republican debate over the enforcement acts went beyond abstract issues of constitutional law. At the core of it lay a growing political dispute over whether the party would be strengthened by continuing to punish recalcitrant white Southerners or if its future lay in seeking reconciliation with former rebels. Given this context, it is not surprising that the trials failed to produce a ringing endorsement of expanded federal jurisdiction over alleged civil rights violations. The government's willingness to expend resources and political capital in the prosecution of violent white supremacists was fading quickly.

Beyond the constitutional problems raised by the enforcement acts, support for Reconstruction was also damaged by a severe and prolonged economic contraction that began in 1873. Caused in part by irresponsible speculation in railroad bonds by tycoon financier Jay Cooke, the panic had a catastrophic effect on a U.S. economy that was still recovering from the war. Over the next three years, the credit system fueling industrial expansion in the Northeast and the West collapsed, demand for agricultural products plummeted, and mass urban unemployment left thousands of working families on the edge of destitution. The most direct impact on freedpeople was the collapse of the Freedmen's Savings and Trust Company, a bank created by Congress in 1865 as a place where former slaves might deposit their wages and earn interest. With 33 branches scattered throughout the South, the bank was intended to assist in the transition from slavery to free labor, teaching freedpeople "a spirit of thrift, frugality, and foresight."[17] Unfortunately for the nearly 100,000 accountholders, the institution was wracked by fraud and mismanagement, and in the early 1870s, control of the bank passed into the hands of Jay Cooke who used it to launder bad assets. When Cooke's bank collapsed in the 1873, the Freedmen's Bank and the hard-earned savings of its depositors went down with it. Although historian Barbara Josiah has shown that some black accountholders had wisely shifted some of their money to other institutions, many lost substantial sums. Black leader Frederick Douglass, who had once served as President of the Bank and lost $10,000 when it collapsed, said that the institution had been "the black man's cow, but the white man's milk."[18]

At the level of national politics, the depression further divided the Republican Party and sapped support for enforcing black rights. Responding to the deflationary effects of the contraction, congressional Democrats joined a few southern and western Republicans to pass currency reform that would have added millions of dollars in paper notes, or greenbacks as they were called, to the money supply. Convinced that the plight of farmers and laborers would improve with monetary stimulus, supporters of the bill urged President Grant to sign it. But this would have been a significant shift in policy, as the federal government had been gradually removing greenbacks from circulation since the war ended, with the intention of returning to a gold standard currency system. Although there was substantial risk that his party would fracture along geographical lines as a result, President Grant vetoed the bill in deference to his own hard-money principles and the financial views of eastern Republicans. "I am not a believer in any artificial method of making paper money equal to coin," Grant wrote in his veto message. Voicing some of the laissez-faire principles that Liberal Republicans had used against him two years earlier, the president insisted that inflationary measures were a "departure from true principles of finance, national interest, [and] national obligations to creditors."[19] But Grant's actions did not prevent a political disaster for the Republicans in the midterm elections, a sweeping defeat that showed that economic issues were increasingly more important to northern and western voters than questions related to Reconstruction.

The impact of the panic on government policy toward the South is especially clear in relation to events in Louisiana, where bitter divisions within the Republican Party prompted white Democrats to launch a violent campaign to retake power. The Republican Party in Louisiana had plunged into chaos in 1872, as radicals and conservatives fought over which faction's candidate had won the gubernatorial election. Convening rival state governments in New Orleans, each group handed out their own patronage appointments to state and local offices, which in turn produced rival claimants for these positions all over the state. The radicals, led by their governor William Kellogg, offered key offices to African Americans, while conservative Republicans, who were increasingly seeking "fusion" with the Democrats, appointed whites as judges and country sheriffs. Although federal authorities would eventually confirm Kellogg as the legitimately elected governor, conservatives regarded his patronage appointments as illegitimate and began arming themselves to depose local black officeholders. Known as the White Leagues or White Lines, these groups were often led by Confederate veterans who believed that violent action against white and black Republicans was a legitimate response to those who would undermine white supremacy and social order. Unlike the clandestine culture of the Ku Klux Klan, moreover, these groups rejected disguises and midnight riding and instead acted openly and with the tacit blessing of state Democratic leaders.

In what might be called the start of a white counterrevolution in the South, White Line militiamen attacked an armed group of blacks who were protecting Republican officeholders at the courthouse at Colfax, Louisiana, on April 13, 1873. As at least 140 White Liners approached

In this *Harper's Weekly* illustration, political car-
toonist Thomas Nast graphically illustrated the
role of white supremacist organizations like the
Ku Klux Klan and the White League in terroriz-
ing African Americans in the South and in reas-
serting white control of social and political life.
(Library of Congress)

Colfax armed with a small artillery piece, blacks in and around the courthouse prepared for battle by building makeshift defenses and practicing
military drills. The battle itself was eerily reminiscent of the Civil War,
as small units of white men led by veterans were skillfully deployed against
defenders who valiantly returned fire but then retreated to what they
hoped was safety inside the building. Soon, however, the shingles of the
courthouse were lit on fire, and when the black men inside attempted to
escape the flames, they were shot down at close range by their enemies or
pursued to their death on the banks of the Red River. Seeing that there
was no escape except death by burning, the remaining blacks surrendered
and were taken prisoner. But after some deliberation, the white men
decided to execute them all, a horrific process that took several hours
and resulted in the killing of between 70 and 165 black men who had surrendered and been disarmed. When family members sought to reclaim the

men's remains, they often found that the bodies had been mutilated and personal belongings stolen. As historian LeeAnna Keith has noted, the men who led the massacre at Colfax were serving notice that the "white men of Louisiana would unite to fight their enemies within, killing and dying for white supremacy and home rule."[20]

The legal case that emerged from the Colfax Massacre played an important role in determining the extent of federal power to protect the civil and political rights of African Americans. Using the Enforcement Act of May 31, 1871, the federal government attempted to prosecute the perpetrators at Colfax, charging them with conspiracy to deprive the victims of their constitutional rights. The validity of the indictment was challenged by defense counsel and the case, *U.S. v. Cruikshank,* made it to the United States Supreme Court, where a unanimous court rejected the indictment and discharged the defendants. In the majority opinion, Chief Justice Morrison Waite restricted the enforcement powers of the federal government to state violations and not the actions of private individuals. Waite argued that the state, not the federal government, had the duty to protect the rights listed in the indictment. For the protection of the people's right to peaceable assembly, for example, Waite stated that "the people must look to the States. The power for that purpose was originally placed there, and it has never been surrendered to the United States."[21] The federal government, therefore, could only intervene when state governments were violating the rights, not in cases where individual citizens were at fault. When it considered the question of whether the victims' voting rights under the Fifteenth Amendment had been violated, the court accepted the reasoning of a lower court and demanded proof of overt racist intent. Because the indictment did not state that the defendants acted with the explicit intent "to deprive the injured persons of their rights on account of their race," the federal government lacked the authority to intervene.[22] While the decision did not declare the enforcement acts unconstitutional, their power had been effectively destroyed. A federal district attorney in South Carolina expressed his sense of powerlessness after *Cruikshank,* frustrated that the federal government could offer no remedy for white violence "unless it can be proved to have been done on account of race. . . . It is hard to sit quietly and see such things."[23]

Conservative southern whites, sensing that the government no longer possessed the resources or the will to enforce the law, intensified their drive for power. In his study of South Carolina, Richard Zuczek has argued that "the North stopped fighting—physically and mentally—in 1865; the South, however, did not."[24] Violence was not scattered or disorganized but was employed as a conscious strategy to overthrow Republican state governments. Voter fraud, economic pressure, death threats, and large-scale attacks like Colfax were used to crush racial equality and Republican power. As James Hogue has stated, "Reconstruction politics became the continuation of civil war by another name."[25] In an 1875 letter to President Grant, General Philip Sheridan estimated that there had been over 3,500 politically motivated killings in Louisiana in a 10-year period. He catalogued nearly 2,000 deaths in 1868 alone, mostly of freedpeople, and no successful prosecutions for murder. By the mid-1870s, the federal government had few resources and even less motivation to deal with the violations of civil and political rights that would soon destroy Reconstruction. The United States military was deployed in specific locations to limit violent outbreaks or preserve the peace at election times, but the number of troops was too small to stem the tide. In 1868, the United States had roughly 17,000 troops stationed in the former Confederacy; one-third of which were in Texas to deal with Indian issues. That number decreased each year, and in 1874, there were only 7,700 troops in the South, more than half in Texas. Most federal troops were stationed near towns and thus away from the rural areas where the majority of Southerners lived and worked.[26]

Though a larger military presence in the South might have been an effective deterrent to paramilitary violence, northern public opinion did not support it. The cost of maintaining troops in the midst of an economic recession was certainly one factor, but more important was the general antipathy to using the power of the bayonet to bring about political change. Northerners increasingly believed that if state governments could only survive with military intervention, then they lacked legitimacy. This discomfort with military occupation gave conservative southern whites the opportunity to use violence to take control of state governments.

Nowhere was this more apparent than in the Deep South. As the 1874 state elections approached in Louisiana, for example, members of the White Leagues disrupted Republican political meetings all over the state and used the implicit threat of Colfax-style violence to force Republican officeholders to resign in large numbers. Although federal troops were called to New Orleans several times to prevent a full-scale seizure of the state government by armed white supremacists, the impact of white violence effectively suppressed the Republican vote and allowed for the return of a Democratic majority in early 1875. Two years would pass before the full "redemption" of Louisiana's government by southern Democrats was complete, but the combination of a determined white-supremacist insurgency and federal government weakness was the key to ending Reconstruction in the South.[27]

In addition to the paramilitary groups that drove Republicans from power in states like Louisiana, the redemption movement also required a new kind of southern Democratic leader, one who could project a moderate, reasonable face in national politics. By the mid-1870s, just such a group, often called Bourbon Democrats, had emerged in the South and they presented themselves to a weary northern public as a conservative, but loyal and public-spirited alternative to the weakened and conflicted Reconstruction state governments. Lucius Quintus Lamar of Mississippi, for example, who had once served as an officer in the Confederate army, was elected as a Democrat to the United States House of Representatives in 1873 where he interacted quite amicably with his Republican opponents, even delivering a glowing eulogy following the death of the radical Republican senator Charles Sumner. Rather than rail openly against Reconstruction, Lamar adopted a statesmanlike acceptance of its current reality while working assiduously to destroy it in Mississippi. Other Bourbons or simple "conservatives" followed suit, keeping violent white supremacist organizations at a distance even as they benefitted from the political conditions that such groups created.[28]

The effectiveness of this strategy was most evident in Mississippi, a state in which African American voting rights had produced Republican majorities in both Houses of the state legislature and the election of Adelbert Ames, a New Englander and former Union general, as governor in 1873. In what became known as the "Mississippi Plan," however, the state's Democrats launched a campaign of intimidation and violence that destroyed the Republican Party and guaranteed the return of white supremacists to power. In the lead up to state elections in 1875, for example, Democrats began to harass both white and black Republicans wherever they attempted to meet and speak. In the face of what one Republican sheriff described as a "perfect organized armed opposition that embraced the entire [D]emocratic [P]arty," many white Republicans simply renounced their party allegiance or withdrew from political activity

L.Q.C. Lamar of Mississippi exemplified the strategy of southern Democratic leaders during the early 1870s in avoiding overt conflict with federal Reconstruction policies while working behind the scenes to destroy them. (Library of Congress)

altogether.[29] When black Republicans gathered for political meetings, moreover, armed white militias provoked conflict and then insisted that they had appeared only to suppress rioting blacks. A conflict of just this kind occurred in Clinton, Mississippi, where blacks who attempted to defend themselves against a white paramilitary group were dispersed and then hunted down and murdered outside the town. In the aftermath of such incidents, white Democratic leaders like Lucius Lamar publicly lamented the use of violence by members of his party but blamed Governor Ames for failing to keep blacks in line. White Republican James Lee of Monroe County told Governor Ames that the level of violence was more extreme than anything he had seen since the Civil War. "They intended to carry the next general election in this state at any cost," he lamented.[30]

Governor Ames found himself in an untenable position. Since the only state militia forces at his disposal were made up exclusively of blacks, any attempt to use them to restore order would further inflame whites. Appealing to President Grant for military assistance would simply reinforce the claims of white Democrats who insisted that he was an incompetent leader unworthy of his office. When no viable alternative had emerged by September 1875, however, Ames finally asked the president for help, pleading that "the power of the U.S. government alone can give the security our citizens are entitled to."[31] Still reeling from the effects of the panic and desperately trying to hold his party together, Grant refused to risk conservative disapproval by intervening in Mississippi. Advisors insisted that any further military action in the South would lead to a Democratic victory in the 1875 gubernatorial election in Ohio, a key state in the national balance of power. Unable or unwilling to see the terrible realities Ames was facing, the president rather blithely suggested that the governor strengthen his "position by exhausting his own resources in restoring order, before he receives government aid."[32] The result of the policy was the utter defeat of Mississippi Republicans in 1875, with the Democrats' strategy turning what had been a huge deficit in the 1873 elections into an overwhelming majority 2 years later, a swing of as many as 50,000 votes. Democrats carried some counties of the state by majorities that were larger than the total number of registered voters, thus adding voter fraud to the party's new approach to taking power. Yet Democratic leaders insisted that theirs was a legitimate victory, representing the state's "redemption" from corruption and misrule. As historian Richard Current has put it, "Mississippi Democrats of 1875 were masters of the Big Lie."[33]

The "Mississippi Plan" became a blueprint for southern Democrats who read Grant's refusal to intervene in Mississippi as a clear signal that the defeat of Reconstruction was at hand. Other states followed aspects of the approach, with South Carolina holding most closely to Mississippi's example. During the 1876 election, for example, Democrats intent on violent intimidation to suppress the Republican vote demanded that black militia companies surrender their weapons in advance of the polling. When a black unit in Hamburg, South Carolina, refused to comply, armed vigilantes surrounded them in a local armory building and threatened them with murderous rifle and artillery fire. After a brief firefight in which both sides suffered casualties, the black troops were captured by the mob

Former Confederate general Wade Hampton became governor of South Carolina after a disputed election in the state was resolved as part of the Compromise of 1877. (Library of Congress)

and at least five of them were shot to death after being told by their captors to flee. Republican governor Daniel Chamberlain's request for military assistance in advance of the election resulted in the dispatch of about 5,000 troops to the state, but South Carolina Republicans were in serious trouble. Highly organized paramilitary units known as Red Shirts brutally intimidated Republican voters and drummed up support for the Democratic candidate for governor, the former secessionist and Confederate general Wade Hampton. Although the result of the election was disputed due to evidence of massive voter fraud in Edgefield and Laurens counties, jubilant white Democrats celebrated victory anyway and proceeded to organize the state government. Similar Democratic successes occurred in other parts of the South, suggesting that "redemption" was a movement whose time had come.[34]

The results of the 1876 election in South Carolina were much closer than those in Mississippi had been a year earlier, and the disputed tallies in two counties became part of a larger national drama in which the future of Reconstruction once again hung in the balance. The presidential election that year, a contest between New York Democrat Samuel Tilden and Ohio Republican Rutherford B. Hayes, had been inconclusive. Tilden won the popular vote by a slim margin, and he appeared to have prevailed narrowly in the Electoral College as well. But returns in three southern states, Louisiana, South Carolina, and Florida, were contested by sitting Republican governors who insisted that Democratic victories resulted from intimidation and fraud. Determined to settle the issue prior to inauguration day in March, Congress appointed a bipartisan election commission to review the evidence and to make a final, and legally binding, decision on the distribution of electoral votes. Although the commission would determine the next occupant of the White House, its decision would also have a bearing on the fate of the Republican Party in the three southern states where it was desperately clinging to power. Would the nation permit the systematic suppression of black voters and allow Democrats to take control of the entire South, or was there some remaining commitment to the Fifteenth Amendment among Republicans and the northern public?

Unfortunately for advocates of biracial democracy, there were clear signs by 1876 that the Republican Party was on the brink of abandoning Reconstruction altogether. In addition to President Grant's refusal to intervene in Mississippi, congressional Republicans had come to regard Reconstruction governments as scandal-ridden embarrassments that could only be maintained through expensive and unpopular military occupation. Having lost control of Congress in the 1874 elections, Republicans attempted to rebrand their party as a bastion of sound economic principles, good government reformism, and Protestant moral virtue. Although they continued to describe Democrats as unpatriotic "copperheads" who had failed to support the nation in its time of dire need, they carefully avoided any support for Reconstruction in the South. Republican journalists in the North recognized that in order to win the election, their presidential candidate would have to distance himself from Reconstruction, making clear his intention to "withdraw the troops" and take a "hands off" policy toward

This Thomas Nast cartoon illustrates the explosive issues at stake in the contested election of 1876. (Library of Congress)

the South.[35] While Hayes was not willing to speak quite so bluntly, careful readers of his speeches could find more than a few hints of his intentions. In accepting the Republican nomination, for example, he emphasized the need for a final sectional reconciliation that would restore "honest and capable local government" in the South, a coded but nonetheless clear indication that he was not interested in vigorous enforcement of civil rights or voting rights laws.[36]

Although elements of the Republican political base remained committed to civil and political equality for blacks, many of them were content with leaders who gave rhetorical rather than substantive support to enforcement. In 1875, for example, Congress passed a new civil rights bill in honor of Senator Charles Sumner who had died from a heart attack in March 1874. The original bill prohibited any form of racial segregation in schools, churches, juries, cemeteries, and other public places, and it received the support of abolitionists and black politicians who argued that "So long as the freedmen are excluded from the public schools, equal seats in the railroad cars and churches, and places of amusement and hotels, our work is not done."[37] Yet by the time it was passed, the sections on school desegregation had been removed and the enforcement provisions of the law had been weakened. A majority of the Republican legislators who voted for the measure, moreover, were either voluntarily retiring from political life or had been defeated in the fall 1874 elections. Sensing that the law was a symbolic gesture rather than a serious attack on inequality, black legislator Henry McNeal Turner described it as "a patched up apology for a Civil Rights Bill."[38]

Given this context, it was unlikely that congressional Republicans would provide any long-term support for Republican governments in Florida, South Carolina, or Louisiana during the negotiations over the disputed 1876 presidential election. The electoral commission, which was to investigate the returns in the contested states, was divided evenly between Republican and Democratic members of Congress, but it also contained five Supreme Court Justices, two Republicans, two Democrats, and one independent, David Davis of Illinois. When Justice Davis was elected to the Senate, however, he was replaced by another Republican justice, Joseph Bradley, giving Republicans effective control of the commission. A major issue that the commission faced was how deeply to scrutinize the results in disputed states. Democrats insisted that the investigation must explore the details of popular vote counts, but Republicans contended that the commission must instead accept results as they were certified by Republican state officials. With a pivotal vote cast by Justice Bradley, the commission took the latter course and as a result awarded all of the contested electoral votes to Hayes, who thereby prevailed over Tilden in the Electoral College by a single vote. Democrats used various parliamentary tactics to prevent Hayes's formal election, but they were unsuccessful and he took office as president in March 1877.

Although many Democrats felt betrayed by what they regarded as a stolen election, they acquiesced in President Hayes's peaceful inauguration because of secret political assurances that had been worked out in advance of the final settlement. In the Compromise of 1877, Democrats agreed to accept the legitimacy of the new president in exchange for certain guarantees: the most important of which were the withdrawal of federal troops from the South and the acceptance of a Democratic takeover in South Carolina, Louisiana, and Florida. Once in office, Hayes was as good as his word, ordering the federal troops protecting Republican governors in South Carolina and Louisiana to stand down and offering no assistance to Republicans in Florida. In New Orleans, federal troops had been protecting the state capitol and the Republican claimant for the governorship after his Democratic rival had seized control of government offices and the police force. Hayes's order that the troops return to barracks ended the nearly four-month siege of New Orleans with the Democrats firmly in control of Louisiana politics. The result of the Compromise of 1877, therefore, was the "redemption" of the last three Reconstruction governments in the South and the beginning of a new era of Jim Crow segregation and political disenfranchisement for blacks in the region. Although it would take the better part of two decades to complete the process of removing African Americans from political power and participation, white southern Democrats now possessed the local and state autonomy they needed to defeat the most basic goals of Reconstruction.[39]

In addition to the political defeat of Reconstruction in the South, the United States Supreme Court also rolled back the scope of change by consistently narrowing Congress's power over state actions and by watering down the substance of the three Reconstruction amendments. Although the 1873 *Slaughterhouse Cases* did not deal specifically with Reconstruction or civil rights issues, the case nevertheless struck an important blow against congressional authority. The court's majority in this decision rejected the argument of Louisiana butchers that a state law granting a monopoly to slaughter animals to one company in New Orleans violated their rights under the Fourteenth Amendment. Writing for the majority, Justice Miller argued that the regulation of slaughterhouses was a traditional power of states and the Fourteenth Amendment was not designed to restrict "the exercise of legislative power by the States, in their most ordinary and usual functions."[40] While much of the Reconstruction-era legislation increased the power of the federal government over states, the court retained a more traditional understanding of federalism.

In the *Civil Rights Cases* in 1883, the court ruled on the constitutionality of the Civil Rights Act of 1875, combining five cases in which African Americans had been denied equal access to restaurants, theaters, railroad cars, and hotels. At issue was whether the act had properly used the enforcement clause of the Fourteenth Amendment to prohibit racial discrimination in public accommodations. In striking down the Civil Rights Act of 1875, the court denied that Congress had jurisdiction over discrimination by private individuals. According to Justice Bradley, the Fourteenth Amendment did not cover private discrimination, but only prohibited state action. "Individual invasion of individual rights," argued Bradley, "is not the subject matter of the amendment." The lone dissenter in the case was John Marshall Harlan who rejected Bradley's narrow reading of the Fourteenth Amendment. Harlan argued that since "railroad corporations, keepers of inns, and managers of places of public amusement are agents or instrumentalities of the State," they were therefore "amenable . . . to governmental regulation." Though the Civil Rights Act of 1875 had been among the weakest of congressional attempts to promote racial equality, Harlan understood that the court's ruling in the case was a major defeat for all of the nation's civil rights laws. He ended his dissent with a reminder that Congress had recognized "the legal right of the black race to take the rank of citizens, and to secure the enjoyment of privileges belonging, under the law, to them."[41] In the post-Reconstruction era, voices like those of Justice Harlan were a distinct minority.

*****

Given the fact of Redemption and the federal government's rapid retreat from the promises of robust citizenship for African Americans, what was the legacy of Reconstruction? For conservative whites in the South, Reconstruction was a threat to their customary power and was therefore something to be resisted, using any means possible. For Republicans, Reconstruction was an opportunity to transform their sectional party into a national one and to support the political equality of freedpeople. For millions of former slaves, Reconstruction represented a chance to throw off the shackles of slavery and to determine for themselves what freedom would mean.

Reconstruction has often been presented primarily as a political event—the moment when the requirements for the readmission of the southern states would be decided. Judged by the limited goal of restoring the political unity of the United States, Reconstruction achieved its objective. Northern and southern white men who had killed one another by the hundreds of thousands during the Civil War years were now reunited in political parties, businesses, and some religious denominations. Although sectional antagonism certainly persisted, as leaders in each region still "waved the bloody shirt" of war from time to time to rally regional political support, the ex-Confederate states had successfully reentered the political and economic life of the nation after four years of truly catastrophic Civil War.

But African Americans, white abolitionists, and radical Republicans had embraced broad principles of equality and social justice at the end of the war, and these groups argued that Reconstruction meant more than restoration. The resistance of white Southerners to even modest demands provoked congressional Republicans to listen to these more radical voices and push for civil and political equality for African Americans. The Fourteenth and Fifteenth Amendments stand as an enduring legacy of the efforts of countless Americans who wanted to make the promise of freedom a reality. Yet as congressional Republicans debated legislation guaranteeing black suffrage and equality before the law, they confronted a plethora of countervailing pressures. The Constitution protected the sovereignty of states, and many in government refused to wipe away these traditional prerogatives in order to expand federal power in the name of justice. Federalism, therefore, created a powerful barrier to the continued enforcement of the Reconstruction amendments, and as time passed, many Northerners grew weary of continued sectional conflict. In agreements such as the Compromise of 1877, northern whites chose reconciliation with their former enemies over equality for former slaves. "[T]he forces of reconciliation overwhelmed the emancipationist vision in the national culture," writes historian David Blight. "For many whites . . . healing from the war was simply not the same proposition as doing justice to the four million emancipated slaves and their descendants."[42]

Could the course of Reconstruction have been different? Some historians have argued that a sustained military occupation of the South would have been enough to counter the determined resistance of white Southerners to racial and political change. Looking back at the events of his presidency, Ulysses S. Grant concluded that "Military rule would have been just to all, to the Negro who wanted freedom, the white man who wanted protection, the Northern man who wanted Union." So why didn't President Grant follow the course he thought was just? "The trouble about military rule in the South," Grant explained, "was that our people did not like it. It was not in accordance with our institutions."[43]

Americans were simply unwilling to rely so heavily on military means to bring about political change. In hindsight, President Grant may have concluded that Thaddeus Stevens's plan to reduce the South indefinitely to a territorial condition would have been a more effective mechanism to change the region, but it was never politically viable. Accepting the political reality, Grant argued that "we made our scheme, and must do what we can with it."[44]

Grant's comments reflect the disappointment of many that Reconstruction did not go far enough. Yet a growing number of historians have shifted our attention away from the partisan battles in Washington and focused instead on the momentous social transition from slavery to freedom. This examination of the social meaning of emancipation has revealed deep, fundamental change to Southern society as blacks and whites sought to reconstruct households and the system of labor. In countless individual acts, freedpeople determined the meaning of emancipation by leaving the land of their former masters or by refusing to work for terms dictated by white planters. As freedpeople sought self-determination, white Southerners did their best to hold onto racial privilege and curtail the meaning of freedom. These negotiations occurred in private spaces, but they nevertheless reflected a profoundly altered environment. After emancipation, white women, for example, were in the unfamiliar and frankly unsettling position of negotiating with black women over domestic labor, and some employers were slow to realize that freedwomen would simply seek employment elsewhere if they did not like the terms. Despite the efforts of white employers, therefore, freedpeople rejected the subjugation they had experienced as slaves. Reflecting the altered consciousness, one freedwoman was overheard saying, "My Mis don't like it because I won't answer, but I ain't got no call to answer now."[45]

Defining freedom as broadly as possible, African Americans took enormous risks to achieve literacy, political rights, economic opportunity, and family security. When possible, they forged alliances with whites and fought back against the reactionary forces that threatened to undo even the most basic meaning of emancipation. In the early years of Reconstruction, when state and national forces appeared on the verge of restoring antebellum political, social, and economic conditions, this alliance proved highly effective in demanding another course. If Congressional Reconstruction did not go far enough in ensuring either economic or political justice, black leaders in the South nevertheless played a critical role in the establishment of public schools and the development of regional infrastructure. At the grass roots level, black Southerners went to the polls, built churches, attended schools, demanded respect from white neighbors, and built lives of purpose and dignity. These strong roots would survive the collapse of Reconstruction and would provide extremely fertile ground for the freedom struggles a century later. "We still live, and while there is life there is hope," Frederick Douglass told an audience in 1880. "Let us, then, wherever we are, whether at the North or at the South, resolutely struggle on in the belief that there is a better day coming."[46]

NOTES

1. Edwards Pierrepont to Adelbert Ames, September 14, 1875, in *The Civil War and Reconstruction: A Documentary Collection*, ed. William E. Gienapp (New York: W.W. Norton, 2001), 407.

2. William Gillette, *Retreat from Reconstruction, 1869–1879* (Baton Rouge: Louisiana State University Press, 1979), 14.

3. James M. McPherson and James K. Hogue, *Ordeal by Fire: The Civil War and Reconstruction* (New York: McGraw-Hill, 2010), 587.

4. Nicholas Lemann, *Redemption: The Last Battle of the Civil War* (New York: Farrar, Straus and Giroux, 2006), 80.

5. Heather Cox Richardson, *The Death of Reconstruction: Race, Labor, and Politics in the Post-Civil War North, 1865–1901* (Cambridge: Harvard University Press, 2001), 68, 94–95; Steven Hahn, *A Nation Under Our Feet: Black Political Struggles in the Rural South from Slavery to the Great Migration* (Cambridge: Harvard University Press, 2003), 262.

6. Godkin quoted in Michael Les Benedict, "Reform Republicans and the Retreat from Reconstruction," in *The Facts of Reconstruction: Essays in Honor of John Hope Franklin*, eds. Eric Anderson and Alfred E. Moss, Jr. (Baton Rouge: Louisiana State University Press, 1991), 70.

7. Carl Schurz speech in U.S. Senate, January 30, 1872, in *Speeches, Correspondence and Political Papers of Carl Schurz*, vol. 2, ed. Frederic Bancroft (New York: G.P. Putnam's Sons, 1913), 326–327.

8. Andrew L. Slap, *The Doom of Reconstruction: The Liberal Republicans in the Civil War Era* (New York: Fordham University Press, 2006), 201.

9. Horatio Seymour to Tilden, October 3, 1872 in *Letters and Literary Memorials of Samuel J. Tilden*, vol. 1, ed. John Bigelow (New York: Harper & Brothers, 1908), 311.

10. Gillette, *Retreat from Reconstruction*, 66–67.

11. Allen W. Trelease, *White Terror: The Ku Klux Klan Conspiracy and Southern Reconstruction* (New York: Harper & Row, 1971), 365.

12. *Testimony Taken by the Joint Select Committee to Inquire into the Condition of Affairs in the Late Insurrectionary States, Vol. 6: Georgia* (Washington, D.C., 1872), 517.

13. Trelease, *White Terror*, 388–389; Xi Wang, *The Trial of Democracy: Black Suffrage & Northern Republicans, 1860-1910* (Athens: University of Georgia Press, 1997), 58–66.

14. Mark S. Weiner, *Black Trials: Citizenship from the Beginnings of Slavery to the End of Caste* (New York: Vintage, 2004), 198.

15. Gillette, *Retreat from Reconstruction*, 52.

16. Xi Wang, *Trial of Democracy*, 83.

17. Philip Dray, *Capitol Men: The Epic Story of Reconstruction through the Lives of the First Black Congressmen* (New York: Houghton Mifflin, 2008), 259.

18. William S. McFeely, *Frederick Douglass* (New York: W.W. Norton, 1991), 286; Barbara Josiah, "Providing for the Future: The World of the African American Depositors of Washington DC's Freedmen's Savings Bank, 1865-1874," *Journal of African American History* 89 (Winter 2004), 7–11.

19. U.S. Grant, veto of the Currency Act, April 22, 1874, in *The Papers of Ulysses S. Grant*, vol. 25, ed. John Y. Simon (Southern Illinois University Press, 2003), 74.

20. LeeAnna Keith, *The Colfax Massacre: The Untold Story of Black Power, White Terror, and the Death of Reconstruction* (New York: Oxford University Press, 2008), 110.

21. *U.S. v. Cruikshank*, 92 U.S. 542 (1876).

22. Keith, *Colfax Massacre*, 145.

23. Xi Wang, *Trial of Democracy*, 126–133, quote, p. 131; Charles Lane, *The Day Freedom Died: The Colfax Massacre, the Supreme Court, and the Betrayal of Reconstruction* (New York: Henry Holt, 2008), 245–246.

24. Richard Zuczek, *State of Rebellion: Reconstruction in South Carolina* (Columbia: University of South Carolina Press, 1996), 6.

25. James K. Hogue, *Uncivil War: Five New Orleans Street Battles and the Rise and Fall of Radical Reconstruction* (Baton Rouge: Louisiana State University Press, 2011), 9.

26. Hogue, *Uncivil War*, 1–2; Mark Grimsley, "Wars for the American South: The First and Second Reconstructions Considered as Insurgencies," *Civil War History* 58 (March 2012), 12.

27. McPherson and Hogue, *Ordeal by Fire*, 640–641.

28. Lemann, *Redemption*, 104–105.

29. James W. Lee to Adelbert Ames, Feb. 7, 1876, in *The Civil War and Reconstruction*, ed. Gienapp, 408.

30. Ibid; Lemann, *Redemption*, 111–114.

31. Eric Foner, *Reconstruction: America's Unfinished Revolution* (New York: Harper & Row, 1988), 560.

32. Pierrepont to Ames, September 14, 1875, in *The Civil War and Reconstruction*, ed. Gienapp, 407.

33. Richard Nelson Current, *Those Terrible Carpetbaggers: A Reinterpretation* (New York: Oxford University Press, 1988), 324.

34. Zuczek, *State of Rebellion*, 159–187.

35. Gillette, *Retreat from Reconstruction*, 317.

36. Rutherford B. Hayes to Edward McPherson, Wm. A. Howard, Jos. H. Rainey, June 8, 1876, in *Major Problems in the Civil War and Reconstruction*, ed. Michael Perman (New York: Houghton Mifflin, 1988), 407.

37. James M. McPherson, "Abolitionists and Civil Rights Act of 1875," *Journal of American History* 52 (December 1965), 506.

38. Douglas Egerton, *The Wars of Reconstruction* (New York: Bloomsbury Press, 2014), 311.

39. Hogue, *Uncivil War*, 165–174.

40. Stanley I. Kutler, *Judicial Power and Reconstruction Politics* (Chicago: University of Chicago Press, 1968), 139.

41. *Civil Rights Cases*, 109 U.S. 3 (1883).

42. David Blight, *Race and Reunion: The Civil War in American Memory* (Cambridge: Harvard University Press, 2001), 2–3.

43. John Russell Young, *Around the World with General Grant*, ed. Michael Fellman (Baltimore: Johns Hopkins University Press, 2002), 336–337.

44. Ibid.

45. Thavolia Glymph, *Out of the House of Bondage: The Transformation of the Plantation Household* (Cambridge: Cambridge University Press, 2008), 163.

46. Frederick Douglass, *Life and Times of Frederick Douglass* (London, 1882), 442.

ANALYTICAL ESSAYS

COUNTERFACTUAL ESSAY: WOULD RECONSTRUCTION HAVE BEEN DIFFERENT IF LINCOLN HAD LIVED?

Andrew Johnson had a profound impact on the course of Reconstruction. In May 1865, President Johnson proposed a plan that offered amnesty to most southern whites who pledged their loyalty and required that some large landholders apply for a presidential pardon. Southern states would be restored to their prewar position once they had ratified the Thirteenth Amendment abolishing slavery and repudiated both secession and the Confederate war debt. Though white Southerners might have thought themselves fortunate to escape harsher demands, they chose instead to resist the president's plan. Southern states, for example, passed a series of discriminatory laws known as black codes that defined the status of African Americans in terms that were not radically different from slavery. In addition, the southern electorate did not select loyal Union men for political office, preferring instead former Confederate officials like Alexander Stephens. When Congress wanted to use the power of the national government to protect freedpeople, Johnson stood in the way. Opposed to using the power of the federal government to remake Southern society or to protect the civil rights of African Americans, Johnson vetoed both an extension of the Freedmen's Bureau Act and the Civil Rights Act of 1866. As a result of Johnson's intransigence toward Congress and Southern refusal to follow the lenient plan the president had offered, radical Republicans took control of Reconstruction, divided the South into military districts, disenfranchised a significant percentage of the white electorate, enfranchised African American men, and provided equality before the law. The intense conflict between Johnson and Congress continued and finally culminated in his impeachment.

Would Reconstruction have followed the same course if Abraham Lincoln had lived? The question invites us to consider how both the process and outcome of Reconstruction were affected by one individual. Lincoln's statements and policies regarding wartime reconstruction provide a starting point, but we must also consider the extent to which postwar political realities might have led Lincoln to modify his wartime plans. While it is impossible to know with certainty how events would have unfolded, scholars have identified important differences between the two leaders. The contrasting political styles of Lincoln and Andrew Johnson, alone, would certainly have had a major impact.

Lincoln's wartime reconstruction plan offers some clues about what Reconstruction would have been like if Lincoln had lived. In December 1863, Lincoln issued "The Proclamation of Amnesty and Reconstruction" in which he advocated pardoning all former Confederates except high-ranking civilian and military officials who would take an oath of future loyalty. As soon as the total number taking the oath in a given state equaled 10 percent of that state's vote total in the 1860 presidential election, this new loyal electorate could reorganize the state government and seek presidential recognition. Congressional opposition emerged both to the specifics of Lincoln's Ten Percent Plan and his assumption that the president would determine the course of Reconstruction. Radical Republican Thaddeus Stevens, for example, argued that the southern states were "conquered provinces" that had lost the privileges of statehood, and Congress could enact sweeping changes as a result. Hoping to slow the pace of wartime reconstruction, radical Republicans offered their own plan. The Wade-Davis Bill required that 50 percent of the electorate swear an oath of allegiance to the United States Constitution and restricted participation in the formation of the new government to individuals who could take an "iron-clad oath," swearing that they had never aided the Confederacy. Under this plan, only Unionists and not Confederates could have taken part in the conventions to create new state governments. After Lincoln's pocket veto of the measure, Benjamin Wade and Henry Winter Davis issued their manifesto, which accused the president of holding the "electoral votes of the Rebel States at the dictation of his personal ambition" and claimed that "[a] more studied outrage on the legislative authority of the people has never been perpetrated."[1]

This conflict over Reconstruction policy suggests certain similarities between the experiences of Lincoln and Johnson. Both devised a plan that favored the speedy restoration of the states that was rejected as too lenient by radicals in Congress. Both Lincoln and Johnson were criticized for assuming presidential prerogative and not including Congress in the formulation of Reconstruction policy. Johnson, himself, sought support by claiming that his policy was an extension of Lincoln's. Yet the dispute over the Wade-Davis Bill also reveals an important difference. Despite the angry and heated rhetoric that went so far as to accuse the president of "dictatorial usurpation," Lincoln did not escalate the conflict with Congress and avoided a break with the radicals in his party. Unlike Andrew Johnson, Lincoln possessed the political skills to navigate through the treacherous water of intraparty disagreements. He retained good personal relationships with members of Congress who criticized him and he understood the importance of not alienating moderates, lessons Johnson would have done well to learn. Lincoln understood how the Republican Party operated and who to call in order to get things done. This fact made him a more effective leader than Johnson, a lifelong Democrat who disagreed with aspects of Republican ideology and who lacked ties to the key party leaders.

Though Andrew Johnson claimed that his May Proclamations merely followed the course set by Abraham Lincoln in states like Louisiana, he ignored the very real fact that Lincoln's plan was proposed in the midst of war and would not have been the only option after the conflict had ended. Noting the fluidity of Lincoln's Reconstruction policy, Eric Foner has argued that "[d]ifferent approaches had operated simultaneously in different parts of the South, all of them conceived as ways to weaken the Confederacy and secure the abolition of slavery rather than as fixed blueprints for the postwar South."[2] Historians have also noted that Lincoln modified his views on a number of key issues as circumstances changed (emancipation being one of the most central), and, as a result, we cannot know what plan Lincoln would have had for Reconstruction once winning the war was no longer an issue. We can safely assume, however, that Lincoln would not have stubbornly held onto a position that was failing and that he would have considered new mechanisms to achieve his objectives if southern whites had refused to cooperate with his initial plan.

Finding it "inconceivable" that Lincoln would have followed Johnson's course, historian William Harris has suggested that Lincoln's political acumen made him more attuned to northern expectations for the postwar settlement. As a result, he would have modified his policies, ceasing to pardon former rebels once evidence of southern defiance was available and restricting their political rights until their cooperation was assured.[3]

When confronted with white southern opposition to black freedom, Lincoln's policies might easily have broadened. In fact, Lincoln's final speech supports the idea that he was moving toward support for black suffrage, the most important issue for radicals. In a speech that defended the wartime Louisiana government against its radical Republican critics, Lincoln publicly endorsed a limited form of black suffrage for the first time: "I would myself prefer that [the vote] were now conferred on the very intelligent and on those who serve our cause as soldiers."[4] With this statement, Lincoln signaled to radical Republicans that he would work with them on some level. If the president during Reconstruction proved able to reconcile the divergent views of Republicans in Congress instead of reflexively rejecting all attempts at protecting the civil rights of African Americans, then he would have removed one of the major catalysts for the radicalization of congressional Republicans that Andrew Johnson provided.

Though we cannot know what program Lincoln would ultimately have endorsed, the powerful differences in the political styles of Lincoln and Johnson suggest that the process of Reconstruction would have been different. Eric Foner has noted that the complexity of Reconstruction required an executive with political dexterity and a willingness to compromise, qualities that were notably absent in Andrew Johnson. Ohio Governor Jacob Cox, for example, presented Johnson as "obstinate without being firm, self-opinionated without being capable of systematic thinking, combative and pugnacious without being courageous." The president, Cox concluded, was "always *worse* than you expect."[5] In 1866, Johnson risked alienating both members of Congress and the general public by his intemperate attacks on radical Republicans like Charles Sumner and Thaddeus Stevens. In a February 1866 speech, Johnson defended his view of Reconstruction as promoting the reunion of North and South but then questioned the loyalty of those Northerners who opposed him, going so far as to equate their actions with the treasonous acts of Southerners like Jefferson Davis and Robert Toombs.

When the audience called out for names, Johnson obligingly replied, "I say Thaddeus Stevens, of Pennsylvania, I say Charles Sumner, I say Wendell Phillips, and others of the same stripe, are among them."[6] A couple of months later Johnson continued his attacks. When a heckler encouraged Johnson to hang Jeff Davis, he responded, "Why don't you hang Thad. Stevens and Wendell Phillips?"[7] Northern Republicans, even those who disagreed with Thaddeus Stevens on the question of black suffrage, might easily have resented the equation of Stevens and Jeff Davis. Certainly the overwhelming support of northern voters for radical Republicans in fall 1866 elections suggests that Johnson had overplayed his hand.

In addition to rhetorical attacks on radicals, Johnson also foolishly alienated moderate Republicans who might have been his allies. When Johnson vetoed the Civil Rights bill sponsored by moderate Illinois senator Lyman Trumbull, he rejected a law that had received broad Republican support and that reflected northern expectations about the meaning of freedom. While the northern public was divided on black suffrage, it did support equality before the law, a principle that was violated by southern states through the black codes. In his veto message, Johnson charged that the bill offered "discriminatory protection to colored persons" and that it raised a "grave question." Johnson asked "whether, where eleven of the thirty-six States are unrepresented in Congress at the time, it is sound policy to make our entire colored population, and all other excepted classes, citizens of the United States. Four millions of them have just emerged from slavery into freedom. Can it be reasonably supposed that they possess the requisite qualifications to entitle them to all the privileges and immunities of citizenship of the United States? Have the people of the several States expressed such a conviction?"[8] Using language that left no room for negotiation, Johnson created a confrontation that resulted in a congressional override of the president's veto, the first time in American history that a major piece of legislation had become law after a presidential veto.

Not only would Lincoln have avoided the cataclysmic collisions that Johnson favored, but Lincoln also supported the principles embedded in the Civil Rights Act of 1866. When he debated Stephen Douglas for the Senate seat in 1858, Lincoln expressed views that were far from racial equality but were also distinct from the overt racism of Douglas (or Johnson). Clarifying his views on racial equality, Lincoln stated that

I hold that . . . there is no reason in the world why the negro is not entitled to all the natural rights enumerated in the Declaration of Independence, the right to life, liberty and the pursuit of happiness. I hold that he is as much entitled to these as the white man. I agree with Judge Douglas he is not my equal in many respects – certainly not in color, perhaps not in moral or intellectual endowment. But in the right to eat the bread, without leave of anybody else, which his own hand earns, *he is my equal and the equal of Judge Douglas, and the equal of every living man.*[9]

Possessing greater sympathy for freedpeople than Johnson, Lincoln might also have been more supportive of the Freedmen's Bureau. Johnson disregarded all efforts of Freedmen's Bureau Commissioner O. O. Howard to moderate his policies and fired agents like Rufus Saxton who sought to help freedpeople. There is no reason to think that Lincoln would have supported land confiscation, but he would have grasped that for freedom to be meaningful, economic opportunity was essential. The president might well have given Freedmen's Bureau agents more leeway to formulate policies that addressed the real economic constraints to freedom that emerged in the postwar South. While it is clear that Lincoln was not a radical, we cannot know how Lincoln might have balanced his belief in free labor and his commitment to the constitutional limits of federal power with the sometimes violent denial of freedom in the South.

In the end, the differences between Lincoln and Johnson on Reconstruction were both of style and substance. The evidence suggests that Lincoln would not only have supported the Republican position of protecting the legal rights of African Americans, but he might well have supported black suffrage. Adept at political negotiation and avoiding vituperative attacks, Lincoln would not have followed Johnson's path of vetoing the Civil Rights Act of 1866. He also would never have advocated southern opposition to the Fourteenth Amendment as Johnson did. When the governor of Alabama encouraged his state to ratify the amendment, Johnson specifically urged him to oppose it. Instead of acting as a mediator, the president fanned the flames of southern intransigence. Unlike Johnson, Lincoln possessed a pragmatic understanding of his political environment that would have allowed him to negotiate the challenges that Reconstruction presented the country. If Johnson had been more flexible, had he been willing to work with the moderates in Congress, then the outcome might have been substantially less far-reaching. With a president and Congress standing behind one policy, the white South might have acquiesced to northern expectations and radical Republicans would have had less power in Congress. While we cannot know what path Reconstruction would have followed if Abraham Lincoln had been able to serve his second term, it is clear that Andrew Johnson left an indelible mark on the history of the period.

Notes

1. The Wade-Davis Manifesto, 1864, in *The Civil War and Reconstruction: A Documentary Collection*, ed. William Gienapp (New York: Norton, 2001), 318.

2. Eric Foner, *The Fiery Trial: Abraham Lincoln and American Slavery* (New York: W. W. Norton, 2010), 333.

3. William C. Harris, *With Charity for All: Lincoln and the Restoration of the Union* (Lexington: University Press of Kentucky, 1997), 274.

4. Abraham Lincoln, April 11, 1865 speech, quoted in Foner, *The Fiery Trial*, 331.

5. Brooks D. Simpson, *The Reconstruction Presidents* (Lawrence: University Press of Kansas, 1998), 110.

6. Andrew Johnson, "Washington's Birthday Address," February 22, 1866 in *Andrew Johnson, His Life and Speeches* by Lillian Foster (New York: Richardson & Co. 1866), 251.

7. Andrew Johnson, "Speech in Cleveland," September 3, 1866, in *The Papers of Andrew Johnson*, vol. 11, ed. Paul H. Bergeron (Knoxville: University of Tennessee Press, 1994), 176.

8. Andrew Johnson, veto of 1866 Civil Rights Bill, in *Andrew Johnson, His Life and Speeches*, 266.

9. Abraham Lincoln's reply to Stephen Douglas, Ottawa Debate, in *The Complete Lincoln-Douglas Debates of 1858*, ed. Paul M. Angle (Chicago: University of Chicago Press, 1991), 117.

DEFINING MOMENTS ESSAY: HOW DID THE PASSAGE OF THE SOUTHERN BLACK CODES CHANGE THE DIRECTION OF RECONSTRUCTION?

Although the Thirteenth Amendment abolished slavery in the United States, Andrew Johnson's Reconstruction policy provided wide latitude for southern states to define what freedom would entail. In August 1865, the *New York Times* warned southern states that they would not be restored to the Union if African Americans were "kept in a state of subordination" and subjected to "peculiar restraints and exactions."[1] Though equal suffrage was not a requirement, the *Times* indicated that certain legal safeguards, especially the right of African Americans to testify against whites, were key preconditions for restoration. Not persuaded by northern sentiment, state legislatures sought to retain white control over black labor and to keep African Americans in a subordinate social position.

In statutes known collectively as black codes, southern legislatures enacted a series of discriminatory laws in 1865–66 that replaced the power of the master with state legislation that controlled freedpeople. The laws of South Carolina and Mississippi were openly discriminatory, applying exclusively to blacks, while other southern states passed laws that omitted overt racial categories but were applied only to African Americans. As the *New Orleans Tribune* noted, the abolition of slavery in Louisiana was not followed by the revocation of the police ordinances to uphold slavery, and as a result, "men are not equal before the law, and not equal before the magistrates as far as Louisiana is concerned."[2] The black codes inflamed northern public opinion against the white South and generated a more radical congressional plan for Reconstruction. As Leon Litwack has argued, the black codes "came to symbolize to the victorious North, white southern intransigence and unrepentance in the face of military defeat."[3]

The purpose of the black codes—whether explicitly or implicitly—was to make legal distinctions between freedpeople and whites. As white Southerners considered how best to restart the southern cotton economy without the slave system that had sustained it for decades, they retained antebellum racial attitudes that included a belief that all blacks would be idle unless compelled to work. The black codes reflected the southern desire to restrict economic options and control the labor of African Americans so that planters would have a predictable, steady labor force.

Since legal emancipation ensured that African Americans no longer be defined as chattel property, southern states needed to create a legal identity for freedpeople, and thus in one sense the mass of black people gained legal personhood for the first time in southern history. In "An Act to Confer Civil Rights on Freedmen," for example, the Mississippi legislature defined the basic rights of freedpeople as being able to sue and be sued, acquire personal property, and testify against whites when an African American was party to the case. Marriage between African Americans would also now be respected in law. But these limited rights should not overshadow the larger purpose of the black codes, which was to minimize the social and economic change brought about by the abolition of slavery.[4]

The most fundamental intent of the black codes was to control and compel black labor at a time when former slaves were seeking greater autonomy. In the aftermath of slavery, freedpeople sought the ability to contract with an employer of their own choosing and to negotiate the terms of their employment. Yet this basic economic freedom would have created a competitive labor market in which wages rose to attract workers. Hoping to minimize day-to-day labor struggles, anxious white employers turned to the state to restrain the economic options available to freedpeople and the result was a variety of vagrancy and apprenticeship laws that could be used "as a means of coercing freedmen into unfair contracts with planters."[5] These provisions of the black codes required that all African Americans sign an annual employment contract. If they left before the year ended, wages were forfeited. To ensure that women and children would also work in the fields, Texas included a provision that compelled the labor of the whole family when the head of household signed an annual contract. In order to limit freedpeople's economic options even further, South Carolina's code restricted freedpeople to the occupational categories of farmer or servant, unless they paid an annual tax. Mississippi denied African Americans the right to rent or lease land, except in urban areas, so that their labor would be available for white planters. To keep wages from increasing, moreover, 10 of the former Confederate states passed anti-enticement laws that prohibited employers from hiring someone already under contract. These codes guaranteed not only that planters would have the labor supply they needed but also that freedpeople would have little bargaining power to negotiate conditions or wages.

While labor contracts were supported by many Northerners as necessary for southern economic growth, some provisions struck observers as too close to slavery and generated support for congressional intervention in the South. A. Watson Webber, the commander of U.S. forces at Columbia, Louisiana, sent a copy of a disturbing labor contract to his superiors. In it, an African American woman promised to work diligently, obediently, and respectfully for her master and to "conduct myself as when I was owned by him as a slave." Her master in turn pledged "to feed clothe,

house and furnish medical attention to her" in the "same quality and quan-
tity as were furnished the employee while she was the slave of the employer."
Emphasizing that this woman's contract was not anomalous, Webber noted
that African American workers in the area were not being adequately com-
pensated for their labor and were "clad in the cast off rags of their slave days."
Based on his observations, Webber concluded, "As it is, the blacks stand just
where they did three years ago as slaves, except that their clothes are more
badly worn, and an officer of the government is their driver. Their proper
freedom is yet a myth."[6] For Northerners who believed that the creation of
a free labor society in the South was a nonnegotiable result of Union victory,
these developments were deeply disturbing.

Vagrancy laws, another common provision in the black codes, were further evidence of southern white recalcitrance. These laws stipulated that
anyone who did not have a labor contract by the second Monday in January would be deemed a vagrant and fined. Those deemed guilty of vagrancy
and unable to pay the fine could then be hired out to a third party who
would pay the fine for them. This often meant six months or, in the case
of Florida, a year's uncompensated labor. A vagrant, however, was not simply defined as an individual without an employment contract. Disrespect
or impudence to an employer could also lead to a sentence as a vagrant
in Florida. Based on his examination of the black codes, Congressman
James Blaine claimed that "no fair man could fail to see" that the effect
of these laws was to reduce blacks to slavery, "a punishment that could be
repeated whenever desired."[7] Like vagrancy laws, apprenticeship laws further
convinced northern observers that the black codes contained too many similarities to the slave system. The arbitrary power assigned to the courts to
apprentice children without the consent of their parents had an obvious parallel to the power of masters to separate families under slavery. Minors in
Mississippi whose parents could not be found or were deemed unable to care
for them were apprenticed to white masters, with a preference given to the
minors' former owners. To control the apprentice, masters were given the
right to inflict "moderate corporeal chastisement." The Freedmen's Bureau
in Mississippi investigated numerous cases of families seeking the return of
children apprenticed without their consent or even knowledge.

Newspaper accounts provided northern audiences with disturbing
descriptions of the racial attitudes that had produced these laws. After an
extended visit to the South, for example, journalist Sidney Andrews stated

that he did not find any southern whites who thought state laws should apply equally to blacks and whites. While some accepted that "the special servitude of man to man" should end, "even the best men hold that each State must have a negro code."[8] Some justified discriminatory laws by appealing to white supremacy. Believing that the abolition of slavery should not mean any alteration of political, economic, or social power, the *Jackson News* ran on its masthead, "This is a white man's country" and argued that the state legislature must keep freedpeople "in the position which God almighty intended," that is, "a position inferior to the white man."[9] The editor of the *Gainesville New Era* stated that "inferiority of social and political position for the Negro race, and superiority for the white race, is the natural order of American Society."[10] The public comments of newspaper editors were also reflected in the private correspondence of southern whites following the war. Edmund Rhett, who offered specific suggestions to a member of South Carolina's convention in October 1865, insisted that "the general interest both of the white man and of the negro requires that he should be kept as near to his former condition as Law can keep him and that he should be kept as near to the condition of slavery as possible, and as far from the condition of the white man as is practicable."[11]

When drafting the black codes, most state legislators in Mississippi and South Carolina ignored the adverse consequences that might result should the North conclude that slavery was being reimposed under a new name. But there were a few voices of caution as some southern politicians worried openly that the rush to impose overtly discriminatory laws like the ones favored by Edmund Rhett was not in the interest of the white South. South Carolina politician James Hemphill, for example, contended that his state's black code would be perceived by the North "as too much of a white man's law."[12] Regretting the path that South Carolina had followed, Julius J. Fleming correctly predicted that the black code would "draw upon us fresh and fierce broadsides from the unfriendly majority which now controls Congress." Understanding the potential fallout, some white Southerners urged greater circumspection and suggested that southern states should have avoided "such ostentatious legal and judicial distinctions between the races."[13]

As Fleming predicted, the passage of the black codes provoked anger in the North. The *Chicago Tribune* proclaimed, "We tell the white men of

Mississippi that the men of the North will convert the State of Mississippi into a frog pond before they will allow any such laws to disgrace one foot of soil in which the bones of our soldiers sleep and over which the flag of free- dom waves."[14] Demanding political consequences for southern actions, the *Tribune* went on to argue that

> We have no words adequate to express our sense of the baseness of such efforts to smuggle slavery back into existence. The North must come up to the position ... that there can be no "Black Codes" whatever in the Southern States, that all laws applicable to one race shall apply to the other, and that no State shall be admitted into the Union until it shall have adopted a provision depriving the Legislature forever of the power to enact one law for blacks and another for whites.[15]

The restoration of southern states, the seating of newly elected southern senators and congressman, and the removal of federal troops from southern soil were impeded by the passage of these laws. Many in the North simply could not agree to the rapid readmission of southern states who were responsible for laws that Congressman James Blaine described as having as reestablished a form of servitude "more heartless and more cruel than the slavery which had been abolished."[16]

In petitions and in the press, moreover, African Americans were among the strongest voices of protest against the many restrictions that black codes imposed upon their freedom. Some petitioners argued that the black codes were incontrovertible evidence that more radical guarantees of equality, especially black suffrage, were necessary. Aware that these dis- criminatory laws revealed the basic intention of white Southerners to con- strict the meaning of freedom, blacks responded by laying claim to a broader spectrum of rights. Refusing to accept the half freedom of the black codes, African American petitioners in South Carolina demanded all of the rights that white American citizens had enjoyed for decades: "The right to assemble in peaceful convention, to discuss the political questions of the day; the right to enter upon all the avenues of agriculture, commerce, trade; to amass wealth by thrift and industry; the right to develop our whole being by all the appliances that belong to civilized society."[17]

While requests for black suffrage did not take root in 1866, the black codes served as evidence that southern states could not be trusted to pro- tect the rights of freedpeople and that strong federal action was required to prevent the return of slavery. Fortunately, many of the provisions of the black codes that explicitly discriminated against blacks never went into effect. The portion of Mississippi's law that prohibited African Americans from renting land outside the city limits, for example, was invalidated by the Freedmen's Bureau. Military leaders also intervened to block the full execution of the black codes. In January 1866, General U.S. Grant ordered southern commanders to protect African Americans from criminal prosecution for "offenses for which white persons are not punished in the same manner and degree."[18] In South Carolina, moderate Governor James Orr worked with General Dan Sickles to suspend all laws that did not apply equally to blacks and whites in the state. The actions of military commanders led Illinois Representative Burton Cook to conclude that "Every act of legislation . . . proves that these people would be again enslaved if they were not protected by the military arm of the Federal Government."[19]

In addition to generating opposition from military commanders, the overtly oppressive character of the black codes also spurred Congress to action. At issue was the meaning of the newly ratified Thirteenth Amendment abolishing slavery. Some in Congress concluded that it did not simply "sever the mere legal ligament by which the person and the service of the slave was attached to the master," but that the amendment conferred basic civil rights to former slaves.[20] By passing the black codes, therefore, southern states made a mockery of emancipation. Burton Cook argued that if freedom meant that a state legislature could pass a law that "a man not supporting himself by labor shall be deemed a vagrant, and that a vagrant can be sold," then "the President had far better never have issued the proclamation of emancipation."[21] As a remedy for the discriminatory black codes, a majority in Congress came to support the federal government guaranteeing a more expansive understanding of freedom and equality before the law through the Civil Rights Act of 1866 and section one of the Fourteenth Amendment. In the end, the black codes played an instrumental role in creating a more radical political climate in which the terms for the restoration of southern states to the Union would be much stricter than President Johnson's moderate plan for Reconstruction.

Notes

1. *New York Times* (August 19, August 29, 1865).
2. *New Orleans Tribune* (July 19, 1865), 4.

3. Leon F. Litwack, *Been in the Storm So Long: The Aftermath of Slavery* (New York: Vintage Books, 1979), 375.

4. *Laws of the State of Mississippi, Passed at a Regular Session of the Mississippi Legislature, Held in the City of Jackson, October, November, and December, 1865* (Jackson, 1866), 82–91.

5. Donald G. Nieman, *To Set the Law in Motion: The Freedmen's Bureau and the Legal Rights of Blacks, 1865–1868* (Millwood, New York: KTO Press, 1979): 72–73.

6. Col A. Watson Webber to Capt S. B. Ferguson, 20 Sept. 1865, enclosing contract between E. W. Reitzell and an unnamed freedwoman, 1 Aug. 1865, Letters Received, ser. 542, Northeastern Dist. of LA, U.S. Army Continental Commands, Record Group 393 Pt. 3, National Archives; reprinted in Freedmen and Southern Society Project, http://www.freedmen.umd.edu/Webber.htm (accessed May 19, 2014).

7. James G. Blaine, *Twenty Years of Congress*, vol. 2 (Norwich, CT: The Henry Bill Publishing Co., 1884), 94.

8. Sidney Andrews, *The South since the War: As Shown by Fourteen Weeks Travel and Observation in Georgia and the Carolinas* (Boston: Ticknor and Fields, 1866), 398.

9. *Jackson News* quoted in William C. Harris, "Formulation of the First Mississippi Plan: The Black Code of 1865," *The Journal of Mississippi History* 29 (September 1967), 185.

10. *Gainesville New Era* quoted in Joe M. Richardson, "Florida Black Codes," *The Florida Historical Quarterly* 47 (April 1969), 367.

11. Rhett letter reprinted in Stephen Budiansky, *The Bloody Shirt: Terror after the Civil War* (New York: Penguin, 2008), 23–24.

12. Joel Williamson, *After Slavery: The Negro in South Carolina during Reconstruction, 1861–1877* (Chapel Hill, University of North Carolina Press, 1965), 76.

13. *Charleston Courier* (December 31, 1865).

14. Quoted in James McPherson and James Hogue, *Ordeal By Fire*, 553; Chicago *Tribune* (December 1), 1865, 2.

15. *Chicago Tribune* editorial reprinted in the *New Orleans Tribune* (December 24 1865).

16. Blaine, *Twenty Years of Congress*, II: 97.

17. State Convention of the Colored People of South Carolina, "Memorial to the Senate and House of Representatives of the United States, November 24, 1865," in *The Civil War and Reconstruction: A Documentary Reader*, ed. Stanley Harrold (Malden, MA: Blackwell Publishing, 2008), 192–193.

18. Nieman, *To Set the Law in Motion*, 78.

19. *Congressional Globe*, 39th Congress, 1st Session, 1125 (March 1, 1866).

20. *Congressional Globe*, 39th Congress, 1st Session, 503 (J. M. Howard speech, January 30, 1866).

21. *Congressional Globe* 39th Congress, 1st Session, 1124 (March 1, 1866).

DOCUMENT ANALYSIS ESSAY: THE FOURTEENTH AMENDMENT

Section 1. All persons born or naturalized in the United States, and subject to the jurisdiction thereof, are citizens of the United States and of the State wherein they reside. No State shall make or enforce any law which shall abridge the privileges or immunities of citizens of the United States; nor shall any State deprive any person of life, liberty, or property, without due process of law; nor deny to any person within its jurisdiction the equal protection of the laws.

Section 2. Representatives shall be apportioned among the several States according to their respective numbers, counting the whole number of persons in each State, excluding Indians not taxed. But when the right to vote at any election for the choice of electors for President and Vice President of the United States, Representatives in Congress, the Executive and Judicial officers of a State, or the members of the Legislature thereof, is denied to any of the male inhabitants of such State, being twenty-one years of age, and citizens of the United States, or in any way abridged, except for participation in rebellion, or other crime, the basis of representation therein shall be reduced in the proportion which the number of such male citizens shall bear to the whole number of male citizens twenty-one years of age in such State.

Section 3. No person shall be a Senator or Representative in Congress, or elector of President and Vice President, or hold any office, civil or military, under the United States, or under any State, who, having previously taken an oath, as a member of Congress, or as an officer of the United States, or as a member of any State legislature, or as an executive or judicial officer of any State, to support the Constitution of the United States, shall have engaged in insurrection or rebellion against the same, or given aid or comfort to the enemies thereof. But Congress may by a vote of two-thirds of each House, remove such disability.

Section 4. The validity of the public debt of the United States, authorized by law, including debts incurred for payment of pensions and bounties for services in suppressing insurrection or rebellion, shall not be questioned. But neither the United States nor any State shall assume or pay any debt or obligation incurred in aid of insurrection or rebellion against the United States, or any claim for the loss or emancipation of any slave; but all such debts, obligations and claims shall be held illegal and void.

Section 5. The Congress shall have power to enforce, by appropriate legislation, the provisions of this article.

*****

The Joint Committee on Reconstruction, composed of 15 members from the House and Senate, was charged with determining the terms by which the former Confederate states would be restored to the Union. After hearing testimony from southern whites, former slaves, and Union soldiers, the committee concluded that a "vindictive and malicious hatred of former slaves" permeated the South. This racial prejudice created an atmosphere in which "acts of cruelty, oppression and murder" were tacitly sanctioned by state and local officials.[1] Civil equality for African Americans was therefore considered essential by the majority of Congress. In light of racial violence and the discriminatory black codes, constitutional guarantees to secure the civil rights of all citizens were needed before the Confederate states could be restored to the Union. The Fourteenth Amendment incorporated a complex assortment of provisions that were before Congress once the Confederacy had been defeated and slavery abolished. Rather than tackling the issues separately, the amendment combined questions of citizenship and equality before the law with reduced representation for the South and the disqualification of former Confederate officials from office holding. While the amendment clearly reflected the Republican Party's egalitarian principles, it also laid the political groundwork for the creation of a party constituency in the South. By favoring Unionists and encouraging the enfranchisement of African Americans, the amendment's architects sought to marry ideals and interests.

Though Republicans dominated Congress, significant intraparty differences existed over specific Reconstruction policies and compromises were necessary to achieve the necessary two-thirds vote in both Houses. The product of intense political negotiation, the Fourteenth Amendment passed Congress on June 13, 1866, and was ratified on July 9, 1868. In the end, they found the language that all but four Republicans in the House and Senate supported, but not all were satisfied with it. Some radical Republicans had hoped that the amendment would include a provision for universal suffrage, but it did not receive the necessary support from moderates. Speaking before the House of Representatives on May 8, 1866, radical Republican Thaddeus Stevens acknowledged that the proposal fell short of his wishes, but he supported it on pragmatic grounds. Assessing northern public opinion, Stevens believed that more radical measures would fail to gain state support. "I shall not be driven by clamor or denunciation to throw away a great good because it is not perfect." Stevens told his colleagues. "I will take all I can get in the cause of humanity and leave it to be perfected by better men in better times."[2] Stevens and other Republicans were motivated by a sense of urgency. Congress and the president were engaged in an escalating conflict, and congressional Republicans wanted to put constitutional safeguards in place before southern states were restored to the Union. To understand this complex and significant document, we must analyze the content of each section, paying specific attention to important changes that were made to the original proposal.

The part of the Fourteenth Amendment that receives the most attention today is the first section, but in fact, it generated less debate at the time than other parts of the amendment. Section 1 begins with a definition of citizenship that included all persons born in the United States, a statement that rejected the Supreme Court's denial of African American citizenship in the 1857 *Dred Scott* case. Congressman James Blaine argued that citizenship needed to be clearly defined in the Constitution to prevent both the states and the judiciary from offering their own interpretation. Section 1 also includes a federal guarantee of equality before the law. Both of these provisions were already present in the Civil Rights Act of 1866, passed over Johnson's veto in April, but section 1 is not simply a restatement of the earlier statute. The language of section 1 of the Fourteenth Amendment is broad and does not include a precise definition of equality before the law: "No State shall make or enforce any law which shall abridge the privileges or immunities of citizens of the United States; nor shall any State deprive any person of life, liberty, or property, without due process of law." Added by Ohio Congressman John Bingham, "privileges and immunities" has an indefiniteness of meaning that stands in marked contrast to the 1866 Civil Rights Act, which specified that all citizens "shall have the same right ... to make and enforce contracts, to sue, be parties, and give evidence, to inherit, purchase, lease, sell, hold, and convey real and personal property, and to full and equal benefit of all laws and proceedings for the security of person and property."[3]

The term "privileges and immunities," used in Article IV, section 2 of the Constitution, might have seemed preferable to a specific list of rights because Republicans in fact disagreed over the specifics. By opting for a statement of broad principle, they minimized acrimonious debate and found common ground. Opening the Senate discussion of the Fourteenth Amendment, Michigan Senator Jacob Howard turned to the Bill of Rights—to freedom of speech and of the press, the right to bear arms, and the right to be exempt from unreasonable searches and seizures—to explain the meaning of "privileges and immunities." Howard went on to argue that the purpose of section 1 was to limit the power of the states to pass discriminatory laws like the black codes and to compel them to "respect great fundamental guarantees" like equal justice.[4] Calling it "a broad statement of principle," historian Eric Foner has argued that the Fourteenth Amendment "challenged legal discrimination throughout the nation and changed and broadened the meaning of freedom for all Americans."[5]

While the first section of the amendment generated little controversy, political leaders struggled to resolve the representation problem caused by the abolition of slavery. Under the original provisions of the U.S Constitution, representation was based on the whole number of free persons in each state and three-fifths of the slave population. With the end of slavery, a state's population would now include all freedpeople, even if those states denied African Americans the right to vote. This change would result in an increase in the number of southern representatives and Electoral College votes. Fearing that "the inevitable effect of the rebellion would be to increase the political power of the insurrectionary states," the Joint Committee on Reconstruction sought a new mechanism to determine representation that would avoid enhancing the political power of southern white Democrats.[6] One possible remedy was to enfranchise African Americans, but even the radical Republicans acknowledged that it was not politically attainable at that time. Republicans instead sought out a compromise measure that would unite the radical and conservative wings of the party.

The Joint Committee initially proposed that representation would be based on the number of qualified voters in each state, but it met with heated opposition from Northern states that did not want their representation decreased because they denied women and immigrants the right to vote. Basing representation on voters instead of population would have benefitted the West and hurt the Northeast. In 1866, California and Vermont had roughly the same population and each had three representatives, but California had more than twice as many voters as Vermont. Similar disparities existed among other states and another mechanism was found to determine representation. As a compromise measure, section two stated that if a state denied suffrage to adult male citizens, then its representation would be reduced by the same proportion. Thaddeus Stevens defended the second section as "the most important" in the amendment because it would encourage states to grant universal suffrage or lose power. He calculated that southern states would have only 37 representatives in Congress, thereby making the region a "hopeless minority," if they failed to enfranchise African Americans. Despite Stevens's optimistic and inaccurate predictions that white Southerners would conquer prejudice and enfranchise African Americans, some Republicans opposed the measure because it accepted that states could deny the right to vote on racial grounds. Radical Republican George Julian argued that section 2 "struck at the very principle of Democracy," and he called it a "scheme of cold-blooded treachery and ingratitude to a people who had contributed nearly two hundred thousand soldiers to the armies of the Union." Most radicals, however, accepted George Boutwell's conclusion that "It was impossible in 1866 to go farther than the provisions of the Fourteenth Amendment."[7]

Women's rights activists like Elizabeth Cady Stanton and Susan B. Anthony opposed the Fourteenth Amendment because it introduced the word "male" into the Constitution for the first time. Section 2 of the amendment did not include any provision that states would lose representation if they denied women the right to vote, only if a state denied suffrage "to any of the *male* inhabitants." In antebellum America, reformers had worked to improve the condition of women and slaves, and Stanton and Anthony were angered when the reform coalition broke down after the war. Former allies like Wendell Phillips had determined that the cause of freedmen was more imperative than that of women. Noting the limitations of the Fourteenth Amendment, Garrett Epps has argued in *Democracy Reborn* that while "black Americans gained formal guarantees of citizenship, women were forced to accept a gender distinction in the reformed Constitution."[8] The combined impact of the Fourteenth and Fifteenth Amendments (which allowed gender to be a legitimate reason to deny a citizen the right to vote) was to sever the reform coalition and lead women's suffrage activists to create an independent movement.

In addition to the controversy surrounding section 2, section 3 also caused debate and revisions to the proposed amendment. In this section, Congress responded to the fact that southern states appeared unwilling to reject the political leaders of the secession movement in favor of loyal men. In the original draft that passed the House, section 3 prohibited anyone who had aided the Confederacy from voting in national elections until 1870. This proposal only covered national elections, so state and local ones would not be affected. While some radicals thought the provision was the "mildest of all punishments ever inflicted on traitors," other Republicans found it too harsh and the section was substantially revised in the Senate.[9] Instead of disenfranchising former Confederate officials, section 3 barred from office anyone who had taken an oath to uphold the U.S. Constitution and then broken it by supporting the Confederacy. The condition was permanent unless two-thirds of Congress voted to remove it. While supporters emphasized that this provision was less vindictive than disenfranchisement, it in fact had a broad impact. Most of the prewar southern political leaders were ineligible to hold office under the Fourteenth Amendment, paving the way for Republican gains in southern states.

The fourth section of the Fourteenth Amendment, which prohibited any interference with pensions for Union soldiers and any repayment of Confederate debt, was not controversial. The inclusion of these provisions into an amendment indicates the concern in Congress that white Southerners, once their states were restored to the Union, might again dominate the government and overturn legislative enactments. James Blaine, for example, worried that if former Confederates united with northern Democrats, they might even object to pensions for wounded soldiers or for the widows of fallen soldiers, if Southerners did not receive the same compensation. For Blaine, therefore, the repudiation of the Confederate war debt needed to be paired with a provision that affirmed the "sacredness" of national pensions. In the final section of the amendment, Congress is formally granted the authority to enforce the provisions of the amendment. This addition was necessary because without it, the Constitution did not delegate to Congress the powers needed to carry out the guarantee of civil equality. The Fourteenth Amendment created a federal guarantee of civil rights, a move that shifted power away from the states and toward the federal government.

Ultimately, the new amendment amounted to a complete plan for Reconstruction. Moderate Republicans argued that if southern states ratified the Fourteenth Amendment, then they would be readmitted. In response, Tennessee quickly ratified the amendment during the summer of 1866 and Congress did readmit the state. While the amendment might have been the basis for readmission, the other 10 southern states defied the will of Congress and roundly rejected it. The amendment received no votes in the state legislatures of Florida, Louisiana, and Mississippi and only a single vote in Virginia and South Carolina. Southern states were encouraged by President Johnson to defy Congress and reject the amendment. The refusal of southern states to acquiesce to civil rights for African Americans led to a more far-reaching plan that included black suffrage. Arguing that white Southerners "brought it upon themselves," James Blaine flatly stated that "The Reconstruction Act would never have been demanded had the Southern States accepted the Fourteenth Amendment in good faith."[10]

Notes

1. *Report of the Joint Committee on Reconstruction* (Washington: Government Printing Office, 1866), xvii.

2. Thaddeus Stevens, May 8, 1866, *Congressional Globe* 39th Congress, 1st Session, 2459.

3. 1866 Civil Rights Act, April 9, 1866, *The Statutes at Large, Treaties, and Proclamations of the* United States of America, vol. 14 (Boston: Little, Brown, and Company, 1868), 27–30.

4. *Congressional Globe*, 39th Congress, 1st Session, 2765–6, May 23, 1866.

5. Eric Foner, *Reconstruction: America's Unfinished Revolution* (New York: Harper & Row, 1988), 257.

6. *Report of the Joint Committee on Reconstruction*, xiii. For analysis of the drafting of the Fourteenth Amendment, see William E. Nelson, *The Fourteenth*

Amendment: From Political Principle to Judicial Doctrine (Cambridge: Harvard University Press, 1988), 45–58.

7. Thaddeus Stevens, May 8, 1866, Congressional Globe 39th Congress, 1st Session, 2459; George W. Julian, *Political Recollections, 1840–1872* (Chicago: A.C. McClurg & Co., 1892), 272; George S. Boutwell, *Reminiscences of Sixty Years in Public Affairs* (New York: McClure, Phillips & Co., 1902), 2 vols, II: 41.

8. Garrett Epps, *Democracy Reborn: The Fourteenth Amendment and the Fight for Civil Rights in Post-Civil War America.* (New York: Holt, 2006), 221.

9. Thaddeus Stevens speech in Congress, May 8, 1866, *Congressional Globe,* 39th Congress, 1st Session, 2460.

10. James G. Blaine, "Ought the Negro To Be Disenfranchised? Ought He To Have Been Enfranchised?—Conclusion," *The North American Review* 128 (March 1879), 278.

PERSPECTIVES ESSAY: HOW RADICAL WAS RADICAL RECONSTRUCTION?

The answer to this question depends in part upon perspective. For many white Southerners, Reconstruction represented an unacceptable, radical intrusion into their most basic rights. Georgia politician and Confederate general Howell Cobb argued that the Military Reconstruction Acts "have deprived us of the protection afforded by our state constitutions and laws, and put life, liberty and property at the disposal of absolute military power." Cobb went on to charge northern "conquerors" with using "their power, both legal and illegal, constitutional and unconstitutional, to make our former slaves *our masters*, bringing these Southern states under the power of *negro supremacy*."[1] White Southerners like Cobb identified a pattern of federal interference with state jurisdiction: The government interfered with their property rights in slaves, and then demanded the ratification of the Fourteenth and Fifteenth Amendments, rewrote state constitutions, and used the military to enforce their vision of a transformed Southern society in which blacks would rule over whites. Congressional action was radical from Cobb's perspective, therefore, not only because the federal government assumed new power, but also because it caused a social transformation where the bottom rail— former slaves—would now be on top.

Most historians do not share Cobb's assessment. Historian Allen Trelease has termed Radical Reconstruction "a halfway revolution." On the side of radical change, Trelease emphasized the granting of political and legal equality to African Americans and the loss of the old planter elite's monopoly on power. The outrage of white conservatives like Howell Cobb confirms that appreciable change did occur, but Trelease argued that "economically and socially there was far less change, and most blacks remained a landless peasantry subject to manifold discrimination."[2] With the ratification of the Thirteenth Amendment, slavery ended in the United States as a legal condition and as a system of labor. But the system of power and privilege that supported slavery persisted and threatened the freedom of former slaves. Reconstruction presented the opportunity for the federal government to revise the allocation of political and social power, and competing visions struggled to win adherents. By and large congressional Republicans rejected radical policies and called for legislation that was in line with traditional understandings of the Constitution. Thus it was the opponents of Reconstruction who presented it as radical, not the supporters.

Congressional Republicans sought instead to extend basic American political rights to African Americans and then leave them alone. When government action did break new ground, it was white supremacist violence and southern intransigence that pushed Republicans to do more. Reflecting back on the passage of the Military Reconstruction Acts, Congressman James Blaine emphasized that "it never could have been accomplished except for the conduct of Southern leaders."[3] Yet even in these instances, concerns about the legitimate exercise of federal power and the use of the army in peacetime limited what the majority of congressional Republicans were willing to support. As a result, former slaves did not receive land during Reconstruction, the military presence in the South was too small and short-lived to bring about equality or even the protection of basic rights, and the text of the constitutional amendments represented significant compromise in principle. In the end, as Michael Les Benedict has argued, " 'Radical Reconstruction' was not very radical after all."[4]

When asked about the meaning of freedom, former slaves often emphasized an economic element, arguing that the ability to be independent and to live by one's own labor would best be achieved through land ownership. Freedpeople had reason to hope that Reconstruction would provide just such a basis for freedom. During the Civil War, land had been confiscated from white planters and the federal government debated whether freedpeople would gain title to this land after the war. In Field Order No. 15, General William T. Sherman reserved confiscated land in the low-country of South Carolina for African Americans, ordering that each family should receive forty acres. But Sherman's field order did not conform to the president's policy, and President Andrew Johnson ordered the immediate return of all confiscated and abandoned land. The sanctity of private property and the demands of federalism made most northern Republicans reluctant to accept widespread redistribution of land. Instead, Republicans subscribed to the free labor ideology, believing that African American freedom could be predicated on their ability to sell their own labor to the highest bidder. Republicans, therefore, promoted the creation of a wage labor system rather than a policy of land redistribution. Only radicals like Thaddeus Stevens of Pennsylvania and Charles Sumner of Massachusetts continued to push for the confiscation and redistribution of land. Thus, when Congress failed to recognize the land claims of freedpeople, it signaled that Reconstruction would not contain a radical economic component. As historians have noted, "freedom defined solely by self-ownership and liberty of contract, without control of productive resources" was narrow and limited.[5] Most freedpeople would remain landless agricultural workers with few options to improve their economic condition.

While congressional Republicans achieved consensus that Reconstruction needed to be rooted in free labor not land redistribution, they debated more strenuously issues of political and civil rights. At the most basic level, the disagreement centered on the proper role of the federal government in reconstructing the former Confederate states. While it had been possible to grant the federal government additional powers in a time of war, many Republicans argued that after the surrender at Appomattox relations between states and the central government should return to prewar patterns as soon as possible. As congressional Republicans defined the political rights of freedpeople, they attempted to expand the reach of the federal government without substantially interfering with traditional state power. The refusal of white Southerners to co-operate with President Johnson's moderate plan led many Republicans to accept the need for increased federal action, but their fundamental adherence to federalism placed limits on what plan they would accept.

The Military Reconstruction Acts, for example, are often presented as evidence of radicalism. The 1868 Democratic Party platform, for instance, called the Military Reconstruction Acts "a flagrant usurpation of power . . . unconstitutional, revolutionary, and void."[6] In response to the violence directed against African Americans in the South and the refusal of southern governments to ratify the Fourteenth Amendment, Congress divided ten southern states into five military districts governed by a military commander. States could only emerge from military occupation by following a series of conditions—ratifying the Fourteenth Amendment, writing new state constitutions, and granting black suffrage. This legislation marked a significant departure from traditional patterns, and states temporarily lost traditional prerogatives. Military commanders, for instance, received the authority to register eligible voters and to remove officials from office who failed to cooperate with the aims of Reconstruction. But these laws also contained limitations on federal power to remake the South. While the most radical members of Congress advocated for an open-ended plan that would allow Reconstruction to continue indefinitely, moderates insisted that readmission to the Union should occur after specific conditions were met. This was a significant blow to radicals, because state readmission severely weakened congressional authority to intervene in southern life.

One of the key achievements of congressional Reconstruction was the Fifteenth Amendment, which addressed black suffrage. After its ratification in 1870, Frederick Douglass equated the Fifteenth Amendment with liberty, equality, and economic independence for African Americans. He contended that the amendment "means that the colored people are now and will be held to be, by the whole nation, responsible for their own existence and their well or ill being. It means that we are placed upon an equal footing with all other men."[7] President Grant shared Douglass's sense of the significance of the amendment, suggesting that it "completes the greatest civil change and constitutes the most important event that has occurred since the nation came into life."[8] With this amendment, Congress took the important step of extending a fundamental political right to a group that had been excluded from the political system, while advancing the electoral chances of southern Republicans at the same time.

The debates in the House and Senate over the Fifteenth Amendment, however, reveal the role of federalism in limiting the effects of Radical Reconstruction. Traditionally, states determined the qualifications for voting, and age, gender, race, and ethnicity were common restrictions.

As Republicans debated whether to enfranchise African Americans, they were also deciding if Congress had the power to supersede traditional state jurisdiction and regulate suffrage. In its final form, the Fifteenth Amendment prohibited states from using "race, color or previous condition of servitude" to restrict voting but allowed them to continue to determine the other qualifications. Historian Xi Wang presents the passage of the Fifteenth Amendment as the work of moderate Republicans, with radicals left hoping for more. Radicals were dissatisfied with the language of the amendment because it did not make a positive guarantee of voting. Massachusetts senator Charles Sumner, for example, had proposed "That the right to vote, to be voted for, and to hold office shall not be denied or abridged anywhere in the United States under any pretense of race or color; and any and all provisions in any State constitutions or in any laws, State, territorial, or municipal, inconsistent herewith are hereby declared null and void."[9] But there was little support for Sumner's proposal because moderates insisted that the authority to determine suffrage remained a state prerogative. As a result, the Fifteenth Amendment stated that race could not be used to restrict voting, but it left open the possibility that other criteria like nativity or gender could be used. Frustrated with the wording of the Fifteenth Amendment, Ohio congressman Samuel Shellabarger argued during congressional debate, "Let it remain possible, under our amendment to still disfranchise the body of the colored race in the late rebel states and I tell you it will be done."[10] Like Sumner, Shellabarger believed that Congress should guarantee equal suffrage.

In the end, the belief in federalism stood in opposition to more radical, affirmative declarations of suffrage and states would continue to determine the qualifications for voting. The *New York Tribune* noted that the Fifteenth Amendment "confers no power whatever on Congress, but only limits the power of the States." Alabama Republican senator Willard Warner was frustrated that the amendment "only provides that certain classes indicated shall not be disfranchised for certain reasons .... For any other reason any State may deprive any portion of its citizens of all share in the Government."[11] Warner's comment correctly identified the limits of the Fifteenth Amendment. Once southern Democrats returned to power, they began to restrict suffrage, using literacy tests, property taxes, poll taxes, and other devices to disqualify the vast majority of African Americans from voting. States also continued to bar women and immigrants from voting. Republicans in the West, for example, had opposed more radical versions of the amendment not because of an opposition to African American suffrage but because it might enfranchise Chinese immigrants. Radicals in both the House and Senate had made alternate proposals in favor of political equality, but a pragmatic concern for compromise carried the day.

Some moderate Republicans hoped that the passage of the Fifteenth Amendment would mark the end of Reconstruction. A growing number of them believed that since equality before the law had been achieved, African Americans should now take care of themselves. The war had been over for five years, the southern states had been restored to the Union, and Congress should stop exceeding its constitutional reach. As one congressman stated, "We are governing the South too much."[12] Yet external pressure did lead to periodic expansion in federal power to protect the rights of former slaves. The murders and assaults committed by groups like the Ku Klux Klan revealed the inability of state and local governments to enforce the law. In the face of a massive amount of violence directed against both white and black Republicans in the South, therefore, Congress decided to assert new powers to enforce both the Fourteenth and Fifteenth Amendments. Historian Xi Wang has argued that the five enforcement acts passed by Congress between 1870 and 1872, "marked the beginning of using national law enforcement to protect citizens' rights in a modern scale."[13]

The enforcement acts represented an unprecedented expansion of the federal government power to protect black voters from terrorist violence. The Enforcement Act of May 31, 1870, for instance, prohibited racial discrimination in voting and made it a federal crime to bribe or intimidate voters. Understanding that discrimination did not simply occur at the polling place, the Enforcement Act also targeted Klan violence. Section 6 made it a felony for two or more people "to injure, oppress, threaten, or intimidate any citizen" or to interfere with "his free exercise and enjoyment of any right or privilege granted or secured to him by the Constitution."[14] The Ku Klux Act of 1871 was designed to enforce the Fourteenth Amendment, penalizing both states and individuals that violated the law. It also expanded the power of the federal government to indict suspected Klansmen and authorized the president to suspend the writ of habeas corpus when he determined that "a condition of lawlessness" existed in a particular county. The Ku Klux Act shifted enforcement power that usually resided with local officials to the federal government, thereby pushing Republicans to what Eric Foner has called "the outer limits of constitutional change."[15] But even here, many Republicans expressed concern about the ramifications of the legislation and stepped back from their support for full equality. Carl Schurz, who had been an early supporter of Radical Reconstruction, opposed the Ku Klux Act, calling it "an encroachment of the national authority upon the legitimate sphere of local self-government."[16] Schurz's comments reveal the intensifying divisions among Republicans over Reconstruction and their growing discomfort with a powerful federal government. Moderates increasingly resisted further action and preferred reunion with white Southerners to continued conflict.

Historians have sometimes argued that a larger military presence would have offered greater protection for Republican voters in the South, but that a prolonged military occupation of the region ran counter to political and economic realities. As southern states were restored to the Union, the number of troops in the South declined markedly. Not only were armies expensive, but Northerners were growing weary of Reconstruction and some concluded that if Republican governments could not exist without military force then they were illegitimate. Although the increased Klan activity in 1870 had prompted President Grant to request greater enforcement powers, he hesitated to use the military to suppress outbreaks of violence. The army could have been used in more instances and military courts could have replaced civilian ones, but this would have altered the balance between civil and military authority. Rejecting Governor Adelbert Ames's request for federal troops in Mississippi to suppress violence against African American voters, Grant's attorney general, Edwards Pierrepont stated that "the whole public are tired out with these annual autumnal outbreaks in the South, and the great majority are ready now to condemn any interference on the part of the Government."[17] By 1875, therefore, the northern interest in active involvement in the suppression of white terror had disappeared.

With the removal of federal troops from the South and the return of southern Democrats to power, the federal government lost vital mechanisms to guarantee its promise of civil and political equality. For historian Hannah Rosen, Reconstruction represented a "promising revolutionary moment," an opportunity for African Americans and northern white politicians to create a biracial coalition committed to legal equality and universal suffrage.[18] Yet it proved ephemeral when conservative whites in the South used violence and intimidation to retake control in the name of white supremacy. Though Republicans dominated Congress during Reconstruction, their moderate view of the Constitution ultimately limited the nature and extent of the change to Southern society. For Reconstruction to bring about a radical transformation, policy makers would have needed to start with a broad definition of freedom for former slaves. Realizing this definition would have required actual and sustained political and legal equality, economic independence, and an end to white supremacy, but these changes did not occur. Conservative whites effectively utilized violence to regain control of state governments and neither the northern public nor the Republican-controlled federal government was willing to vitiate traditional state prerogatives. As Allen Trelease has noted, "National authority and military rule were applied only partially and temporarily after 1865, and often reluctantly at that."[19] Arguments in favor of an enlarged, activist federal government met with opposition not just from Democrats, but from Republicans as well. When drafting the Fifteenth Amendment, Congress rejected more radical proposals that the federal government and not the states should set qualifications for voting. This particular change did not occur until the mid-twentieth century.

Overall, a belief in federalism combined with the need for political compromise and a desire for reunion limited how much authority the federal government would claim during Reconstruction. The widespread violence against African Americans in the South fell within state jurisdiction, and Republicans hesitated before exercising federal power. In the 1870s, a growing number of Republicans believed that the time had come for southern governments to stand or fall on their own and not depend on federal troops for their existence. Southern white conservatives effectively capitalized on this growing discomfort with bayonet government to discredit Republican officeholders as inept. In the end, Howell Cobb was wrong in his assessment: Freedpeople did not become masters and Reconstruction dented but did not overthrow white supremacy.

Notes

1. Howell Cobb to J. D. Hoover, January 4, 1868, in *For the Record: A Documentary History of America*, vol. 1, eds. David R. Shi and Holly A. Mayer (New York: W. W. Norton, 1999), 644.

2. Allen W. Trelease, *White Terror: The Ku Klux Klan Conspiracy and Southern Reconstruction* (New York: Harper & Row, 1971), xxxviii.

3. James G. Blaine, *Twenty Years of Congress: From Lincoln to Garfield*, vol. 2 (Norwich, CT: The Henry Bill Publishing Company, 1886), 262.

4. Michael Les Benedict, *A Compromise of Principle: Congressional Republicans and Reconstruction, 1863–1869* (New York: W. W. Norton, 1974), 13.

5. *Freedom a Documentary History of Emancipation, 1861–1867: Land and Labor, 1865*, series 3, volume 1, ed. Steven Hahn et al. (Chapel Hill: University of North Carolina Press, 2008), 69.

6. James M. McPherson and James K. Hogue, *Ordeal by Fire: The Civil War and Reconstruction* (New York: McGraw-Hill, 2010), 587.

7. Xi Wang, *The Trial of Democracy: Black Suffrage and Northern Republicans, 1860–1910* (Athens, University of Georgia Press, 1997), 51.

8. William Gillette, *Retreat from Reconstruction, 1869–1879* (Baton Rouge: Louisiana State University Press, 1979), 22.

9. *Congressional Globe* 40th Congress, 3rd Session, 1041.

10. Benedict, *A Compromise of Principle*, 332.

11. Warner and the *Chicago Tribune* quoted in Benedict, 331.

12. Gillette, *Retreat from Reconstruction*, 53.

13. Xi Wang, *Trial of Democracy*, 57.

14. *Statutes at Large* 16, (1870): 140–141.

15. Eric Foner, *Reconstruction: America's Unfinished Revolution* (New York: Harper & Row, 1988), 455.

16. Xi Wang, *Trial of Democracy*, 84.

17. Edwards Pierrepont to Gov. Adelbert Ames, Sept 14, 1875, in *The Civil War and Reconstruction: A Documentary Collection*, ed. William E. Gienapp (New York: W. W. Norton, 2001), 407.

18. Hannah Rosen, *Terror in the Heart of Freedom: Citizenship, Sexual Violence, and the Meaning of Race in the Postemancipation South* (Chapel Hill: University of North Carolina Press, 2008), 15–16.

19. Trelease, *White Terror*, xxxviii.

Biographical Essays

ADELBERT AMES (1835–1933)

Adelbert Ames was born in Maine and graduated from West Point in 1861. A decorated Civil War general, he fought in 16 battles, including Gettysburg and Antietam. After the war, Ames served as provisional governor of Mississippi and was then elected as senator from the state in 1870. In the eyes of the white South, Ames was a carpetbagger, an opportunist who favored blacks and alienated white Mississippians. With the support of African American voters, Ames defeated James Alcorn and was elected governor in 1873. The election also resulted in a large Republican majority in both the state House and Senate, with African Americans holding nearly 50 percent of the house seats. Beginning in 1874, state Democrats developed their "Mississippi Plan" to pressure white Republicans to switch parties and then to intimidate black voters. In September 1875, for example, armed whites attacked Republicans at a barbeque in Clinton and then went on to shoot about 30 blacks in the surrounding area. As the violence continued, Governor Ames proved unable to control the situation and asked President Ulysses S. Grant to send troops to the state. Grant ultimately refused, encouraging Ames to use Mississippi's resources to quell the violence. Without federal intervention, the "Mississippi Plan" worked, the Republican vote declined, and Democrats took control of the state legislature. In 1876, the legislature then forced Ames to resign and leave the state rather than face impeachment.

SUSAN B. ANTHONY (1820–1906)

Susan B. Anthony was an educator, public lecturer, and a supporter of the temperance, antislavery, and women's rights movements. Born in Massachusetts, Anthony moved to Rochester, New York, in 1845, where she met a group of abolitionists, including Frederick Douglass. The friendship between Anthony and Elizabeth Cady Stanton began in 1851, and the two women would work together for five decades. They founded the American Equal Rights Association and edited its newspaper, *The Revolution*. Stanton and Anthony opposed the passage of the Fourteenth and Fifteenth Amendments because women were excluded from both measures. Stanton and Anthony formed the National Woman Suffrage Association in 1869 to create a separate movement for women to advocate for a suffrage amendment to the U.S. Constitution. In 1872, Anthony was arrested for trying to vote. She was convicted and fined, but because the judge did not imprison her for refusing to pay the fine, she could not appeal. She served as the president of the National American Woman Suffrage Association from 1892–1900, and the Nineteenth Amendment, which granted women the right to vote in 1920, was named the Susan B. Anthony Amendment.

WILLIAM G. BROWNLOW (1805–1877)

William "Parson" Brownlow was a Methodist circuit rider and political leader in Tennessee during the Civil War and Reconstruction period. He was born into a yeoman family in western Virginia, but lost both parents by the time he was 11 years old. Like many orphaned children of the period, he and his siblings were divided up amongst various relatives. Experiencing a conversion at a Methodist camp meeting in 1825, he decided upon a career as a preacher. Although his education was very limited, Brownlow was by all accounts an intense and quite successful revival preacher. By the 1840s, however, he had left the itinerant ministry for a career in politics and journalism in the eastern region of his adopted state of Tennessee. His newspapers, located in Jonesboro and Knoxville, were fierce in their Whig partisanship and in their denunciation of Jacksonian Democrats. Although Brownlow shared some values with northern evangelical reformers, especially in his support for temperance laws, he opposed abolition and believed that slavery was supported by biblical law. Well before the war, Brownlow developed a reputation as an extremely effective, but utterly unrestrained, debater who used personal invective as a rhetorical weapon. Brownlow's Whig nationalism led him to oppose secession in Tennessee and his persistent, vituperative denunciations of it landed him in prison just months after the state left the Union. Rumors circulated that Brownlow would be executed and he did witness the killings of other Tennessee Unionists during his imprisonment. But in 1862, Confederate authorities in Tennessee escorted Brownlow to Union lines and he spent the following year in the North where he continued to denounce the Confederacy in books, lectures, and newspapers. Appointed as a U.S. Treasury agent in occupied Tennessee in 1863, the "parson" reestablished his newspaper in Knoxville and remained there until the end of the war.

In 1865, Brownlow was elected to the first of two terms as a Republican governor of Tennessee. A longtime and bitter enemy of Andrew Johnson, Brownlow was extremely critical of the new president's policies and proved to be an ally of Congressional Republicans during Presidential Reconstruction. Perhaps most significant was his support for the Fourteenth Amendment, which, when it was ratified by Tennessee in 1866, led to the state's full restoration to the Union. Despite his racism and support for slavery before the war, moreover, Brownlow regarded former slaves as essential to the survival of the Tennessee Republican Party and thus supported legal and political rights for blacks. After his second term as governor, Brownlow served a single term in the United States Senate.

BLANCHE K. BRUCE (1841–1898)

Blanche Bruce was born a slave in Virginia in 1841; his mother was a slave and his father his master. Like many slaves, Bruce used the circumstances of the Civil War to escape from slavery, and in 1861, he settled in Kansas. After the war, he attended Oberlin College for two years before seeking economic opportunity working on a steamboat along the Mississippi River. After settling in Mississippi in 1869, he quickly advanced economically and politically. Bruce became a large landowner and served in many public positions, including tax collector, school superintendent, and sheriff. As school superintendent in Bolivar County, Bruce gained the support of both black and white Mississippians, and by 1872, he had built 21 schools for African Americans. In 1875, Blanche Bruce was sworn in as senator from Mississippi, the first African American to serve a full term in the U.S. Senate. In 1878, Bruce married Josephine Willson from a wealthy Cleveland, Ohio, family, and their Washington parties were well attended by Republican notables and much talked of in the press. James Garfield appointed Bruce Register of the Treasury, a position he held until 1885.

RICHARD "DADDY" CAIN (1825–1887)

An African Methodist Episcopal minister, alderman in Charleston, South Carolina, and the first black clergyman to serve in the U.S. House of Representatives, Richard Cain supported a radical Republican agenda, especially arguing for land ownership for freedpeople. Cain was one of 76 black delegates to South Carolina's 1868 state constitutional convention and impressed those in attendance with the power of his rhetoric. His proposal to create a federally subsidized land commission that would allow freedpeople to buy small parcels of land met with opposition in Washington. The land commission was created, and it purchased roughly 93,000 acres of land, which were then sold to 2,000 black families. Cain personally promoted land ownership by purchasing 2,000 acres of land in Lincolnville, which he then sold to one hundred black families. Cain served two terms in the United States House of Representatives, 1873–1875 and 1877–1879.

FREDERICK DOUGLASS (1818–1895)

Born a slave in Maryland, Frederick Douglass escaped in 1838 and wrote of his experiences and his opposition to slavery in his famous 1845 narrative. In the North, Douglass became an abolitionist orator and author who argued eloquently for freedom and equality. During the Civil War, he supported African American participation in the Union army. After the war ended and slavery was abolished, Douglass continued to advocate for the advancement of African Americans. Freedpeople had been left destitute and powerless, and the answer, for Douglass, was black suffrage. In speech after speech, Douglass carefully refuted the reasons commonly given against enfranchising African Americans as he argued for its necessity. In addition to public speeches, Douglass's advocacy for equality included face-to-face meetings with politicians. Hoping to persuade the president to reconsider his opposition to black suffrage, Douglass joined a delegation of African American men who met with Andrew Johnson in February 1866. The meeting failed to convince President Johnson that black political rights should play any role in Reconstruction. Turning his attention to Congress, Douglass had more success convincing Republicans to accept black suffrage as part of their policy of reconstructing the South.

ULYSSES S. GRANT (1822–1885)

Celebrated as a great Union general, U. S. Grant has received much less praise as a two-term president of the United States. After the Civil War ended, Grant became the General of the Army, and as the nation's top military leader, he advised President Johnson about Reconstruction policy. Grant initially favored the speedy restoration of the South into the Union and advocated for the pardon of top Confederate military and political officials like General James Longstreet and Confederate Vice President Alexander Stephens. Johnson asked Grant to tour the South in 1865 and report on conditions in the region. Grant's letter to the president, which suggested greater loyalty on the part of the white South than expected, was used by Johnson to offset Carl Schurz's negative picture of southern loyalty. Like many moderates in the North, the actions of the white South in 1865–66 made Grant more skeptical of southern loyalty, and he found the hostility expressed in the southern press toward Northerners and the U.S. Army in particular quite disturbing. As the fight between the president and Congress intensified after the vetoes of the Freedmen's Bureau and Civil Rights Bills in 1866, Grant attempted to create a middle ground between the two positions. He opposed Johnson's removal of the district commanders who were carrying out the Military Reconstruction Act and pleaded with the president not to remove Philip Sheridan. When Johnson removed Edwin Stanton as Secretary of War, Grant accepted the position on an interim basis. The popular war hero won the 1868 presidential election, using the slogan "Let Us Have Peace." Demonstrating that the White House and Congress would no longer be at odds, Grant supported black suffrage and worked for the ratification of the Fifteenth Amendment. In response to growing Klan violence in the South, President Grant encouraged Congress to pass legislation that would strengthen the powers of the federal government to combat it. Scandal, not Reconstruction policy, however, has dominated the memory of the Grant administration. In 1875, the "Whiskey Ring," a scandal involving government agents and liquor distillers who defrauded the government of tax dollars, caused trouble for the president when his own private secretary was implicated in the ring.

CHARLOTTE FORTEN GRIMKÉ (1837–1914)

Charlotte Forten Grimké, an educator and essayist, was born in Philadelphia to a prominent free black family. She devoted her life to abolitionism, racial equality, and education. Initially, Charlotte Forten was educated by tutors in her home, but when her father heard that Salem, Massachusetts, had quality schools that were racially integrated, he sent her there to finish her studies. After graduating from the Salem Normal School in 1856, she began teaching at a grammar school in the city. Respiratory illness, however, would plague her throughout her life and on several instances forced her to resign her teaching position. In 1862, she traveled to Union-occupied Port Royal, South Carolina, to aid the progress of her race by teaching former slaves. Charlotte Forten was the first African American to teach on St. Helena Island and wrote of feeling isolated in the first months after her arrival until military personnel, fellow teachers, and the island's black residents accepted her. During her time on the island, she met prominent antislavery military leaders, such as Colonel Robert Gould Shaw, General Rufus Saxton, and Colonel T. W. Higginson. For nearly two years, she worked on St. Helena Island teaching reading, writing, math, and history, until ill health forced her to return to the North. She published an essay about her experiences on the Sea Islands in *The Atlantic Monthly* in 1864. Her writings influenced northern readers as they formulated their attitudes about the willingness and aptitude of freedpeople to learn. In 1878, Forten married Francis J. Grimké, a Presbyterian minister and nephew of the well-known abolitionists Angelina and Sarah Grimké.

WADE HAMPTON III (1818–1902)

Born into a wealthy South Carolina family, Wade Hampton graduated from South Carolina College in 1836 and served in the state legislature from 1852 to1861. Emerging as an able cavalry commander in the Confederate army, Hampton was promoted several times, ending as a lieutenant general. He was wounded three times and saw action at many important battles, including First Bull Run, Fredericksburg, and Gettysburg. After the death of J. E. B. Stuart in 1864, Hampton took command of Lee's cavalry. His military record made him a popular figure among southern whites after the war had ended. Though he offered qualified support for Johnson's plan, Hampton opposed Congressional Reconstruction, in particular black suffrage, and advocated for the restoration of white supremacy. In 1871, he organized a legal defense fund to protect accused Klansmen from prosecution under the Enforcement Acts. During Hampton's 1876 campaign for the governorship of South Carolina, the Red Shirts, a paramilitary organization that supported the Confederate hero, ensured his victory by suppressing the black vote through violence and murder. The results of the gubernatorial election were disputed, but Hampton took office as part of the Compromise of 1877. In addition to serving as governor of South Carolina, Wade Hampton served as a U.S. senator for two terms.

GEN. OLIVER O. HOWARD (1830–1909)

Born in Maine, O. O. Howard graduated from West Point in 1854 and began a career in the U.S. Army. During the Civil War, he commanded troops at Fredericksburg, Gettysburg, and Antietam. Due to injuries sustained at the 1862 Battle at Fair Oaks, Howard's arm was amputated. During Sherman's March to the Sea, he received the command of the Army of Tennessee. To assist in the transition from slavery to freedom, Congress created the Bureau of Refugees, Freedmen, and Abandoned Lands, commonly known as the Freedmen's Bureau, in March 1865, and President Johnson named Howard the commissioner. The Freedmen's Bureau was given broad authority to supervise abandoned lands and address the needs of freedpeople by sponsoring schools, providing food relief and healthcare, and enforcing written contracts between black workers and white landowners. While many scholars have praised Howard as an able leader of the bureau, he has received some criticism for failing to fight effectively for freedpeople, especially over land. Howard supported making confiscated lands available for purchase by former slaves, and he tried to moderate President Johnson's desire to return land to the white land-owners. In the end, he implemented the president's policy. When Johnson ordered that confiscated land be returned to planters, Howard hoped that land already turned over to African Americans could be exempted. As a result, he urged bureau agents to move slowly in the return of land, hoping that the extra time would give Congress an opportunity to pass legislation granting freedpeople title to the property. Congress did not act, and none of Howard's compromise plans found favor with the president. After the Freedmen's Bureau closed, Howard continued in the military, with much of his time spent in the West during conflicts with Native Americans.

ANDREW JOHNSON (1808–1875)

Born in Raleigh, North Carolina, Andrew Johnson began his life in pov-erty, and those early experiences shaped his political career. A Jacksonian Democrat, Johnson criticized southern planters and championed small farmers. During the 1840s and 1850s, he served in the House of Represen-tatives and the Senate. When Tennessee seceded from the Union in 1861, Johnson remained in the Senate, the only Southerner not to follow his state. In 1862, President Lincoln appointed Johnson the provisional gov-ernor of Tennessee, and in 1864, he was selected as Lincoln's vice president for the second term. After Lincoln's assassination in 1865, John-son assumed the presidency, and he made it clear that he wanted to restore the 11 states to the Union before Congress could have any say in Reconstruction policy. An advocate of leniency, Johnson asked only that southern states ratify the Thirteenth Amendment abolishing slavery, repu-diate the Confederate war debt, and repudiate secession. Once states had done these things and individuals had taken loyalty oaths, then Reconstruction would be at an end. He opposed the federal government granting political or civil equality to African Americans. He vetoed the extension of the Freedmen's Bureau and the Civil Rights Act of 1866, claiming that Congress did not have the authority to pass legislation that affected the South until its representatives had been admitted to Congress. These two vetoes alienated moderate Republicans and allowed more radical plans for Reconstruction to win support in Congress. A complete break between the two branches soon occurred. Johnson continued to use the veto in a vain attempt to halt the radicals in Congress, and when that failed, he encouraged southern states to be uncooperative. In addition, he removed officials, like Dan Sickles from the Second Military District of South Carolina and Philip Sheridan from the Fifth Military District of Louisiana and Texas, who were willing to execute congressional legislation. The breach between the president and Congress culminated with Johnson's impeachment for violating the Tenure of Office Act. The Senate voted 35:19, one short of the necessary two-thirds needed to remove the president from office.

LUCIUS QUINTUS LAMAR (1825–1896)

Lucius Q. Lamar, a lawyer, supporter of secession, and Confederate general, was elected to the U.S. Congress in 1873, representing the first district of Mississippi. In a private letter at the time of his election, Lamar expressed his opposition to Governor Adelbert Ames's Reconstruction plans. An advocate of "home rule," Lamar argued that the enfranchisement of African Americans in Mississippi effectively excluded southern whites, whom he cast as the repository of virtue and enlightened public opinion, from the political system. In Lamar's first speech in Congress, however, he recast himself as a national statesman. In a eulogy for radical Republican Charles Sumner, Lamar spoke positively of the Massachusetts senator and encouraged Congress to embrace sectional reconciliation. An astute political operative, he stayed clear of the violence employed by conservative whites to destroy Republicans in the 1875 elections. From this position, Lamar formed alliances with northern Republicans that allowed him to derail bills opposed by white Mississippians. The Democratic-controlled state legislature chose Lamar as U.S. Senator in 1875, but he was not seated until 1877. He was the first ex-Confederate to return to the Senate. Lamar was appointed to the U.S. Supreme Court in 1888.

P. B. S. PINCHBACK (1837–1921)

Pinckney Benton Stewart Pinchback was born in Georgia in 1837. His father had manumitted and then married his mother, and as a result, P. B. S. Pinchback had never been a slave. After the death of his father, the family was left without funds, and P. B. S. Pinchback left school and began working on canal and riverboats in Ohio. As a cabin boy, Pinch-back joined forces with a group of card sharks who hustled passengers. In 1862, he left riverboat life and settled in Union-controlled New Orleans, Louisiana. There Pinchback became an advocate for black civil rights, focusing first on segregated streetcars. Pinchback refused to sit in the "star cars" marked for blacks, sitting instead in those reserved exclusively for whites. Other African Americans, including soldiers, also opposed the discriminatory practice. District Commander Philip Sheridan supported their campaign and met with the streetcar company, advising them to stop making distinctions between passengers. The system of segregated cars was soon abandoned. Elected to the Louisiana state senate in 1868, Pinchback supported two important civil rights bills, one legalizing marriages between people who lived together, regardless of race, and the other fining businesses that discriminated against blacks in public accommodations. When the lieutenant governor of Louisiana, Oscar Dunn, died in 1871, Pinch-back, as president of the senate, assumed office. He also served as acting governor of Louisiana for 36 days when Governor Warmouth was removed from office in 1872. P. B. S. Pinchback was the first African American to be governor of a state and the only one until the late twentieth century.

HIRAM REVELS (1827–1901)

Hiram Revels was the first African American to serve in the U.S. Senate, finishing 13 months of an unexpired term. Born in North Carolina in 1822 to free parents, Revels left the South after Nat Turner's rebellion in 1831. He attended a series of schools, including Knox College in Illinois, and became an ordained pastor of the African Methodist Episcopal church in 1845. He served as a chaplain during the Civil War in a black regiment and worked for the Freedmen's Bureau. In 1866, Hiram Revels settled in Mississippi and soon held a number of political offices, including alderman and state senator. After being appointed by the Mississippi state legislature to the U.S. Senate in 1870, Revels needed Senate approval before he could be seated. The opposition organized their forces to reject Revels, as they had successfully foiled the election of an African American from Louisiana to the U.S. House in 1869. Democrats challenged Revels's appointment, claiming that African Americans had not been citizens for the constitutionally required nine years, but Republicans like Charles

Sumner offered support and the Senate approved his appointment. In his first Senate speech, Revels opposed the readmission of Georgia because it had stopped African Americans from serving in the state legislature. After serving in the U.S. Senate, Revels became president of Alcorn College in Mississippi. He later left the Republican Party and became a Democrat.

CARL SCHURZ (1829–1906)

Born in Germany, Carl Schurz fled his home after participating in the failed Revolution of 1848. Once settled in the United States, he joined the Republican Party and supported Abraham Lincoln for president in 1860. During the Civil War, he served as a major general in the Union army. After the war ended, he toured the South and sent a report on the conditions there to Congress in December 1865. His report emphasized that white Southerners were resisting the emancipation of slaves and the introduction of free labor. To counteract this opposition, Schurz argued that black suffrage should be introduced and that the federal government should keep troops in the South to control the region. These positions placed him in line with the radical wing of the Republican Party. After Schurz moved to Missouri in 1867 to edit a German newspaper, he rose in political power. He was elected senator from Missouri in 1869 and championed civil service reform as a mechanism to prevent political corruption. Moving away from the radicals, Schurz advocated removing the disabilities that had been placed on former rebels so that they could once again vote and hold office. He also opposed the continued use of the military to achieve a republican form of government in the South. Formally breaking with President Grant in the 1870s, Schurz supported Horace Greeley, the Liberal Republican candidate for president, in the 1872 election. From 1877 to 1881, he served as Rutherford B. Hayes's secretary of the interior.

PHILIP SHERIDAN (1831–1888)

The child of Irish immigrant parents, Philip Sheridan grew up in Ohio and graduated from West Point in 1853. During the Civil War, he rose through the ranks of the Union army and is best known for his command of the Union cavalry during the 1864 campaign in the Shenandoah Valley. After the war, he supervised the occupation of Louisiana and Texas and secured the border with Mexico. In July 1866, members of the New Orleans police participated in a brutal attack on an equal rights convention in which approximately 40 people were killed. In his report to the president, Sheridan described the actions of the police as murder. In 1867, he was appointed commander of the Fifth Military District of Louisiana and Texas, where he set about carrying out the Military Reconstruction Acts. In particular, Sheridan removed a number of public officials who would not cooperate with Reconstruction, starting first with those he held responsible for the New Orleans riot and for the failure to prosecute those involved. During his brief tenure as district commander, Sheridan removed the mayor of New Orleans, the attorney general, a judge, members of the New Orleans city council, the governor of Louisiana, and the governor of Texas. He reorganized the New Orleans police department, dismissing officials in the process, and supervised the registration of thousands of African American voters. Sheridan also supported the integration of the New Orleans streetcars after black soldiers were prohibited from sitting in "white" cars. After being removed by Johnson for carrying out the Military Reconstruction Acts too zealously, he then went west where he led attacks on the Plains Indians. He became commanding general of the United States Army in 1883, a position he held until his death.

ROBERT SMALLS (1839–1915)

Robert Smalls, a former slave and Civil War hero, served as a member of the U.S. House of Representatives from Beaufort, South Carolina, during Reconstruction. In May 1862, Smalls engineered his freedom by commandeering the *Planter*, a Confederate steamer filled with ammunition and artillery pieces, and piloting it through Charleston Harbor to the Union line. The vessel, with its shallow draft, was useful to the Union, and Smalls provided important military and geographic intelligence. Northern periodicals ran stories of Smalls's heroic exploits, but white South Carolinians had long memories and tried to destroy Smalls's political career after the war. He was a delegate to the state's 1868 constitutional convention and was subsequently elected to three terms in the South Carolina General Assembly. He was elected to the U.S. House of Representatives in 1875.

When Democrats took the South Carolina statehouse in 1877, Smalls was accused of corruption and encouraged to resign his seat in the U.S. House. After he refused, Smalls was convicted of bribery but pardoned after a deal was made between the federal government and South Carolina. Even after most of the state had been restored to home rule, Beaufort County remained in Republican control. In 1878, 800 armed Red Shirts descended on Gillisonville to harass Smalls, only to be met by African American men and women in the community armed with guns, axes, and hoes. Because of Democratic gerrymandering and Red Shirt violence, Smalls lost the 1878 election for the House of Representatives.

ELIZABETH CADY STANTON (1815–1902)

Stanton was the foremost advocate of women's rights in the nineteenth century. She organized the 1848 Seneca Falls convention that demanded women's suffrage and authored *The Woman's Bible* that criticized traditional religious interpretations of women's status. Often the center of controversy, Stanton broke from her antebellum abolitionist allies and opposed the passage of the Fourteenth and Fifteenth Amendments. In particular, Stanton and Susan B. Anthony disliked the use of the word "male" in the Fourteenth Amendment, noting that for the first time the Constitution specifically restricted citizenship and voting rights to men. Angered that former allies like Charles Sumner, Wendell Phillips, and Frederick Douglass would not budge on the wording of the amendment, Stanton and Anthony submitted a petition to Congress that included over 10,000 signatures. Stanton also opposed the Fifteenth Amendment because it prohibited discrimination on the basis of race, but not gender. In her statements against the amendment, Stanton often resorted to racist and antidemocratic arguments. She resented that men of the "lower orders" would make laws that women of wealth and education would have to follow. The fight over the Fifteenth Amendment led to a split within the women's suffrage movement.

THADDEUS STEVENS (1792–1868)

Thaddeus Stevens was a member of the U.S. House of Representatives from Pennsylvania. As the leader of the radical Republicans in the House,

Stevens supported emancipation, the use of black troops in the Union army, the confiscation and redistribution of rebel land to former slaves, civil equality, and black suffrage. As demonstrated in the debates over the Fourteenth Amendment, Stevens was also a skilled politician, adept at negotiation and compromise. In addition to the Fourteenth Amendment, Stevens also directed the Military Reconstruction Acts through the House and pushed tirelessly for the impeachment of President Johnson. Stevens defended his stringent plan for the readmission of the southern states and his opposition to Johnson's policies by suggesting that ex-Confederate states should be treated as "conquered provinces." He argued that the 11 states had in fact seceded from the Union and, as a result, had severed their constitutional ties to the Union. Because they had been defeated on the battlefield, the 11 southern states had to submit to congressional dictates. The conquered provinces theory and his call for the redistribution of land from former Confederates to ex-slaves were too radical for most Republicans and earned him a reputation among many as vindictive.

CHARLES SUMNER (1811–1874)

Charles Sumner was the leader of the radical Republicans in the U.S. Senate and well-known for his eloquent oratory. Like Thaddeus Stevens in the House, he advocated for black suffrage and equality before the law, denounced President Johnson, and called for his impeachment. Prior to the Civil War, Sumner was an antislavery politician and advocate for the integration of Boston's public schools. His provocative 1856 speech, "The Crime against Kansas," led Preston Brooks to attack him with a cane on the floor of the Senate. Sumner nearly died from the severe, repeated blows to the head, and he did not return to the Senate for three years. He did not support Stevens's theory of the South as conquered provinces, arguing instead for "state suicide," a theory that presented the ordinances of secession as justification for moving the 11 states to the status of territories and allowing Congress to set the rules for their readmission. His commitment to black suffrage led Sumner to voice opposition to the Fourteenth Amendment because it did not mandate black voting rights. He was among the staunchest supporters of civil rights legislation and enforcement during the Reconstruction period. Although the final version of the Civil Rights Act of 1875 was weakened by legislative compromise, its passage was regarded as a memorial to the senator's lifetime of opposition to slavery and inequality.

ELLA GERTRUDE CLANTON THOMAS (1834–1907)

Born in Columbia County, Georgia, Ella Gertrude Clanton grew up with all the privileges that a wealthy planter family could provide. Her formal education was completed at Georgia's Wesleyan Female College in 1851, and the next year she married Jefferson Thomas, the older brother of a school friend. Over the next two decades, Gertrude Thomas gave birth to 10 children. When the Civil War ended, the Thomas family experienced catastrophic financial change. Prior to the war, they had been wealthy southern planters, but afterwards they lost their slaves, their plantations in Burke County, their social prestige, and ultimately their Augusta residence. Jefferson Thomas had invested heavily in Confederate bonds that became worthless once the Confederacy was defeated, and he was forced to declare bankruptcy after his retail business failed. In response to their economic difficulties, Gertrude Thomas began teaching and her salary provided needed family income. Gertrude Thomas chronicled the meaning of these events in a journal she kept from 1848 to 1889. Her writings vividly convey the disorienting change that accompanied emancipation from the perspective of white planters. In particular, her recently published journal reveals the challenges that elite white women faced as they sought to preserve their class identity while confronting the need to work.

ALBION TOURGÉE (1838–1905)

A Union army veteran and native of Ohio, Albion Tourgée settled in North Carolina after the war. Active in the state's Republican Party, Tourgée was elected as a delegate to North Carolina's constitutional convention in 1868 and became a leading advocate of black suffrage. Out of his role in the convention, Tourgée was elected district judge of the state superior court. He demanded that African Americans be allowed to sit on juries and he fined lawyers for using racial epithets. In the press, Tourgée repeatedly defended his judicial record against attacks from Democrats. Ku Klux Klan violence increased within the Seventh District in 1870, and Wyatt Outlaw, an African American Republican town councilman, was hanged near Tourgée's courthouse. After the Klan murdered a friend, State Senator John Stevens, Tourgée pursued both cases but was unable to bring the murderers to justice. In his 1879 novel, *A Fool's Errand*, Tourgée used his own experiences to express his frustration with Reconstruction. Concluding that Northern and Southern society were irreconcilably different, he argued that it was foolish to presume that the North could make the South in its own image.

LAURA TOWNE (1825–1901)

Laura Towne was a northern white teacher in the Sea Islands beginning in 1862. Supported by the Freedmen's Aid Society of Pennsylvania, she traveled to St. Helena Island, South Carolina, after the area was occupied by the Union army as a free labor experiment. Towne, who had studied at the Woman's Medical College in Philadelphia, treated patients as well as distributing supplies and running a school. Unlike many of the northern white teachers who traveled to the Sea Islands, Towne did not return to the North during the summer, the time when disease was most prevalent. With the help of her close friend Ellen Murray, Towne founded the Penn School and taught there for 38 years. After northern interest in educating African Americans waned, Towne had trouble keeping the school afloat financially and used her own money to pay teachers when needed. She wrote about her experiences on St. Helena, and after her death, *The Letters and Diary of Laura M. Towne* was published.

PRIMARY DOCUMENTS

DEFINING FREEDOM
1. The Thirteenth Amendment

The Thirteenth Amendment passed the U.S. Senate (38–6) on April 8, 1864, but failed to achieve the necessary two-thirds majority in the House vote on June 15, 1864. After the 1864 elections, President Lincoln decided not to wait for the new Congress, where a two-thirds majority could easily be achieved, but worked for its passage in the lame-duck House. The amendment passed the House on January 31, 1865, by a vote of 119:56, and the amendment was ratified on December 6, 1865. Emancipation would be one requirement of any plan submitted to the 11 Confederate states, but the meaning of freedom would still have to be determined.

Section 1 Neither slavery nor involuntary servitude, except as a punishment for crime whereof the party shall have been duly convicted, shall exist within the United States, or any place subject to their jurisdiction.

Section 2 Congress shall have power to enforce this article by appropriate legislation.

Source: The House Joint Resolution proposing the 13th amendment to the Constitution, January 31, 1865; Enrolled Acts and Resolutions of Congress, 1789–1999; General Records of the United States Government; Record Group 11; National Archives.

2. Address from the Colored Citizens of Norfolk, Virginia, to the People of the United States

In 1865, African Americans throughout the South held meetings and drafted petitions arguing that emancipation meant not just an end of slavery but also equality, citizenship, and suffrage. Seven African American residents of Norfolk and Henry Highland Garnet, a black abolitionist and minister in Washington D.C., drafted this statement about the meaning of emancipation and the need for action. In particular, this source emphasized that the Thirteenth Amendment, once it was ratified, would not wipe out the countless discriminatory laws that had supported slavery. To justify civil and political equality, this group recalled African American participation in major historical events from the American Revolution through the Civil War.

June 26, 1865

We do not come before the people of the United States asking an impossibility; we simply ask that a Christian and enlightened people shall, at once, concede to us the full enjoyment of those privileges of full citizenship which, not only, are our undoubted right, but are indispensable to that elevation and prosperity of our people which must be the desire of every patriot.

The legal recognition of these rights of the free colored population, in the past, by State legislation, or even by the Judiciary and Congress of the United States, was, as a matter of course, wholly inconsistent with the existence of slavery; but now that slavery has been crushed, with the rebellion, sprung from it, on what pretext can disabilities be perpetuated that were imposed only to protect an institution which has now, thank God, passed away forever? It is a common assertion, by our enemies, that "this is a white man's country, settled by white men, its government established by white men, and shall therefore be ruled by white men only." How far are these statements true and conclusion reasonable? ...

Again, is it true that this government owes its existence entirely to white men? Why, the first blood shed in the Revolutionary war was that of a colored man, Crispus Attucks.... Who has forgotten Andrew Jackson's famous appeal to the colored "citizens" of Louisiana, and their enthusiastic response, in defence of liberty, for others, which was denied themselves?... Then what has been the behavior of our people during the past struggle? Have we in any way embarrassed the government by unnecessary outbreaks on the one hand, or thwarted it by remissness or slackness in response to its calls for volunteers on the other? Let the fact that, in the short space of nine months, from what was called the contra-band camp at Hampton, near Fortress Monroe, and from the other parts of this State alone, over *twenty-five thousand* colored men have become soldiers in the army of the United States, attest our devotion to our country. Over 200,000 colored men have taken up arms on behalf of the Union, and at Port Hudson, Olustee, Milliken's Bend, Fort Wagner, and in the death-haunted craters of the Petersburg mine, and on a hundred well-fought fields, have fully proved their patriotism and possession of all the manly qualities that adorn the soldier.

Such, as everyone knows, have been the relations and attitude of the colored people to the nation in the past, but we believe our present position is by no means so well understood among the loyal masses of the country, otherwise there would be no delay in granting us the express relief which the nature of the case demands. It must not be forgotten that it is the general assumption in the South that the effects of the immortal Emancipation Proclamation of President Lincoln go no further than the emancipation of the negroes then in slavery, and that it is only construc-tively even that that Proclamation can be said, in any legal sense, to have abolished slavery, and even the late Constitutional amendment, if duly ratified, can go no further; neither touch, nor can touch, the slave codes of the various southern States . . . which having been passed before the act of secession, are presumed to have lost none of their vitality, but exist as a convenient engine for our oppression until repealed by special acts of the State legislatures. By these laws, in many of the southern States, it is still a crime for colored men to learn or be taught to read, and their chil-dren are doomed to ignorance; there is no provision for insuring the legal-ity of our marriages; we have no right to hold real estate; the public streets and the exercise of our ordinary occupations are forbidden us unless we can produce passes from our employers, or licenses from certain officials; . . . we have no right to testify before the courts in any case in which a white man is one of the parties to the suit; we are taxed without representation, and, in short, so far as legal safeguards of our rights are concerned, we are defenceless before our enemies. . . . In Richmond, during the three days' sway of the rebel Mayor Mayo, over 800 colored people were arrested, sim-ply for walking the streets without a pass; in the neighboring city of

Portsmouth, a mayor has just been elected on the avowed platform that this is a white man's government, and our enemies have been heard to boast openly that soon not a colored man shall be left in the city; in the greater number of counties in this State, county meetings have been held at which resolutions have been adopted *deploring,* while accepting, the abolition of slavery, but going on to pledge the planters composing the meeting to employ no negroes save such as were formerly owned by themselves without a written recommendation from their late employers, and threatening violence towards those who should do so, thereby keeping us in a state of serfdom, and preventing our free selection of our employers; they have also pledged themselves, in no event, to pay their late adult slaves more than $60 per year for their labor in the future, out of which, with characteristic generosity, they have decided that we are to find clothes for ourselves and families, and pay our taxes and doctors' bills, in many of the more remote districts, individual planters are to be found who still refuse to recognized their negroes as free, forcibly retaining the wives and children of their late escaped slaves; cases have occurred, not far from Richmond itself, in which an attempt to leave the plantation has been punished by shooting to death; and finally, there are numbers of cases known to ourselves in the immediate vicinity of this city in which a faithful performance, by colored men, of the duties or labor contracted for, has been met by a contemptuous and violent refusal of the stipulated compensation. . . .

Fellow citizens, the performance of a simple act of justice on your part will reverse all this; we ask for no expensive aid from military forces stationed throughout the South, overbearing State action, and rendering our government republican only in name; give us the suffrage, and you may rely upon us to secure justice for ourselves, and all Union men, and to keep the State forever in the Union.

Source: The Liberator, September 8, 1865, p. 144.

3. Mississippi Black Codes

In November 1865, Mississippi became the first southern state to define the legal status of freedpeople in a series of laws that have been known as the black codes. Mississippi's black code granted legal rights to freedpeople that they had not possessed under slavery, but they also explicitly discriminated against African Americans. In "An Act to Confer Civil Rights on Freedmen," freedpeople were granted the right to marry, own property, and testify in court. Yet these laws also limited their freedom in fundamental ways. Mississippi used labor contracts, vagrancy laws, and apprenticeship laws to ensure that African Americans would be a cheap source of agricultural labor. All of the other former Confederate states soon followed the lead of Mississippi. The most discriminatory provisions of Mississippi's code never went into effect.

An Act to Confer Civil Rights on Freedmen, and for other Purpose

Section 1. *Be it enacted by the Legislature of the State of Mississippi,* That all freedmen, free negroes and mulattoes may sue and be sued, implead and be impleaded in all the courts of law and equity of this State, and may acquire personal property, . . . by descent or purchase, and may dispose of the same, in the same manner, and to the same extent that white persons may: Provided that the provisions of this section shall not be so construed as to allow any freedman, free negro or mulatto to rent or lease any lands or tenements except in incorporated towns or cities in which places the corporate authorities shall control the same.

SEC. 2. Be it further enacted, That all freedmen, free negroes and mulattoes may intermarry with each other, in the same manner and under the same regulations that are provided by law for white persons: Provided, that the clerk of probate shall keep separate records of the same.

SEC. 3. Be it further enacted, That all freedmen, free negroes or mulattoes, who do now and have heretofore lived and cohabited together as husband and wife shall be taken and held in law as legally married, and the issue shall be taken and held as legitimate for all purposes. That it shall not be lawful for any freedman, free negro or mulatto to intermarry with any white person; nor for any white person to intermarry with any freedman, free negro or mulatto; and any person who shall so intermarry shall be deemed guilty of felony, and on conviction thereof, shall be confined in the State Penitentiary for life; and those shall be deemed freedmen, free negroes and mulattoes who are of pure negro blood, and those descended from a negro to the third generation inclusive, though one ancestor of each generation may have been a white person.

SEC. 4. Be it further enacted, That in addition to cases in which freedmen, free negroes and mulattoes are now by law competent witnesses, freedmen, free negroes or mulattoes shall be competent in civil cases when a party or parties to the suit, either plaintiff or plaintiffs, defendant or defendants, also in cases where freedmen, free negroes and mulattoes is or are either plaintiff or plaintiffs, defendant or defendants, and a white person or white persons is or are the opposing party or parties. They shall also be competent witnesses in all criminal prosecutions where the crime charged is alleged to have been committed by a white person upon or against the person or property of a freedman, free negro or mulatto: Provided, that in all cases said witnesses shall be examined in open court on the stand; except however, they may be examined before the grand jury, and shall in all cases be subject to the rules and tests of the common law as to competency and credibility.

SEC. 5. Be it further enacted, That every freedman, free negro and mulatto shall, on the second Monday of January, one thousand eight hundred and sixty-six, and annually thereafter, have a lawful home or employment, and shall have written evidence thereof, as follows, to-wit: if living in any incorporated city, town, or village, a license from the mayor thereof; and if living outside of an incorporated city, town, or village, from the member of the board of police of his beat, authorizing him or her to do irregular and job work, or a written contract, as provided in section sixth of this act, which licenses may be revoked for cause, at any time, by the authority granting the same. . . .

SEC. 7. Be it further enacted, That every civil officer shall, and every person may arrest and carry back to his or her legal employer any freedman, free negro or mulatto who shall have quit the service of his or her employer before the expiration of his or her term of service without good cause, and said officer and person shall be entitled to receive for arresting and carrying back every deserting employee aforesaid, the sum of five dollars, and ten cents per mile from the place of arrest to the place of delivery. . . .

SEC. 8. Be it further enacted, That upon affidavit made by the employer of any freedman, free negro or mulatto, or other credible person, before any justice of the peace or member of the board of police, that any freedman, free negro or mulatto, legally employed by said employer, has illegally deserted said employment, such justice of the peace or member of the board of police, shall issue his warrant or warrants, returnable before himself, or other such officer, directed to any sheriff, constable or special deputy, commanding him to arrest said deserter and return him or her to said employer. . . .

SEC. 9. Be it further enacted, That if any person shall persuade or attempt to persuade, entice or cause any freedman, free negro or mulatto, to desert from the legal employment of any person, before the expiration of his or her term of service, or shall knowingly employ any such deserting freedman, free negro or mulatto, or shall knowingly give or sell to any such deserting freedman, free negro or mulatto, any food, rayment or other thing, he or she shall be guilty of a misdemeanor, and upon conviction, shall be fined not less than twenty-five dollars and not more than two hundred dollars and costs, and if said fine and costs shall not be immediately paid, the court shall sentence said convict to not exceeding two months imprisonment in the county jail.

Approved November 25, 1865

An Act to Regulate the Relation of Master and Apprentice, as Relates to Freedmen, Free Negroes, and Mulattoes

Section 1. *Be it enacted by the Legislature of the State of Mississippi,* That it shall be the duty of all sheriffs, justices of the peace, and other civil officers of the several counties in this State, to report to the probate courts of their respective counties semi-annually, at the January and July terms of said courts, all freedmen, free negroes and mulattoes, under the age of eighteen, within their respective counties, beats or districts, who are orphans, or whose parent or parents have not the means, or who refuse to provide for and support said minors, and thereupon it shall be the duty of said probate court, to order the clerk of said court to apprentice said minors to some competent and suitable person, on such terms as the court may direct, having a particular care to the interest of said minor: Provided, that the former owner of said minors shall have the preference, when in the opinion of the court, he or she shall be a suitable person for that purpose.

Approved November 22, 1865

An Act to Amend the Vagrant Laws of the State

SEC. 2. Be it further enacted, That all freedmen, free negroes and mulattoes in this State, over the age of eighteen years, found on the second Monday in January, 1866, or thereafter, with no lawful employment or business, or found unlawful assembling themselves together either in the day or night time, and all white persons so assembling themselves with freedmen, free negroes or mulattoes, or usually associating with freedmen, free negroes or mulattoes, on terms of equality, or living in adultery or fornication with a freed woman, free negro or mulatto, shall be deemed vagrants, and on conviction thereof, shall be fined in the sum of not exceeding, in the case of a freedman, free negro or mulatto, fifty dollars, and a white man two hundred dollars, and imprisoned at the discretion of the court, the free negro not exceeding ten days, and the white man not exceeding six months.

Approved November 24, 1865

An Act to Punish Certain Offences therein named, and for other purposes

Section 1. *Be it enacted by the Legislature of the State of Mississippi,* That no freedman, free negro or mulatto, not in the military service of the United States Government, and not licensed so to do by the board of police of his or her county, shall keep or carry fire-arms of any kind, or any ammunition, dirk or bowie knife, and on conviction thereof, in the county court, shall be punished by fine, not exceeding ten dollars, and pay the costs of such proceedings, and all such arms or ammunition shall be forfeited to the informer, and it shall be the duty of every civil and military officer to arrest any freedman, free negro or mulatto found with any such arms or ammunition, and cause him or her to be committed to trial in default of bail.

Approved November 29, 1865

Source: Laws of the State of Mississippi, Passed at a Regular Session of the Mississippi Legislature, Held in the City of Jackson, October, November, and December, 1865 (Jackson, 1866), 82–91, 165.

4. Circular No. 2, by the Mississippi Freedmen's Bureau Assistant Commissioner, Samuel Thomas

To restart the southern economy, the Freedmen's Bureau supported labor contracts between freedpeople and employers. The Bureau would act as an intermediary, ensuring the fairness of the contracts. In this source, the assistant commissioner presents the values the Freedmen's Bureau hoped to inculcate— the value of hard work and the sanctity of contracts. But Samuel Thomas also wanted to counteract the impression that the government would distribute land to former slaves. He assured black Mississippians "that you must labor for what you get like other people."

Vicksburg, Miss. Jan. 2d 1866.

To the Colored People of Mississippi.

Having been charged with the affairs of the Freedmen's Bureau in Mississippi, I am your lawful protector and adviser; and, to some extent, am held responsible for your conduct. If you suffer, or become idle or vicious, blame is attached to me or my officers, even when the fault is not our's.

With the end of 1865 your contracts expire. My officers approved the contracts, and did all they could to compel both you and your employer's to live up to them. In many places these contracts did not secure you more than food and clothes, because you contracted so late that it was impossible to raise a crop.

Many complaints are made, that you did not regard a contract as sacred: that you failed to work as you agreed; acted as you pleased; and visited at a distance, deserting the crop when you knew that your employer would lose all by your failure to keep your contract. On the other hand, it is said by you that the planters have failed to pay and treat you as agreed upon.

This is all wrong. Your contracts were explained to you, and their sacredness impressed upon you, again and again. You knew that when you make a contract, you are bound to give all the labor for which your employer agrees to pay. Efforts have been made by my officers to compel you to perform labor according to agreements, that employers might have no excuse for failing to do their part.

The time has arrived for you to contract for another year's labor. I wish to impress upon you the importance of doing this at once. You know that if a crop of cotten is raised, the work must begin soon, and the hands employed for the year. If you do not contract with the men who wish to employ you, what do you propose to do? You cannot live without work of some kind. Your houses and lands belong to the white people; and you cannot expect that they will allow you to live on them in idleness. It would be wrong for them to do so; and no officer of the Government will protect you in it. If you stay on the plantations where you are, you must agree to work for the owners of them. If not, move out of the way, and give place for more faithful laborers.

I hope you are all convinced that you are not to receive property of any kind from the Government; and that you must labor for what you get like other people. I often hear that you are crowding into towns, refusing to hire out, and are waiting to see what the Government will do for you. As the representative of the Government I tell you that is very foolish; and your refusal to work is used by your enemies to your injury. I know you can get good wages with considerate employers, who will treat you well, and pay for all you do. Everything possible shall be done to secure you good treatment. Make contracts for the year, and go to work; and you will secure homes. The Government hopes you will do your duty; and in return will secure you all the rights of freemen. The season in which planters will think it worth while to employ you, will soon be passed: and if then you are found idle, you may be taken up and set to work where you will not like it. The State cannot and ought not to let any man lie about idle, without any property, doing mischief. A vagrant law is right in principle. I cannot ask the civil officers to leave you idle, to beg or steal. If they find any of you without business and means of living, they will do right if they treat you as bad persons, and take away your misused liberty.

Some of you have the absurd notion, that if you put your hands to a contract, you will somehow be made slaves. This is all nonsense, made up by some foolish or wicked person. There is no danger of this kind to fear; nor will you be branded when you get on a plantation. Any white man treating you so would be punished. Your danger lies exactly in the other direction. . . .

You must be obedient to the law. I do not think the people of Mississippi have made all laws that relate to you as they ought to have done. But, even if there be some things denied to you as yet, which you wish to gain, you can not get them by disobedience and idleness. You cannot make people treat you well, by showing that you do *not* deserve it. If you wish for rights, do right yourselves. If you desire privileges, show that they may be safely entrusted to you. Such a course, with patience, will make you happy and prosperous.

Source: Circular No. 2, Freedmen's Bureau. *Executive Documents Printed by Order of The House of Representatives, During the First Session of the Thirty-Ninth Congress, 1865–66.* Washington: Government Printing Office, 1866, pp. 263–264.

THE POWER TO DECIDE RECONSTRUCTION POLICY
5. Andrew Johnson, "Proclamation of Amnesty and Reconstruction," May 29, 1865

An advocate of sectional reconciliation and limited government, President Andrew Johnson set out his Reconstruction policy without calling Congress into special session in 1865. He favored a lenient plan that would quickly restore southern states and grant amnesty to most individuals. Make note of which groups were not covered by the blanket amnesty.

To the end, therefore, that the authority of the Government of the United States may be restored and that peace, order, and freedom may be established, I, Andrew Johnson, President of the United States, do proclaim and declare that I hereby grant to all persons who have, directly or indirectly, participated in the existing rebellion, except as hereinafter excepted, amnesty and pardon, with restoration of all rights of property, except as to slaves and except in cases where legal proceedings under the laws of the United States providing for the confiscation of property of persons engaged in rebellion have been instituted; but upon the condition, nevertheless, that every such person shall take and subscribe the following oath (or affirmation) and thenceforward keep and maintain said oath inviolate, and which oath shall be registered for permanent preservation and shall be of the tenor and effect following, to wit:

I, _____ _____, do solemnly swear (or affirm), in presence of Almighty God, that I will henceforth faithfully support, protect, and defend the Constitution of the United States and the Union of the States thereunder, and that I will in like manner abide by and faithfully support all laws and proclamations which have been made during the existing rebellion with reference to the emancipation of slaves. So help me God.

The following classes of persons are excepted from the benefits of this proclamation:

First. All who are or shall have been pretended civil or diplomatic officers or otherwise domestic or foreign agents of the pretended Confederate government.

Second. All who left judicial stations under the United States to aid the rebellion.

Third. All who shall have been military or naval officers of said pretended Confederate government above the rank of colonel in the army or lieutenant in the navy.

Fourth. All who left seats in the Congress of the United States to aid the rebellion.

Fifth. All who resigned or tendered resignations of their commissions in the Army or Navy of the United States to evade duty in resisting the rebellion.

Sixth. All who have engaged in any way in treating otherwise than lawfully as prisoners of war persons found in the United States service as officers, soldiers, seamen, or in other capacities.

Seventh. All persons who have been or are absentees from the United States for the purpose of aiding the rebellion.

Eighth. All military and naval officers in the rebel service who were educated by the government in the Military Academy at West Point or the United States Naval Academy.

Ninth. All persons who held the pretended offices of governors of States in insurrection against the United States.

Tenth. All persons who left their homes within the jurisdiction and protection of the United States and passed beyond the Federal military lines into the pretended Confederate States for the purpose of aiding the rebellion.

Eleventh. All persons who have been engaged in the destruction of the commerce of the United States upon the high seas and all persons who have made raids into the United States from Canada or been engaged in destroying the commerce of the United States upon the lakes and rivers that separate the British Provinces from the United States.

Twelfth. All persons who, at the time when they seek to obtain the benefits hereof by taking the oath herein prescribed, are in military, naval, or civil confinement or custody, or under bonds of the civil, military, or naval authorities or agents of the United States as prisoners of war, or persons detained for offenses of any kind, either before or after conviction.

Thirteenth. All persons who have voluntarily participated in said rebellion and the estimated value of whose taxable property is over $20,000.

Fourteenth. All persons who have taken the oath of amnesty as prescribed in the President's proclamation of December 8, A.D. 1863, or an oath of allegiance to the Government of the United States since the date of said proclamation and who have not thenceforward kept and maintained the same inviolate.

Provided, That special application may be made to the President for pardon by any person belonging to the excepted classes, and such clemency will be liberally extended as may be consistent with the facts of the case and the peace and dignity of the United States.

Source: A Compilation of the Messages and Papers of the Presidents, 1789–1897, Volume 6. Ed. James D. Richardson. Washington, D.C.: Government Printing Office, 1897, 310–312.

6. Speech of Thaddeus Stevens, December 18, 1865

Radical Republican Congressman Thaddeus Stevens of Pennsylvania delivered this speech in the House of Representatives as it debated how to proceed with Reconstruction. Stevens began by discussing whether the "rebel states" had in fact left the Union and whether, as President Johnson maintained, they could quickly resume their old position in the government. Stevens argued that Congress had the authority to decide when and how the southern states would be restored to the Union. Concerned that white Southerners would band together with northern Democrats and dominate the political system, he argued that black suffrage would serve as a counterweight and strengthen the Republican Party in the South. Stevens also advocated for federal support, including land, for former slaves.

The President assumes, what no one doubts, that the late rebel States have lost their constitutional relations with the Union, and are incapable of representation in Congress, except by permission of the Government. It matters but little, with this admission, whether you call them States out of the Union, and now conquered territories, or assert that because the Constitution forbids them to do what they did do, that they are therefore only dead as to all national and political action, and will remain so until the Government shall breathe into them the breath of life anew and permit them to occupy their former position. In other words, that they are not out of the Union, but are only dead carcasses lying within the Union. In either case, it is very plain that it requires the action of Congress to enable them to form a State government and send representatives to Congress. Nobody, I believe, pretends that with their old constitutions and frames of government they can be permitted to claim their old rights under the Constitution. They have torn their constitutional States into atoms, and built on their foundations fabrics of a totally different character. Dead men cannot raise themselves. Dead States cannot restore their own existence "as it was." Whose especial duty is it to do it? In whom does the Constitution place the power? Not in the judicial branch of the Government, for it only adjudicates and does not prescribe laws. Not in the Executive, for he only executes and cannot make laws. Not in the Commander-in-Chief of the armies, for he can only hold them under military rule until the sovereign legislative power of the conqueror shall give them law....

Unless the law of nations is a dead letter, the late war between two acknowledged belligerents severed their original compacts, and broke all the ties that bound them together. The future condition of the conquered power depends on the will of the conqueror. They must come in as new States or remain as conquered provinces. Congress – the Senate and House of Representatives, with the concurrence of the President – is the only power that can act in the matter....

The theory that the rebel States, for four years a separate power and without representation in Congress, were all the time here in the Union, is a good deal less ingenious and respectable than the metaphysics of Berkeley, which proved that neither the world nor any human being was in existence. If this theory were simply ridiculous it could be forgiven;

but its effect is deeply injurious to the stability of the nation. I cannot doubt that the late Confederate States are out of the Union to all intents and purposes for which the conqueror may choose so to consider them. . . .

It is obvious from all this that the first duty of Congress is to pass a law declaring the condition of these outside or defunct States, and providing proper civil governments for them. Since the conquest they have been governed by martial law. Military rule is necessarily despotic, and ought not to exist longer than is absolutely necessary. As there are no symptoms that the people of these provinces will be prepared to participate in constitutional government for some years, I know of no arrangement so proper for them as territorial governments. There they can learn the principles of freedom and eat the fruit of foul rebellion. Under such governments, while electing members to the Territorial Legislatures, they will necessarily mingle with those to whom Congress shall extend the right of suffrage. In Territories Congress fixes the qualifications of electors; and I know of no better place nor better occasion for the conquered rebels and the conqueror to practice justice to all men, and accustom themselves to make and obey equal laws. . . .

According to my judgment they ought never to be reorganized as capable of acting in the Union, or of being counted as valid States, until the Constitution shall have been so amended as to make it what its framers intended. . . . The first of those amendments is to change the basis of representation among the States. . . . Now all the colored freemen in the slave States, and three fifths of the slaves, are represented, though none of them have votes. . . . With the basis unchanged, the eighty-three southern members, with the Democrats that will in the best time be elected from the North, will always give them a majority in Congress and in the Electoral College. They will at the very first election take possession of the White House and the halls of Congress. I need not depict the ruin that would follow. Assumption of the rebel debt or repudiation of the Federal debt would be sure to follow. The oppression of the freedmen; the reamendment of their State constitutions, and the reestablishment of slavery would be the inevitable result. That they would scorn and disregard their present constitutions, forced upon them in the midst of martial law, would be both natural and just. No one who has any regard for freedom of elections can look upon those governments, forced upon them in duress, with any favor.

If they should grant the right of suffrage to persons of color, I think there would always be Union white men enough in the South, aided by the blacks, to divide the representation, and thus continue the Republican ascendency. If they should refuse to thus alter their election laws it would reduce the representatives of the late slave States to about forty-five and render them powerless for evil.

It is plain that this amendment must be consummated before the defunct States are admitted to be capable of State action, or it never can be. . . .

But this is not all that we ought to do before these inveterate rebels are invited to participate in our legislation. We have turned, or are about to turn, loose four million slaves without a hut to shelter them or a cent in their pockets. The infernal laws of slavery have prevented them from acquiring an education, understanding the commonest laws of contract, or of managing the ordinary business of life. This Congress is bound to provide for them until they can take care of themselves. If we do not furnish them with homesteads from forfeited rebel property, and hedge them around with protective laws; if we leave them to the legislation of their late masters, we had better have left them in bondage. Their condition would be worse than that of our prisoners at Andersonville. If we fail in this great duty now, when we have the power, we shall deserve and receive the execration of history and of all future ages.

Source: Congressional Globe, 39th Congress, 1st Session, 1865, pp. 72–4.

7. 1866 Civil Rights Act

Passed in response to the southern black codes, the Civil Rights Act of 1866 guaranteed equality before the law for all citizens and defined the meaning of freedom by listing specific rights that all citizens possessed. The act invalidated laws in both the North and South that discriminated against African Americans. The Civil Rights Act reflected the approach of moderate Republicans who wanted to expand the scope of Reconstruction and avoid a complete break with President Johnson. To that end, Illinois senator Lyman Trumbull met with President Johnson and believed that he would sign the measure.

CHAP. XXXI.—*An Act to protect all Persons in the United States in their Civil Rights, and furnish the Means of their Vindication.*

Be it enacted by the Senate and House of Representatives of the United States of America in Congress assembled, That all persons born in the United States and not subject to any foreign power, excluding Indians not taxed, are hereby declared to be citizens of the United States; and such citizens, of every race and color, without regard to any previous condition of slavery or involuntary servitude, except as a punishment for crime whereof the party shall have been duly convicted, shall have the same right, in every State and Territory in the United States, to make and enforce contracts, to sue, be parties, and give evidence, to inherit, purchase, lease, sell, hold, and convey real and personal property, and to full and equal benefit of all laws and proceedings for the security of person and property, as is enjoyed by white citizens, and shall be subject to like punishment, pains, and penalties, and to none other, any law, statute, ordinance, regulation, or custom, to the contrary notwithstanding.

Sec. 2. *And be it further enacted,* That any person who, under color of any law, statute, ordinance, regulation, or custom, shall subject, or cause to be subjected, any inhabitant of any State or Territory to the deprivation of any right secured or protected by this act, or to different punishment, pains, or penalties on account of such person having at any time been held in a condition of slavery or involuntary servitude, except as a punishment for crime whereof the party shall have been duly convicted, or by reason of his color or race, than is prescribed for the punishment of white persons, shall be deemed guilty of a misdemeanor, and, on conviction, shall be punished by fine not exceeding one thousand dollars, or imprisonment not exceeding one year, or both, in the discretion of the court. . . .

In the Senate of the United States, April 6, 1866.

The President of the United States having returned to the Senate, in which it originated, the bill entitled "An act to protect all persons in the United States in their civil rights, and furnish the means of their vindication," with his objections thereto, the Senate proceeded, in pursuance of the Constitution, to reconsider the same; and,

Resolved, That the said bill do pass, two-thirds of the Senate agreeing to pass the same.

Attest: J.W. Forney,

Secretary of the Senate.

In the House of Representatives U.S. April 9th, 1866.

The House of Representatives having proceeded, in pursuance of the Constitution, to reconsider the bill entitled, "An act to protect all persons in the United States in their civil rights, and furnish the means of their vindication," returned to the Senate by the President of the United States, with his objections, and sent by the Senate to the House of Representatives, with the message of the President returning the bill:

Resolved, That the bill do pass, two-thirds of the House of Representatives agreeing to pass the same.

Attest: Edward McPherson, Clerk,

by Clinton Lloyd, Chief Clerk.

Source: The Statutes at Large, Treaties, and Proclamations of the *United States of America,* vol. 14. Boston: Little, Brown, and Company, 1868, 27–30.

8. Andrew Johnson, Veto of the Civil Rights Bill, March 27, 1866

The Civil Rights Bill passed Congress with overwhelming support from Republicans, and they urged the president to sign it. When Andrew Johnson instead vetoed the measure, moderates were shocked by the president's action, and a complete rupture between the executive and legislative branches soon occurred. In his veto message, President Johnson included numerous reasons to reject black citizenship. He questioned whether the measure was necessary, whether Congress had the authority to act, and, expressing his racist views, whether African Americans had the "requisite qualifications" for citizenship. Johnson suggested that immigrants were more deserving of citizenship than African Americans and that the measure discriminated against white men. He also cautioned against the expansion of federal power that would accrue from the measure. In particular, Johnson tried to inflame fears by suggesting that the bill might invalidate state laws that prevented intermarriage between whites and blacks. Johnson was confident that freedpeople would be adequately protected by existing laws. On April 9, 1866, the Civil Rights Act became law, the first time in American history that a major piece of legislation passed over a presidential veto.

To the Senate of the United States:

I regret that the bill which has passed both Houses of Congress, entitled "An Act to protect all persons in the United States in their civil rights, and furnish the means of their vindication," contains provisions which I cannot approve, consistently with my sense of duty to the whole people, and my obligations to the Constitution of the United States. I am, therefore, constrained to return it to the Senate (the House in which it originated) with my objections to its becoming law.

By the first section of the bill, all persons born in the United States, and not subject to any foreign power, excluding Indians not taxed, are declared to be citizens of the United States. This provision comprehends the Chinese of the Pacific States, Indians subject to taxation, the people called Gipsies, as well as the entire race designated as blacks, people of color, negroes, mulattoes, and persons of African blood. Every individual of these races, born in the United States, is by the bill made a citizen of the United States.... If ... such persons are not citizens, as may be assumed from the proposed legislation to make them such, the grave question presents itself whether, where eleven of the thirty-six States are unrepresented in Congress at the time, it is sound policy to make our entire colored population, and all other excepted classes, citizens of the United States. Four millions of them have just emerged from slavery into freedom. Can it be reasonably supposed that they possess the requisite qualifications to entitle them to all the privileges and immunities of citizenship of the United States? ... It may also be asked, whether it is necessary that they should be declared citizens in order that they may be secured in the enjoyment of the civil rights proposed to be conferred by the bill? Those rights are, by Federals as well as by State laws, secured to all domiciled aliens and foreigners, ... and it may safely be assumed that the same enactments are sufficient to give like protection and benefits to those for whom this bill provides special legislation. Besides, the policy of the Government, from its origin to the present time, seems to have been that persons who are strangers to and unfamiliar with our institutions and laws, should pass through a certain probation; at the end of which, before attaining the coveted prize, they must give evidence of their fitness to receive and to exercise the rights of citizens as contemplated by the Constitution of the United States. The bill in effect proposes a discrimination against large numbers of intelligent, worthy and patriotic foreigners, and in favor of the negro, to whom, after long years of bondage, the avenues to freedom and intelligence have just now been suddenly opened.... Yet it is now proposed by a single legislative enactment to confer the rights of citizens upon all persons of African descent, born within the excluded limits of the United States, while persons of foreign birth, who make our land their home, must undergo a probation of five years, and can only then become citizens upon proof that they are of good moral character, attached to the principles of the Constitution of the United States, and well disposed to the good order and happiness of the same. The first section of the bill also contains an enumeration of the rights to be enjoyed by those classes so made citizens in every State and Territory of the United States. Thus a perfect equality of the white and colored races is attempted to be fixed by a Federal law in every State of the Union, over the vast field of State jurisdiction covered by these enumerated rights. In no one of them can any State exercise any power of discrimination between different races. In the exercise of State policy over matters exclusively affecting the people of each State, it has frequently been thought expedient to discriminate between the two races. By the statutes of some of the States, North as well as South, it is enacted, for instance, that no white person shall intermarry with a negro or mulatto.... I do not say that this bill repeals State laws, on the subject of marriage between the two races.... I take this discrimination, however, as an instance of the State policy as to discrimination, and to inquire whether, if Congress can abrogate all State laws of discrimination between the two races, in the matter of real estate, of suits, and of contracts generally, Congress may not also repeal the State laws as to the contract of marriage between the races? Hitherto, every subject embraced in the enumeration of rights contained in the bill has been considered as exclusively belonging to the States; they all relate to the internal policy and economy of the respective States. They are matters which, in each State, concern the domestic condition of its people, varying in each according to its peculiar circumstances and the safety and well-being of its own citizens.... If Congress shall declare by law who shall hold lands, who shall testify, who shall have capacity to make a contract in a State, that Congress can also declare by law who, without regard to race or color, shall have the right to act as a juror or as a judge, to hold any office, and finally to vote, in every State and Territory of the United States. ...

I do not propose to consider the policy of this bill. To me the details of the bill are fraught with evil. The white race and black race of the South have hitherto lived together under the relation of master and slave— capital owning labor. Now that relation is changed; and as to ownership, capital and labor are divorced. They stand now, each master of itself. In this new relation, one being necessary to the other, there will be a new adjustment, which both are deeply interested in making harmonious. Each has equal power in settling the terms; and, if left to the laws that regulate capital and labor, it is confidently believed that they will satisfactorily work out the problem. . . . This bill frustrates this adjustment. It intervenes between capital and labor, and attempts to settle questions of political economy through the agency of numerous officials, whose interest it will be to foment discord between the two races. . . . In all our history, in all our experience as a people living under Federal and State law, no such system as that contemplated by the details of this bill has ever before been proposed or adopted. They establish for the security of the colored race safeguards which go indefinitely beyond any that the General Government has ever provided for the white race. In fact, the distinction of race and color is by the bill made to operate in favor of the colored against the white race. They interfere with the municipal legislation of the States; with relations existing exclusively between a State and its citizens, or between inhabitants of the same State; an absorption and assumption of power by the General Government which, if acquiesced in, must sap and destroy our federative system of limited power, and break down the barriers which preserve the rights of the States. It is another step, or rather stride, towards centralization and the concentration of all legislative powers in the National Government. The tendency of the bill must be to resuscitate the spirit of rebellion, and to arrest the progress of those influences which are more closely drawing around the States the bonds of union and peace.

My lamented predecessor, in his proclamation of the 1st of January, 1863, ordered and declared that all persons held as slaves within certain States and parts of States therein designated, were, and thenceforward should be free; and further, that the Executive Government of the United States, including the military and naval authorities thereof, would recognize and maintain the freedom of such persons. This guaranty has been rendered especially obligatory and sacred by the amendment of the Constitution abolishing slavery throughout the United States. I, therefore, fully recognize the obligation to protect and defend that class of our people whenever and wherever it shall become necessary, and to the full extent, compatible with the Constitution of the United States. Entertaining these sentiments, it only remains for me to say that I will cheerfully cooperate with Congress in any measure that may be necessary for the preservation of civil rights of the freedmen, as well as those of all other classes of persons throughout the United States, by judicial process under equal and impartial laws, or conformably with the provisions of the Federal Constitution.

Source: Lillian Foster. *Andrew Johnson, His Life and Speeches*. New York: Richardson & Co., 1866, 265–270, 277–280.

MILITARY RECONSTRUCTION ACTS
9. First Reconstruction Act, March 2, 1867

The Military Reconstruction Acts of 1867 applied to 10 of the 11 states that had passed ordinances of secession. Tennessee was exempted from military reconstruction because it had ratified the Fourteenth Amendment in 1866. The first act divided the ten southern states into five military districts and spelled out what the states needed to do to be readmitted to the Union. In subsequent acts, Congress gave additional power to the military commanders of the five districts, including the ability to register eligible voters and remove political officials who interfered with Reconstruction.

An Act to provide for the more efficient Government of the Rebel States

WHEREAS no legal State governments or adequate protection for life or property now exists in the rebel States of Virginia, North Carolina, South Carolina, Georgia, Mississippi, Alabama, Louisiana, Florida, Texas, and Arkansas; and whereas it is necessary that peace and good order should be enforced in said States until loyal and republican State governments can be legally established: Therefore,

Be it enacted . . ., That said rebel States shall be divided into military districts and made subject to the military authority of the United States as hereinafter prescribed, and for that purpose Virginia shall constitute the first district; North Carolina and South Carolina the second district; Georgia, Alabama, and Florida the third district; Mississippi and Arkansas the fourth district; and Louisiana and Texas the fifth district.

SEC. 2. *And be it further enacted,* That it shall be the duty of the President to assign to the command of each of said districts an officer of the army, not below the rank of brigadier-general, and to detail a sufficient military force to enable such officer to perform his duties and enforce his authority within the district to which he is assigned.

SEC. 3. *And be it further enacted,* That it shall be the duty of each officer assigned as aforesaid, to protect all persons in their rights of person and property, to suppress insurrection, disorder, and violence, and to punish, or cause to be punished, all disturbers of the public peace and criminals; and to this end he may allow local civil tribunals to take jurisdiction of and to try offenders, or, when in his judgment it may be necessary for the trial of offenders, he shall have power to organize military commissions or tribunals for that purpose, and all interference under color of State authority with the exercise of military authority under this act, shall be null and void. . . .

SEC. 5. *And be it further enacted,* That when the people of any one of said rebel States shall have formed a constitution of government in conformity with the Constitution of the United States in all respects, framed by a convention of delegates elected by the male citizens of said State, twenty-one years old and upward, of whatever race, color, or previous condition, who have been resident in said State for one year previous to the day of such election, except such as may be disfranchised for participation in the rebellion or for felony at common law, and when such constitution shall provide that the elective franchise shall be enjoyed by all such persons as have the qualifications herein states for electors of delegates, and when such constitution shall be ratified by a majority of the persons voting on the question of ratification who are qualified as electors for delegates, and when such constitution shall have been submitted to Congress for examination and approval, and Congress shall have approved the same, and when said State, by a vote of its legislature elected under said constitution, shall have adopted the amendment to the Constitution of the United States, proposed by the Thirty-ninth Congress, and known as article fourteen and when said article shall have become a part of the Constitution of the United States said State shall be declared entitled to representation in Congress, and senators and representatives shall be admitted therefrom on their taking the oath prescribed by law, and then and thereafter the preceding sections of this act shall be inoperative in said State: *Provided*, That no person excluded from the privilege of holding office by said proposed amendment to the Constitution of the United States, shall be eligible to election as a member of the convention to frame a constitution for any of said rebel States, nor shall any person vote for members of such convention.

SEC. 6. *And be it further enacted*, That, until the people of said rebel States shall be by law admitted to representation in the Congress of the United States, any civil governments which may exist therein shall be deemed provisional only, and in all respects subject to the paramount authority of the United States at any time to abolish, modify, control, or supersede the same; and in all elections to any office under such provisional governments all persons shall be entitled to vote, and none others, who are entitled to vote, under the provisions of the fifth section of this act; and no persons shall be eligible to any office under any such provisional governments who would be disqualified from holding office under the provisions of the third *article* of said constitutional amendment.

Source: The Statutes at Large, Treaties, and Proclamations of the *United States of America*, vol. 14. Boston: Little, Brown, and Company, 1868, 428–29.

10. Andrew Johnson, Veto of the First Military Reconstruction Act, March 2, 1867

In his veto of the Military Reconstruction Act, Andrew Johnson argued that the measure was unconstitutional and that the military district commanders were granted despotic power over the states. He maintained Congress did not have the authority to mandate changes to state constitutions. Southern states had been in rebellion, but now that it had ended, they should be restored to their former position in the Union. He also argued against black suffrage and accused the Congress of "Africanizing" the South. His argument did not sway Congress and the bill was quickly passed over Johnson's veto by a vote of 135 to 48 in the House and 38 to 10 in the Senate.

The bill places all the people of the ten States therein named under the absolute domination of military rulers; and the preamble undertakes to give the reason upon which the measure is based and the ground upon which it is justified. It declares that there exists in those States no legal governments and no adequate protection for life or property, and asserts the necessity of enforcing peace and good order within their limits. . . .

The bill, however, would seem to show upon its face that the establishment of peace and good order is not its real object. The fifth section declares that the preceding sections shall cease to operate in any State where certain events shall have happened. . . . All these conditions must be fulfilled before the people of any of these States can be relieved from the bondage of military domination; but when they are fulfilled, then immediately the pains and penalties of the bill are to cease, no matter whether there be peace and order or not, and without any reference to the security of life or property. The excuse given for the bill in the preamble is admitted by the bill itself not to be real. The military rule which it establishes is plainly to be used, not for any purpose of order or for the prevention of crime, but solely as a means of coercing the people into the adoption of principles and measures to which it is known that they are opposed, and upon which they have an undeniable right to exercise their own judgment.

I submit to Congress whether this measure is not in its whole character, scope, and object without precedent and without authority, in palpable conflict with the plainest provisions of the Constitution, and utterly destructive to those great principles of liberty and humanity for which our ancestors on both sides of the Atlantic have shed so much blood and expended so much treasure. . . .

The power thus given to the commanding officer [of each military district] over all the people of each district is that of an absolute monarch. His mere will is to take the place of all law. The law of the States is now the only rule applicable to the subjects placed under his control, and that is completely displaced by the clause which declares all interference of State authority to be null and void. He alone is permitted to determine what are rights of person or property, and he may protect them in such way as in his discretion may seem proper. It places at his free disposal all the lands and goods in his district, and he may distribute them without let or hindrance to whom he pleases. Being bound by no State law, and there being no other law to regulate the subject, he may make a criminal code of his own; and he can make it as bloody as any recorded in history, or he can reserve the privilege of acting upon the impulse of his private passions in each case that arises. He is bound by no rules of evidence; there is, indeed, no provision by which he is authorized or required to take any evidence at all. Everything is a crime which he chooses to call so, and all persons are condemned whom he pronounces to be guilty. He is not bound to keep any record or make any report of his proceedings. He may arrest his victims wherever he finds them, without warrant, accusation, or proof of probable cause. If he gives them a trial before he inflicts the punishment, he gives it of his grace and mercy, not because he is commanded so to do. . . .

It is plain that the authority here given to the military officer amounts to absolute despotism. . . .

Some persons assume that the success of our arms in crushing the opposition which was made in some of the States to the execution of the Federal laws reduced those States and all their people – the innocent as well as the guilty – to the condition of vassalage and gave us a power over them which the Constitution does not bestow or define or limit. No fallacy can be more transparent than this. Our victories subjected the insurgents to legal obedience, not to the yoke of an arbitrary despotism. . . .

Invasion, insurrection, rebellion, and domestic violence were anticipated when the Government was framed, and the means of repelling and suppressing them were wisely provided for in the Constitution; but it was not thought necessary to declare that the States in which they might occur should be expelled from the Union. Rebellions, which were invariably suppressed, occurred prior to that out of which these questions grow; but the States continued to exist and the Union remained unbroken. . . .

The purpose and object of the bill - the general intent which pervades it from beginning to end - is to change the entire structure and character of the State governments and to compel them by force to the adoption of organic laws and regulations which they are unwilling to accept if left to themselves. The negroes have not asked for the privilege of voting; the vast majority of them have no idea what it means. This bill not only thrusts it into their bands, but compels them, as well as the whites, to use it in a particular way. If they do not form a constitution with prescribed articles in it and afterwards elect a legislature which will act upon certain measures in a prescribed way, neither blacks nor whites can be relieved from the slavery which the bill imposes upon them. Without pausing here to consider the policy or impolicy of Africanizing the southern part of our territory, I would simply ask the attention of Congress to that manifest, well-known, and universally acknowledged rule of constitutional law which declares that the Federal Government has no jurisdiction, authority, or power to regulate such subjects for any State. To force the right of suffrage out of the hands of the white people and into the hands of the negroes is an arbitrary violation of this principle.

Source: A Compilation of the Messages and Papers of the Presidents, 1789–1897, Volume 6. Ed. James D. Richardson. Washington, D.C., Government Printing Office, 1897, 498–507.

11. Editorial Response to the Veto of the Military Reconstruction Bill

In "The Veto of the Reconstruction Bill," Harper's Weekly *rejects the assumptions that form the basis of Johnson's veto message. In particular, the editorial argues that the rebellion is not over and that the country is not at peace. From that starting point, it accepts the assertion of congressional authority over the southern states. In the end, the editorial claims that northern voters have repudiated Johnson's position on Reconstruction and that he should consider resigning the presidency.*

The veto of the Reconstruction bill . . . is a long paper, but it begs the whole question from beginning to end. There is not a good suggestion in it which is not wholly inapplicable. Being asked what he thinks of an eagle, the President proceeds to prove that a buzzard is not a nightingale. He makes an assertion contradicting the fundamental assertion of the bill, and goes on with his argument from premises which no one but himself concedes. The bill declares that there is no lawful government in any of the late rebel States. The President replies that "to pronounce the supreme law-making power of an established State illegal is to say that law itself is unlawful." What is an established State? Did the President's will establish South Carolina? If not, how is there any establishment there which is valid in the view of the National Government? And if the President's will established the State, where does the Constitution, which he so earnestly commends, grant him the authority? Having thus assumed the whole case the President sweeps on with generalizations which have no relation to the facts, and statements which are disproved by the most ample evidence....

Throughout this long document there is no sign of the least consciousness that the country is not at peace, but is settling the conditions of peace.... The President has proclaimed that the rebellion has ceased, but that no more makes peace than his appointment of Provisional Governors establishes States. Congress alone can declare war and raise and support armies and navies, and Congress alone therefore can say when war has ceased. The President as usual returns to the Congressional declaration of July, 1861, that the war was not for subjugation, and he argues that it was merely the suppression of an insurrection. But the Supreme Court, upon which he relies, has decided that it was a war, and when an insurrection has proceeded upon the scale of the late war it is for Congress, and Congress alone, to decide when it has ended.... The President who says that the rebellion of a State does not destroy or interrupt its relations in the Union is the same President who, within two years, required the rebel States to adopt the Emancipation Amendment, to repudiate their rebel debt, and to disavow their secession ordinances as conditions of their return to the Union.

Every argument of the Veto Message is fatal to the policy which the President has pursued; every assertion is contrary to the express evidence, and every appeal to the Constitution is futile from a man who denies to the people in Congress a power which he alone has not hesitated to exercise. It is plain that the President has nothing more to say. His position has been as fully and ably explained as it can be, and it is utterly and indignantly repudiated by the people. Since, then, his oath binds him to execute the laws, and since the most vital laws, in his judgment, are unconstitutional, why does he consent to be an instrument of what he considers fatally destructive measures? He tells us that he is a patriot. Do patriots remain in place when they think that they are to be used to destroy the liberties of their country?

Source: *Harper's Weekly*, March 16, 1867, p 162.

SUFFRAGE
12. Frederick Douglass, "What the Black Man Wants"

Douglass delivered this speech in 1865 at the annual meeting of the Massachusetts Anti-Slavery Society. Like others in the Equal Rights movement in the North, Douglass believed that suffrage was essential to achieving full citizenship. Yet the achievement of this goal was fraught with difficulties. In 1865, African Americans were fully enfranchised in only five states, and a small percentage of African Americans who met the state's property qualifications were eligible in New York. A referendum to enfranchise African Americans failed in Connecticut in 1866. African Americans, North and South, pressured Republicans to support black suffrage. Compare Douglass's arguments in this speech with those made in Source 2. Consider how both of these sources can be used to contradict Andrew Johnson's claim about black suffrage in his veto of the Military Reconstruction Act.

I am for the "immediate, unconditional, and universal" enfranchisement of the black man, in every State in the Union. Without this, his liberty is a mockery; without this, you might as well almost retain the old name of slavery for his condition; for, in fact, if he is not the slave of the individual master, he is the slave of society, and holds his liberty as a privilege, not as a right. He is at the mercy of the mob, and has no means of protecting himself.

It may be objected, however, that this pressing of the negro's right to suffrage is premature. Let us have slavery abolished, it may be said, let us have labor organized, and then, in the natural course of events, the right of suffrage will be extended to the negro. I do not agree with this. . . . This is the hour. Our streets are in mourning, tears are falling at every fireside, and under the chastisement of this rebellion we have almost come up to the point of conceding this great, this all-important right of suffrage. I fear that if we fail to do it now, if Abolitionists fail to press it now, we may not see, for centuries to come, the same disposition that exists at this moment. Hence, I say, now is the time to press this right.

It may be asked, "Why do you want it? Some men have got along very well without it. Women have not this right." Shall we justify one wrong by another? That is a sufficient answer. Shall we at this moment justify the deprivation of the negro of the right to vote, because some one else is deprived of that privilege? I hold that women, as well as men, have the right to vote, and my heart and my voice go with the movement to extend suffrage to woman; but that question rests upon another basis than that on which our right rests. We may be asked, I say, why we want it. I will tell you why we want it. We want it because it is our right, first of all. No class of men can, without insulting their own nature, be content with any deprivation of their rights. We want it, again, as a means for educating our race. Men are so constituted that they derive their conviction of their own possibilities largely from the estimate formed of them by others. If nothing is expected of a people, that people will find it difficult to contradict that expectation. By depriving us of suffrage, you affirm our incapacity to form an intelligent judgment respecting public men and public measures; you declare before the world that we are unfit to exercise the elective franchise, and by this means lead us to undervalue ourselves, to put a low estimate upon ourselves, and to feel that we have no possibilities like other men. Again, I want the elective franchise, for one, as a colored man, because ours is a peculiar government, based upon a peculiar idea, and that idea is universal suffrage. If I were in a monarchical government, or an autocratic or aristocratic government, where the few bore rule and the many were subject, there would be no special stigma resting upon me, because I did not exercise the elective franchise. . . . [B]ut here, where universal suffrage is the rule, where that is the fundamental idea of the government, to rule us out is to make us an exception, to brand us with the stigma of inferiority, and . . . therefore, I want the franchise for the black man.

There are, however, other reasons, not derived from any consideration merely of our rights, but arising out of the condition of the South, . . . considerations which must arrest the attention of statesmen. I believe that when the tall heads of this rebellion shall have been swept down, as they will be swept down, when the Davises and Toombses and Stephenses, and others who are leading in this rebellion shall have been blotted out, there will be this rank undergrowth of treason, . . . growing up there, and interfering with, and thwarting the quiet operation of the federal government in those States. You will see those traitors handing down, from sire to son, the same malignant spirit which they have manifested, and which they are now exhibiting, with malicious hearts, broad blades, and bloody hands in the field, against our sons and brothers. That spirit will still remain; and whoever sees the federal government extended over those southern States will see that government in a strange land, and not only in a strange land, but in an enemy's land. A post-master of the United States in the South will find himself surrounded by a hostile spirit; a collector in a Southern port will find himself surrounded by a hostile spirit; a United States marshal or United States judge will be surrounded there by a hostile element. That enmity will not die out in a year, will not die out in an age. . . . They will endeavor to circumvent, they will endeavor to destroy, the peaceful operation of this government. Now, where will you find the strength to counterbalance this spirit, if you do not find it in the negroes of the South? They are your friends, and have always been your friends. They were your friends even when the government did not regard them as such. . . . They are our only friends in the South, and we should be true to them in this their trial hour, and see to it that they have the elective franchise. . . .

What have you asked the black men of the South, the black men of the whole country, to do? Why, you have asked them to incur the deadly enmity of their masters, in order to befriend you and to befriend this Government. You have asked us to call down, not only upon ourselves, but upon our children's children, the deadly hate of the entire Southern people. You have called upon us to turn our backs upon our masters, to abandon their cause and espouse yours; to turn against the South and in favor of the North; to shoot down the Confederacy and uphold the flag – the American flag. You have called upon us to expose ourselves to all the subtle machinations of their malignity for all time. And now, what do you propose to do when you come to make peace? To reward your enemies, and trample in the dust your friends? Do you intend to sacrifice the very men who have come to the rescue of your banner in the South, and incurred the lasting displeasure of their masters thereby? Do you intend to sacrifice them and reward your enemies? Do you mean to give your enemies the right to vote, and take it away from your friends? Is that wise policy? Is that honorable? Could American honor withstand such a blow? I do not believe you will do it. I think you will see to it that we have the right to vote. There is something too mean in looking upon the negro, when you are in trouble, as a citizen, and when you are free from trouble, as an alien. When this nation was in trouble, in its early struggles, it looked upon the negro as a citizen. In 1776 he was a citizen. At the time of the formation of the constitution the negro had the right to vote in eleven States out of the old thirteen. In your trouble you have made us citizens. In 1812 General Jackson addressed us as citizens – "fellow-citizens." He wanted us to fight. We were citizens then! And now, when you come to frame a conscription bill, the negro is a citizen again. He has been a citizen just three times in the history of this government, and it has always been in time of trouble. In time of trouble we are citizens. Shall we be citizens in war, and aliens in peace? Would that be just? . . .

What I ask for the negro is not benevolence, not pity, not sympathy, but simply justice. . . . Everybody has asked the question, . . . "What shall we do with the negro?" I have had but one answer from the beginning. . . . Do nothing with us! If the apples will not remain on the tree of their own strength, if they are worm-eaten at the core, if they are early ripe and disposed to fall, let them fall! I am not for tying or fastening them on the tree in any way, except by nature's plan, and if they will not stay there, let them fall. And if the negro cannot stand on his own legs, let him fall also. All I ask is, give him a chance to stand on his own legs! Let him alone! If you see him on his way to school, let him alone, – don't disturb him! If you see him going to the dinner table at a hotel, let him go! If you see him going to the ballot-box, let him alone, – don't disturb him! . . . If you will only untie his hands, and give him a chance, I think he will live. He will work as readily for himself as the white man. A great many delusions have been swept away by this war. One was, that the negro would not work; he has proved his ability to work. Another was, that the negro would not fight; that he possessed only the most sheepish attributes of humanity; was a perfect lamb, or an "Uncle Tom;" disposed to take off his coat whenever required, fold his hands, and be whipped by anybody who wanted to whip him. But the war has proved that there is a great deal of human nature in the negro, and that "he will fight," as. . .said, in earlier days than these, "when there is a reasonable possibility of his whipping anybody."

Source: Mayo W. Hazeltine, ed. *Orations from Homer to William McKinley*, vol. 18. New York: P.F. Collier and Son, 1902, 7667–7676.

13. The Fifteenth Amendment

The Fifteenth Amendment passed Congress on February 26, 1869, and was rati- fied on February 3, 1870. The effect of the amendment, along with the Military Reconstruction Acts, was that African Americans voted and held political office. After Reconstruction ended, southern states used a number of means, especially literacy tests, poll taxes, and the grandfather clause, to disenfranchise African Americans. The court upheld these measures. African American political partici- pation would not return to 1870s' levels for nearly one hundred years.

Section 1 The right of citizens of the United States to vote shall not be denied or abridged by the United States or by any State on account of race, color, or previous condition of servitude.

Section 2 The Congress shall have power to enforce this article by appro- priate legislation.

Source: The House Joint Resolution proposing the 15th amendment to the Constitution, December 7, 1868; Enrolled Acts and Resolutions of Congress, 1789–1999; General Records of the United States Government; Record Group 11; National Archives.

14. Elizabeth Cady Stanton on Suffrage

The wording of the Fifteenth Amendment, which did not prohibit discrimination on the basis of gender, caused a split between former allies. When Susan B. Anthony asked abolitionist Gerrit Smith to sign a petition in 1868 calling for a suffrage amend- ment that did not distinguish between men and women, he declined, predicting that in his view it would fail. Smith argued that his first priority was to enfranchise African American men, and though he supported women's suffrage, it came second. Eliza- beth Cady Stanton responded to Smith's letter in January 1869.

To the Senate and House of Representatives in Congress assembled:
The undersigned, citizens of the State of New York, earnestly but respectfully request, that in any change or amendment of the Constitution

you may propose to extend or regulate suffrage, there shall be no distinctions made between men and women. . . .

The above is the petition to which our friend Gerrit Smith, as an abolitionist, can not conscientiously put his name, while Republicans and Democrats are signing it all over the country. He does not clearly read the signs of the times, or he would see that there is to be no reconstruction of this nation, except on the basis of universal suffrage, as the natural, inalienable right of every citizen. . . . As the aristocracy in this country is the "male sex," and as Mr. Smith belongs to the privileged order, he naturally considers it important for the best interests of the nation, that every type and shade of degraded, ignorant manhood should be enfranchised, before even the higher classes of womanhood should be admitted to the polls. This does not surprise us. Men always judge more wisely of objective wrongs and oppressions, than of those in which they are themselves involved. Tyranny on a Southern plantation is far more easily seen by white men at the North than the wrongs of the women of their own households. . . . Hence, in criticizing such good and noble men as Gerrit Smith and Wendell Phillips for their apathy on woman's enfranchisement at this hour, it is not because . . . we have the least hope of influencing them, but simply to rouse the women of the country to the fact that they must not look to these men as their champions at this hour.

Again; Mr. Smith refuses to sign the petition because he thinks to press the broader question of "universal suffrage" would defeat the partial one of "manhood suffrage"; in other words, to demand protection for woman against her oppressors, would jeopardize the black man's chance of securing protection against his oppressors. If it is a question of precedence merely, on what principle of justice or courtesy should woman yield her right of enfranchisement to the negro? If men can not be trusted to legislate for their own sex, how can they legislate for the opposite sex, of whose wants and needs they know nothing? It has always been considered good philosophy in pressing any measure to claim the uttermost in order to get something. . . . But their intense interest in the negro blinded our former champions so that they forsook principle for policy, and in giving woman the cold shoulder raised a more deadly opposition to the negro than any we had yet encountered, creating an antagonism between him and the very element most needed to be propitiated in his behalf. It was this feeling that defeated "negro suffrage" in Kansas.

But Mr. Smith abandons the principle clearly involved, and intrenches himself on policy. He would undoubtedly plead the necessity of the ballot for the negro at the south for his protection, and point us to innumerable acts of cruelty he suffers to-day. But all these things fall as heavily on the women of the black race, yea far more so, for no man can ever know the deep, the damning degradation to which woman is subject in her youth, in helplessness and poverty. The enfranchisement of the men of her race, Mr. Smith would say, is her protection. Our Saxon men have held the ballot in this country for a century, and what honest man can claim that it has been used for woman's protection? Alas! we have given the very hey day of our life to undoing the cruel and unjust laws that the men of New York had made for their own mothers, wives, and daughters. . . .

Politicians will find, when they come to test this question of "negro supremacy" in the several States, that there is a far stronger feeling among the women of the nation than they supposed. We doubt whether a constitutional amendment securing "manhood suffrage" alone could be fairly passed in a single State in this Union. Women everywhere are waking up to their own God-given rights, to their true dignity as citizens of a republic, as mothers of the race.

Although those who demand "woman's suffrage" on principle are few, those who would oppose "negro suffrage" from prejudice are many, hence the only way to secure the latter, is to end all this talk of class legislation, bury the negro in the citizen, and claim the suffrage for all men and women, as a natural, inalienable right. The friends of the negro never made a greater blunder than when, at the close of the war, they timidly refused to lead the nation in demanding suffrage for all. If even Wendell Phillips and Gerrit Smith, the very apostles of liberty on this continent, failed at that point, how can we wonder at the vacillation and confusion of politicians at this hour. We had hoped that the elections of '67, with their overwhelming majorities in every State against negro suffrage, would have proved to all alike, how futile is compromise, how short-sighted is policy.

Source: The Revolution, January 14, 1869; reprinted in Elizabeth Cady Stanton, Susan B. Anthony, and Matilda Joslyn Gage, eds. *History of Woman Suffrage*, volume 2. New York, 1881, 317–9.

15. Charles Sumner on the Impeachment Trial of Andrew Johnson, May 26, 1868

The House of Representatives passed eleven articles of impeachment in March 1868, nine of which focused on President Johnson's violation of the Tenure of Office Act, a measure that required Senate approval before the president could remove an appointed official from office. Charles Sumner, a Massachusetts senator and radical Republican, had been a vocal advocate of impeachment for years. The Senate failed to remove the president from office by one vote. In this speech to the Senate explaining his enthusiastic support for removal, Charles Sumner discussed not simply the Tenure of Office Act, but expressed much deeper concerns about the president.

This is one of the last great battles with Slavery. Driven from these legislative chambers, driven from the field of war, this monstrous power has found a refuge in the Executive Mansion, where, in utter disregard of Constitution and law, it seeks to exercise its ancient domineering sway. All this is very plain. Nobody can question it. Andrew Johnson is the impersonation of the tyrannical Slave Power. In him it lives again. He is lineal successor of John C. Calhoun and Jefferson Davis, and he gathers about him the same supporters. Original partisans of Slavery, North and South, habitual compromisers of great principles, maligners of the Declaration of Independence, politicians without heart, lawyers for whom a technicality is everything, and a promiscuous company who at every stage of the battle have set their faces against Equal Rights, – these are his allies. It is the old troop of Slavery, with a few recruits, ready as of old for violence, cunning in device, and heartless in quibble. With the President at their head, they are now intrenched in the Executive Mansion. . . .

I would not in this judgment depart from the moderation proper to the occasion; but God forbid, that, when called to deal with so great an offender, I should affect a coldness I cannot feel! Slavery has been our worst enemy, assailing all, murdering our children, filling our homes with mourning, darkening the land with tragedy; and now it rears its crest anew, with Andrew Johnson as its representative. Through him it assumes once more to rule and to impose its cruel law. The enormity of his conduct is aggravated by his bare faced treachery. He once declared himself the Moses of the colored race. Behold him now the Pharaoh! With such treachery in such a cause there can be no parley. Every sentiment, every conviction, every vow against Slavery must now be directed against him. Pharaoh is at the bar of the Senate for judgment. . . .

Slavery in all its pretensions is a defiance of law; for it can have no law in its support. Whoso becomes its representative must act accordingly; and this is the transcendent crime of Andrew Johnson. For the sake of Slavery, and to uphold its original supporters in their endeavors to continue this wrong under another name, he has set at defiance the National Constitution and the laws of the land; and he has accompanied this unquestionable usurpation by brutalities and indecencies in office without precedent. . . . This usurpation . . . became manifest as long ago as the winter of 1866, when . . . he assumed legislative powers in the reconstruction of the Rebel States, and, in carrying forward this usurpation, nullified an Act of Congress, intended as the corner-stone of Reconstruction, by virtue of which Rebels are excluded from office under the National Government, and thereafter, in vindication of this misconduct, uttered a scandalous speech, in which he openly charged members of Congress with being assassins, and mentioned some by name. Plainly he should have been impeached and expelled at that early day. The case against him was complete. . . .

Meanwhile the President proceeded in transgression. There is nothing of usurpation he has not attempted. . . . Timid at first, he grew bolder and bolder. . . . On two separate occasions, in July and September, 1865, he confessed the power of Congress over the subject [of Reconstruction]; but when Congress came together in December, the confessor of Congressional power found that he alone had this great prerogative. According to his new-fangled theory, Congress had nothing to do but admit the States with the governments instituted through his will alone. . . .

Had this assumption of power been incidental, for the exigency of the moment, as under pressure of war, and especially to serve human rights, to which before his elevation the President had professed such vociferous devotion, it might have been pardoned. It would have passed into the chapter of unauthorized acts which a patriot people had condoned. But it was the opposite in every particular. Beginning and continuing in usurpation, it was hateful beyond pardon, because it sacrificed Unionists, white and black, and was in the interest of the Rebellion, and of Rebels who had been in arms against their country.

More than one person was appointed provisional governor who could not take the oath of office required by Act of Congress. . . . Rebels crawled forth from their retreats. Men who had hardly ventured to expect life were candidates for office, and the Rebellion became strong again. The change was felt in all gradations of government, in States, counties, towns, and villages. Rebels found themselves in places of trust, while true-hearted Unionists . . . were driven into hiding-places. All this was under the auspices of Andrew Johnson. It was he who animated the wicked crew. He was at the head of the work. Loyalty was persecuted. White and black, whose only offence was that they had been true to country, were insulted, abused, murdered. . . . More than two thousand murders have been reported in Texas alone since the surrender of Kirby Smith. . . . All this is directly traced to Andrew Johnson. . . .

The Freedmen's Bureau, that sacred charity of the Republic, was despoiled of its possessions for the sake of Rebels, to whom their forfeited estates were given back after they had been vested by law in the United States. . . . Rebels were allowed to fill the antechambers of the Executive Mansion and to enter into the counsels. The pardoning power was prostituted, and pardons were issued in lots to suit Rebels, thus grossly abusing that trust whose discreet exercise is so essential to the administration of justice. . . . The veto power, conferred by the National Constitution as a remedy for ill-considered legislation, was turned by him into a weapon of offence against Congress, and into an instrument to beat down the just opposition which his usurpation had aroused. . . . Laws enacted by Congress for the benefit of the colored race, including that great statute for the establishment of the Freedmen's Bureau, and that other great statute for the establishment of Civil Rights, were first attacked by Presidential veto, and, when finally passed by requisite majority over the veto, were treated by him as little better than dead letters, while he boldly attempted to arrest a Constitutional Amendment by which the right of citizens and the national debt were placed under the guaranty of irrepealable law. . . .

All these things from beginning to end are plain facts, recorded in our annals and known to all. And it is further recorded in our annals and known to all, that . . . untold calamities have been brought upon our country, disturbing business and finance, diminishing the national revenues, postponing specie payments, dishonoring the Declaration of Independence in its grandest truths, arresting the restoration of the Rebel States, reviving the dying Rebellion, and, instead of that peace and reconciliation so much longed for, sowing strife and wrong, whose natural fruit is violence and blood.

Source: Charles Sumner. *His Complete Works*, vol. 16. Boston: Lee and Shepard, 1900, 134–5, 164–171.

CONDITIONS IN THE SOUTH
16. Case of *Fanny Tipton v. Richard Sanford,* Huntsville, Alabama, March 24, 1866

Workers hoped to control their labor—by choosing an employer, negotiating the terms of employment, and leaving an employer if circumstances were not as promised. Employers, by contrast, attempted to limit the ability of workers to determine their wages and working conditions. In between these two groups stood the Freedmen's Bureau, whose agents investigated complaints from both workers and employers and settled disputes. Fanny Tipton, for example, resisted attempts by her employer's son to expand her work, refusing to do kitchen work because she had been hired as a field hand. After being whipped, Tipton quit and a suit was brought against Richard Sanford. This case serves as an example of how freedpeople asserted their own interests and resisted the efforts of employers to control their labor. Workers like Tipton, who quit in the early part of the year, risked losing only a couple of month's wages and stood a reasonable chance of finding other employment.

Cause of Action: Assault & Battery 30 Stripes

Proceedings in case

Commenced Saturday March 24, Sent Order for def[endan]t.

F[anny] T[ipton] Sworn. Deposes.

Hired to defdts Father since christmas 1865. Had no Contract in writing, he promised one, but never gave me one. He agreed to give me $40 for years work. Quarters & Fuel. Left him last. Tuesday morning 20ᵗʰ March. Left him because defendts. son whipped me. He whipped me Tuesday morning. He whipped me because I had not cleaned a Rabbit for him on Monday night. I was not the cook. and had no place in the Kitchen. I was hired for a Field hand. He called me out on Tuesday morning, and asked me if I had cleaned the Rabbit I said, No! and that I did not intend to. He said he would clean me, and I said "clean away" and started off after Water. He picked up a Stick and called me to stop. I did not stop. and he struck me with the stick – A Stick as thick as my thumb. He struck me 30 licks I counted thirty up to the place where I crossed the Fence. I kept jawing, and he told me to hush. Said if I did not he would give me as much more. I said come ahead whenever you get ready. I then went to my House and Mr. S – Richards Father and said it was against his will, that he would not have allowed it. and told his wife if I was fool enough to leave for Richards striking me – I might go – I then left.

Richard Sanford sworn deposes.

Fanny came to our place January 15th and left 19th of March, She was to get $40 – per year we have paid her $8 – She agreed to do whatever she was told to do. she has refused several times to obey orders. I told her to clean the Rabbit, and she talked about in such a way, as to show she did not intend to obey. I told her to stop she refused I then picked up a little switch and struck her a few times and left her

Edie Sanford Sworn deposes.

On Tuesday the fuss happened. On monday night defendant. sent Fannie word to clean a Rabbit for his sick brother. she had not been doing anything all day, and so she was asked to do this, She told me to tell them that she would not do it. He told me to go back & tell her if she did not he would clean her next morning. she then said that after that message, she would not anyhow. Next morning she heard def.t talking – very loud and heard some blows struck, stepped to door and looked out and saw him strike her two or three times – dont know how many times he did strike her it was about 100 ft. from where I was, to them.

Samuel Hollingsworth sworn deposes.

I live in the place with def.t was present on Tuesday morning when the fuss occurred, I first saw def.t walking up to plaintiff talking, I was some 30 Yds off I kept going on to the house; I saw def.t pick up a stick, not a large stick & saw him strike her but once. I was walking off did not go up as it was none of my business.

Fined – def.t Richard Sanford $15 and gave him a severe reprimand – Paid it March 26th 1866.

Source: Reprinted in *Freedom: A Documentary History of Emancipation, 1861–1867*, series 3, volume 2, *Land and Labor, 1866–1867*, ed. Rene Hayden, Anthony E. Kaye, Kate Masur, Steven F. Miller, Susan E. O'Donovan, Leslie S. Rowland, and Stephen A. West (Chapel Hill: University of North Carolina Press, 2013), 401–2.

17. The letter of Phebe Trotter to Provost Marshal and the affidavit of Eliza Avant were enclosed in a letter that Chaplain L. S. Livermore sent to Lt. Col. R. S. Donaldson, January 10, 1866

After emancipation, former slaves wanted to reunite their families to reclaim parental authority over their children. Former slaveholders, who did not want to relinquish control over the labor of children, employed a variety of techniques to minimize the impact of the Thirteenth Amendment. Some masters were slow to accept that slavery had ended and did not release minors from their control, ignoring the entreaties of parents. In an instance like the one involving Phebe Trotter, the Freedmen's Bureau represented one avenue to secure the release of her children when their former master attempted to coerce them into signing an employment contract. In addition to the use of force, employers also used apprenticeship laws to maintain control. As seen in the Mississippi black codes, local officials could bind out minors in cases where they believed parents were unwilling or unable to care for their children. Eliza Avant hoped that the Freedmen's Bureau would intercede and block a former slaveholder from binding out her children.

Greenwood Miss Jan. 6th, 1866

Provost Marshal I send you a few lines concerning my Chrildren they have worked for Colonel Walton their former owner ever since the Surrender without any liberties at all or any pay or Clothing And in Cristmas week they wanted to come and see me and they would not allow them to come unless they would sign a piece of writing to stay this year and they would not do it and come off just so to Greenwood and sent for me I went for I had good homes for them where they would be well treated and next morning Col Walton sent a crowd of men there and took them off to McNutt to scare them into writing all with guns and pistols my Children dont want to sine and they are trying to make them I hope to hear from you soon let me what I can do I am able to take care of them and I want them with me Yours Respectfully

Phebe Trotter

Affidavit of Miss Eliza Avant of Coffevill

Deposeth and Saith

That Wm Avant my formor owner has had my Children Leah, Hagar, Tom, Demp, and Pink, bound to him. He told me that I had to go. I tried to hire the oldest two to him, but he would not hire. He wanted no free niggers around him he said. I signed no paper. Begged them not to bind them. I told Massah if he would hire the two oldest I could easy suppor[t] the two youngest but he would not. I suppose the papers were completed. My husband is a soldier in the army. I have not heard from him in a year. I have a son also in the army. I have a son in Memphis about 20 years old He sent me word he would be home after Christmas. I have been the slave of Avant for nine or ten years. But he drove me off last week on friday morning. while I told him I did not think he would treat me so, as good a slave as I had been for him I dont realy know whether he bound Demp or not I don't know where demp is now. Sworn to before me [L.S. Livermore] this 8 day of January 1866 at Grenada Miss

Source: Reprinted in *Freedom: A Documentary History of Emancipation, 1861–1867*, series 3, volume 2, *Land and Labor, 1866–1867*, ed. Rene Hayden, Anthony E. Kaye, Kate Masur, Steven F. Miller, Susan E. O'Donovan, Leslie S. Rowland, and Stephen A. West. Chapel Hill: University of North Carolina Press, 2013, 572.

18. Testimony of Isaac A. Postle

After a surge of Klan violence in the South that made both life and property inse-cure, President Grant asked Congress to investigate and to intervene.

In March 1871, members of the House and Senate formed a joint committee to investigate Klan violence, and it took testimony from witnesses around the South that filled 13 volumes. In 1871, Congress passed the Enforcement Act that expanded the power of the federal government to indict suspected Klansmen. Events in nine counties in South Carolina prompted the president to invoke the military provisions of the Enforcement Acts, declaring "a condition of lawlessness" and suspending the writ of habeas corpus. Federal troops made 500 arrests. Isaac Postle testified about events in York county, South Carolina. After the arrests and trials in 1871–1872, Klan violence decreased in the South.

Examined by Mr. Corbin:

I live in York County, near Rock Hill, about four miles from Mr. James Smith's place; I have been a preacher for about five years; I have lived in York County ever since the days of emancipation; the Ku-Klux came to my house last spring; it was on Friday night, and I judge it was between three and four o'clock; they came and called for Postle to come out; thinking I might be killed, and being quick to wake, I jumped up, and my judgment was to get out of the way, and there being a loose plank in the house, I got under the floor; my wife she put the plank back, and after she had gathered the baby off the bed she just went and opened the door; all this time they were knocking and calling out to open the door; when they got in they began with her, to find out where I was; some said, "He is under the house," and my wife told them he had gone away; that I had gone up the river for some meal; they cursed her and told her it was a d —d lie; some of them made for the loose plank, and cried out: "Here's where he went;" they turned up the plank and looked and commenced beating and knocking about; I heard my wife screaming and hallooing, and after they had got through with her and knocking her over, and putting the rope around her neck, they called for a light, and they got two or three pine torches; some of them went on one side of the house with their torches, and the others stood on the other side, and I could see them looking round and under the house; then one of them, that I took to be the captain, saw me and pointed his pistol at me, and said: "Come out; if you don't I'll kill you;" then I came out as far as the top of the floor, when he grasped me by the hair, and one of the men struck me with something like a club; it was a thing that tapers off at one end, and people call it a sling-shot; the man who had hold of me asked if I knew him; I said, "No, sir;" but he still had my hair; he then put a line round my neck and gathered it up in his hand and took me out of the house; they took me about two hundred and fifty yards till we struck the woods; then the crowd got round me and questioned me, and asked me if I hadn't been preaching up burning and corruption, and telling the people to set fire to the gin-houses and barns; said I, "No sir; I never did;" said I, "I have never preached nothing but peace and harmony," and they repeated their questions over and over again; said I: "We have had no disturbances in this part of the country; no burnings nor anything like that in this part of the country; said he: "Do you know who set any of these barns on fire?" Said I: "I do not; I have been traveling up and down the river, preaching in my circuit, and don't know anything about it;" then they called me a d—d liar, and said I could tell them if I liked; then they began to question me about guns, and I told them that I knew nothing about them; then they said, "Jerk him with the line," and they made one of them go up a tree, and, said they, "We will have the truth directly;" I thought then they were going to hang me; the one that went up, he drew me up till I had to stand on tip-toe; only my toes touched the ground, so that I was choked and could not tell them anything; then they slackened the line a bit and put all these questions to me over again; said I: "I know nothing about any of these burnings or disturbances;" then the captain told each of the men to hit me two licks apiece, and they stepped up and he handed them something like a halter, an inch and a half wide, and with that they gave me two licks apiece as hard as they could; my flesh was cut so much that it bled, for I had nothing on but my shirt and slips; then the man that had been up in the tree came down and took the strap, and he hit me his two licks; the captain then took the line and loosed it off my neck, and questioned me something about my children, and said: "Didn't you say that you would raise your children as good and as nice as anybody's children?" Said I: "No, sir; I cannot raise my children so well, because I am not able;" with that he took the line off my neck, and, said he, "If there is any more burning of gin-houses in the country, we intend to kill ten niggers for every one burned, and you'll be the first one," he said it just so; then they asked me about my politics, and if I did not belong to the League society, and wasn't I for Grant; and I says, "No sir;" and I told them I was sick at the election time and couldn't vote, and at another time I was away preaching; then they asked me again if I did not preach corruption and burning, and I told them I didn't; I preached only peace and harmony, and I didn't advise or instruct anything that was wrong; I said that ever so many times, but it didn't seem to have any impression.

Question. Did you recognize any of the party?

Answer. Up to the time they took the rope off my neck I didn't recognize any one, for up to that time it wasn't my expectation that they would let me off; but when they took the rope off my neck it kindled hope in my mind; and the man they called captain talked with me, and said that they were men of peace, of justice, and of right; and then it was that I believed that Mr. Avery was one of the men; I had no knowledge of any man up to that time, because from the time they took me from the house they kept jerking at the rope that was round my neck, and when they took the rope off I gathered some hope; and then I judged that Mr. Avery was the man, and that Howard White was another, and James Matthews another.

The witness had told his story up to this point with a good deal of repetition. He was here interrupted by Mr. Wilson, who said that the witness ought to be instructed to state the facts upon which he based his assertions.

Judge BRYAN. The witness must be allowed to state his testimony in his own way.

The witness continued: These men I have spoken of I believe were in the party; Howard White is a colored man and, I believe, a democrat; he has left our part of the country, and I don't know where he is now; I didn't recognize anybody else in the crowd; the men appeared to be dressed in different colors; when I was under the house I looked at the captain, and his dress appeared to be blue and yellow; he had horns on his head over a foot long, and something over his face that appeared to be of different colors; I didn't hardly know what it looked like, but I believe it was blue and yellow; he had a long gown that came pretty much down toward his feet; some of them had on dresses, as I saw while I was under the house, that appeared to be short dresses like half-grown girls wear, and seemed to come down to their knees; some of them had old handkerchiefs over their faces, with holes in them for their eyes; I think there were about twelve in the company, but I did not count them.

Source: US Congress, *Testimony Taken by the Joint Select Committee to Inquire into the Condition of Affairs in the Late Insurrectionary States: South Carolina,* vol. 3. Washington, D.C.: Government Printing Office, 1872, 1952–3.

19. Laura Towne Letters on Election Violence in South Carolina

This source was written by Laura Towne, a northern white teacher in the Sea Islands. She discusses the attempt of a paramilitary group, the Red Shirts in South Carolina, to suppress black voting and black office holding through violence and intimidation. Hundreds of armed Red Shirts supported Democrat Wade Hampton's successful bid for governor in 1876. The center of this story is Robert Smalls, an African American congressman from Beaufort, South Carolina.

October 29, 1878

Political times are simply frightful. Men are shot at, hounded down, trapped, and held till certain meetings are over, and intimidated in every possible way. It gets worse and worse as election approaches. Mr. French of the Beaufort *Tribune*, says, "In order to prevent our county falling into such hands (Republican), *any* measures that will accomplish the end will be justifiable, *however wicked* they might be in other communities." Upon this plan is the whole campaign conducted.

November 6, 1878

The election was a most quiet one. It was opposite our school, but so still that we said it was impossible to believe that hundreds of people were just outside.... On Saturday I went to a Republican meeting at the church. Robert Smalls told of his mobbing at Gillisonville. He was announced to speak there, and when ten o'clock – the hour – came, he was on the spot and with him about forty men. The stand was in front of a store in the street, and men and women were coming up the street to attend the meeting, when eight hundred red-shirt men, led by colonels, generals, and many leading men of the state, came dashing into the town, giving the "real rebel yell," the newspaper said. Robert Smalls called it "whooping like Indians." They drew up, and as body stood still, but every few minutes a squad of three or four would scour down street on their horses, and reaching out would "lick off the hats" of the colored men or slap the faces of the colored women coming to the meeting, whooping and yelling and scattering the people on all sides. This made the colored men so mad that they wanted to pitch right into a fight with the eight hundred, but Robert Smalls restrained them, telling them what folly it was. Then the leader, Colonel somebody, came up and demanded half-time. Robert S. said there would be no meeting. Then they said he *should* have a meeting and *should* speak. He refused to say a word at a Democratic meeting, and as there was no Republican one, he said he would not speak at all. They gave him ten minutes to make up his mind. Then he withdrew into the store with his forty men and drew them all up around it behind the counters. They had guns. He told them to aim at the door, and stand with finger on trigger, but on no account to shoot unless the red-shirts broke in. Meantime, when the ten minutes were over, the outsiders began to try to break down the door. They called Smalls and told him they would set fire to the house and burn him up in it. They fired repeatedly through the windows and walls. He showed us two balls he had picked up inside. He would not come out, and the leaders led off part of the red-shirts and began to make speeches, leaving the store surrounded, however, for fear Smalls should escape.

The people who had come to the meeting meanwhile ran to raise the alarm in every direction, and in an incredibly short time the most distant parts of the county heard that their truly beloved leader was trapped in a house surrounded by red-shirts, and that his life was in danger. Every colored man and woman seized whatever was at hand – guns, axes, hoes, etc., and ran to the rescue. By six o'clock afternoon a thousand negroes were approaching the town, and the red-shirts thought best to gallop away. They left twenty armed men to meet the train upon which Smalls was to return to Beaufort and to "attend to him." He had to go away ahead of the train and jump on the tender in the dark, and so he got back safely. At every station they met troops of negroes, one and two hundred together, all on their way to Gillisonville to the rescue. Smalls thinks this attack was caused by Hampton's saying in a public speech that there was but one man he now thought *ought* to be out of the way, and that man was Robert Smalls, who, by giving the Republicans one more vote in the

House, would strengthen them in the choice of the next President, which would probably take place in the House of Representatives. I think if Robert S. does meet with any violence there will be hot times between blacks and rebs, but of course it is not likely they will touch him, after the election, – unless he is elected, – when I do not think his life would be worth a button. . . .

November 10, 1878

Our election was quiet, of course. The people seemed thoroughly in earnest, and voted steadily and silently without the usual play and laughter. . . .The count of the vote at night was specially attended to. The result on this island was nine hundred and eighteen votes, only nine of them Democratic and only one of the nine a colored man's vote. This is much fewer than at the election two years ago, and shows that here Democracy does not gain ground. Of course, Robert Smalls was defeated, and the people are greatly grieved about it, and are not reconciled to the result.

Source: Letters and Diary of Laura M. Towne Written from the Sea Islands of South Carolina, 1862–1884. Rupert Sargent Holland, ed. Cambridge: The Riverside Press, 1912, 288–293.

CONFLICTING ATTITUDES ON RECONSTRUCTION
20. Representative James M. Leach's Opposition to the Ku Klux Act, 1871

James Madison Leach (1815–1891) was born in North Carolina, and he attended the United States Military Academy in West Point, New York, before studying law. Entering politics, he served in the North Carolina state house and one term in the United States House of Representatives before the Civil War. During the war, Leach served as a lieutenant colonel in the Confederate army and two years in the Confederate congress. During Reconstruction, Leach was a member of the U.S. Congress for two terms, 1871–1875. The following source is an excerpt from Representative Leach's speech during the House debate over the Ku Klux Act on April 5, 1871. In the speech, Leach expressed his profound opposition to the Ku Klux Act, claiming that it was an abuse of power, destroyed state sovereignty, and signaled the rise of despotism. While he acknowledged that violent attacks on African Americans were wrong, he simply denied that they were occurring at all. Instead, he suggested that Reconstruction was a partisan power grab by the Republican Party.

I undertake to say that this bill puts on trial, so to speak, the Constitution of the United States; that in its monstrous provisions it, in effect, annihilates the States of this Union, and if passed and practically carried out it will overthrow the liberties of the people of all the States of this Republic.... [T]his bill establishes ... executive irresponsibility in the fullest sense of the term. All the powers of the Government ... will be absorbed in the hands of one man; and all history, with fatal uniformity, shows that ... this in itself is a long and most dangerous stride toward despotism....

[T]his bill proposes to delegate to the President the power to suspend the sacred writ of *habeas corpus*; ... and thereby transforming the President of the United States into a dictator, and entirely destroying the sovereignty of the States. This is a grant of power without authority of law, that the Father of his Country never would have allowed himself to have been invested with – a power he never should have been invested with....

I come now to some of the circumstances of the origin of this bill, and the arguments used in its favor, as it appears to be in a large degree aimed at North Carolina.... [I]n North Carolina we have been cursed with an administration of the State government without a parallel for stupidity, recklessness, and corruption.... Now, sir, when will our countrymen of the North learn to condemn the stories of these shameless slanderers? When will the honest and intelligent people of the North be able to see, what is so manifest, that these wonderful tales of outrage and horror are almost entirely base falsehoods, manufactured by unscrupulous politicians for the purpose of "arousing the northern mind and firing the northern heart," all for party and personal aggrandizement?

Why, sir, after the most searching investigation ... not a single case of what is coming to be technically denominated "outrage" was shown to have occurred in the counties of Alamance and Caswell, the counties and localities where such things are mainly charged to exist.... And in my district I have never known or heard of one instance of attempts by [white] employers to influence [African American] votes – not one.... [E]verybody of sense knows that these acts of lawlessness were the unfortunate outgrowth of a great social revolution in the South, together with the natural demoralization consequent upon the war; and as we recede from that fearful period the impossibility of reviving such acts and conduct will become more and more absolute. I protest, therefore, against this attempt to go back to the dead past and seek to get up an artificial and fictitious horror and pretended dread of events which have no reality in North Carolina, and are as little likely to occur there as another deluge.

If I must speak of "outrages," may I not call this bill an outrage – an outrage upon the Constitution, an outrage upon liberty and free government, an outrage upon the good name of a noble State and a law-loving people, and an outrage upon the whole history of the State whose heroic deeds and glorious prestige of the past cannot be taken from her, thank God, neither by bad men or wicked partisans, whether within her borders or without? . . .

What is needed, and all that is needed, to restore perfect harmony and universal affection for the Federal Government in the South, is a final cessation from this whole policy of jealous and penal legislation, which looks so much like it was meant to benefit party and not country, and the adoption of a truly fraternal and kindly policy which will prove to that section that you have ceased to regard it as a province, to be held in subjection by the iron hand of tyranny, and that you once more love it as a noble and beautiful part of our grand heritage. . . .

I suppose there are those who may hope and think that this bill, if passed, will redound to the advantage of the Republican party. Why, sir, their own party in the North are tired of it. . . . I tell this House that the inevitable result of all this penal and oppressive legislation, founded as it is, upon exaggeration, irresponsible testimony, and base falsehood, even with the military added and sent South and the writ of *habeas corpus* suspended, will finally . . . result in implanting in the hearts of southern people the true idea of the whole matter, that the party in power hopes to retain it by oppression and injustice, that it is not able to rehabilitate the States and restore harmony to the Union. . . .

[L]ook at the brutal oppression in my State . . . and ponder the result. Insurrection was proclaimed, though there was not one insurgent in the State; martial law was declared, though nobody was resisting the civil laws; troops in large number . . . were recruited . . . though there was nothing to make war upon; a hundred good citizens, many of them the purest and best men of the State . . . were seized on by arrest, with no charges against them, and imprisoned . . . without lawful warrant. . . .

Alas, that this body cannot see these things as they really are, not as party men, but in the interests of truth and justice, and then, in the exercise of an enlarged statesmanship, comprehending the whole country, legislate accordingly!

Source: *Congressional Globe*, 42nd Congress, 1st Session, 1871, 479–481.

21. Hiram Revels to President U.S. Grant, November 6, 1875

Hiram Revels, the first African American to serve in the United States Senate, wrote a public letter to the president explaining the Democratic victory in the 1875 elections in Mississippi. A former Republican, Revels had broken from the state's Republican Party and in particular its carpetbagger governor, Adelbert Ames. To take back control of the state, Mississippi Democrats had engaged in violent attacks on Republican voters. Like the Red Shirts in South Carolina, this violence occurred openly, not under the cover of darkness and Klan hoods. Unable to quell the violence with the state's resources, Governor Ames appealed to President Grant to send troops. Grant declined to intervene and black turnout decreased precipitously in the November elections. Revels, however, focused not on white attacks on black voters, but on corrupt Republican officials as the source of the Democratic victory. He blamed the violence in Mississippi on unprincipled or incompetent Republicans who stirred up racial hatred instead of promoting reconciliation.

Since reconstruction, the masses of my people have been . . . enslaved in mind by unprincipled adventurers, who, caring nothing for country, were willing to stoop to anything no matter how infamous, to secure power to themselves, and perpetuate it. My people are naturally Republicans, and always will be, but as they grow older in freedom so do they in wisdom. A great portion of them have learned that they were being used as mere tools, and, as in the late election . . . they determined by casting their ballots against these unprincipled adventurers, to overthrow them. . . . My people have been told by these schemers, when men have been placed on the ticket who were notoriously corrupt and dishonest, that they must vote for them; that the salvation of the party depended upon it; that the man who scratched a ticket was not a Republican. This is only one of the many means these unprincipled demagogues have devised to perpetuate the intellectual bondage of my people. To defeat this policy, at the late election men, irrespective of race, color, or party affiliation, united and voted together against men known to be incompetent and dishonest. I cannot recognize, nor do the mass of my people who read, recognize the majority of the officials who have been in power for the past two years as Republicans. . . .

The great mass of the white people have abandoned their hostility to the general government and Republican principles, and to-day accept as a fact that all men are born free and equal, and I believe are ready to

guarantee to my people every right and privilege guaranteed to an American citizen. The bitterness and hate created by the late civil strife has, in my opinion, been obliterated in this state, except perhaps in some localities, and would have long since been entirely obliterated, were it not for some unprincipled men who would keep alive the bitterness of the past, and inculcate a hatred between the races, in order that they may aggrandize themselves by office, and its emoluments, to control my people, the effect of which is to degrade them. . . . If the state administration had adhered to Republican principles, . . . appointed only honest and competent men to office, and sought to restore confidence between the races, bloodshed would have been unknown, peace would have prevailed, Federal interference been unthought of, harmony, friendship and mutual confidence would have taken the place of the bayonet.

Source: James W. Garner. *Reconstruction in Mississippi.* New York: Macmillan, 1902, 399–400.

22. Adelbert Ames to the U.S. House of Representatives and Senate, January, 4, 1876

Republican Senator George Boutwell chaired a select committee to investigate the 1875 Mississippi election. The group was charged with determining if fraud or violence had been directed against African Americans in the state. After taking considerable testimony, the committee concluded that white employers had compelled their employees to vote for Democratic candidates and that armed groups of Democrats operated throughout the state, regularly breaking up Republican meetings. The riots in Vicksburg in December 1874 and in Clinton in September 1875 were more violent examples of a regular pattern of behavior. The "Mississippi Plan" was to terrorize African American voters in the months leading up to the election, so that voter turnout for Republicans would diminish. By this strategy, the Democrats regained control of both local government and the state legislature. Governor Adelbert Ames, who was impeached by the Democratic-controlled state legislature, was one of the witnesses who testified in 1876. Contrast Ames's presentation of conditions in Mississippi with Revels's letter to President Grant in the entry above. Ames hoped that the federal government would act to defend political equality, when in fact the nation was moving away from Reconstruction.

On the fourth day of September last a political meeting at Clinton, Hinds County, was interfered with and dispersed by violence, which resulted in the death of a number of persons, and which was followed, subsequently, by the pursuit and shooting of others, by armed men riding through the country. Impelled, through fear of violence, men abandoned their homes and fled by hundreds to [Jackson, Mississippi] for safety. . . .

At this juncture, business was suspended, and disquiet or terror existed in the minds of all. The authority of the county was paralyzed. The sheriff reported his utter helplessness to give the needed protection. . . . The State was without a militia or constabulary force. . . .

Under such a combination of circumstances, . . . I was constrained to call upon the National Government for assistance to protect against domestic violence. This call was unsuccessful. It was followed by a succession of demonstrations by the armed part of the people toward the unarmed, causing a feeling of insecurity and danger, which continued until and after the day of the election. . . .

The deeds of violence already alluded to . . . in various parts of the State, had the effect to intimidate many voters. . . . The character of the events which have transpired compel the conclusion that the evil is to be attributed to a race question. . . . The inhabitants of the State are somewhat equally divided between the two races. They have, until recent years, borne the relation of master and slave. By a power external to the State, the slave has been made the civil and political equal of the master. The withdrawal of this restraining force leaves the formerly dominant race to re-assert its supremacy. Though the complete supremacy of former days may not be possible, still the tendency is toward supremacy. The effort in this direction has heretofore and elsewhere resulted, as in this election, in violence, loss of life, and intimidation. How far this effort has resulted in the virtual disfranchisement of the one race, and revolutionized the State government, is a question worthy [of] the most patient and careful inquiry.

Unless every class of citizens be thoroughly protected in the exercise of all their rights and privileges, our Government proves unequal to its pretensions. The nation, recognizing the race-antagonisms, has anticipated them in the interest of liberty and equality by modifications of the fundamental law of the land, and I recommend, as both right and expedient, action in harmony with such modifications.

Source: Mississippi in 1875: Report of the Select Committee to Inquire into the Mississippi Election of 1875, vol. 1. Washington, D.C.: Government Printing Office, 1876, 6–7.

ANNOTATED
BIBLIOGRAPHY

Ash, Stephen V. *A Massacre in Memphis: The Race Riot that Shook the Nation One Year After the Civil War*. New York: Hill and Wang, 2013.

    This study of the 1866 Memphis race riot focuses attention on the role of violence in the debate over citizenship and equality. Combining both analytical and narrative styles, Stephen Ash provides readers with a highly detailed description of early-Reconstruction Memphis and a deeply researched account of the three terrible days of riots that began on May 1, 1866. The opening section of the book explores the increasingly dangerous divisions that had emerged in the city as a result of the war. Under a Union occupation that began in June 1862, Memphis had become a haven for escaped slaves and an important destination for northern Protestant reformers who supported the struggling black community. By 1865, however, the city's Irish immigrant population was determined to preserve its hard-won status through violent defenses of white supremacy. Ash clearly demonstrates that the presence of armed and uniformed black soldiers was regarded as an intolerable assertion of African American autonomy and citizenship. Since the city's Irish-dominated municipal government and police force were responsible for maintaining order, their hostility to uniformed black soldiers played a central role in the violence.

Baggett, James Alex. *The Scalawags: Southern Dissenters in the Civil War and Reconstruction*. Baton Rouge: Louisiana State University Press, 2003.

    Baggett uses a collective biography approach to study white Southerners who supported Congressional Reconstruction and the Republican Party. This group was called scalawags and they were vilified as corrupt opportunists who betrayed their community and race. Rejecting this caricature, Baggett collected data on over 700 scalawag leaders to determine their background and to explain what drew them to the Republican Party. Covering the entire South, he determined that scalawags shared many similarities with their Democratic counterparts in terms of wealth and racial attitudes. One of the main distinctions, however, was that many scalawags had been Unionists before the Civil War. They had overwhelmingly opposed secession and only reluctantly supported the Confederacy.

Benedict, Michael Les. *A Compromise of Principle: Congressional Republicans and Reconstruction, 1863–1869*. New York: Norton, 1974.

Benedict's carefully researched book provides a thorough examination of the political history of Reconstruction. Benedict studies the passage of specific pieces of legislation as well as the impeachment of Andrew Johnson. In the process, he argues that Reconstruction was not very radical. Instead, conservatives and moderates shaped policy and limited the impact of radical positions. In particular, Benedict highlights that the radicals failed to achieve majority support for land confiscation and that the drafting of the Fifteenth Amendment preserved the right of states to determine qualifications for voting. In the end, Benedict argues that political expediency trumped principle.

Carter, Dan T. *When the War Was Over: The Failure of Self-Reconstruction in the South, 1865–1867*. Baton Rouge: Louisiana State University Press, 1985.

This book examines the role of white southern political leaders during the period of Presidential Reconstruction. The author contends that many of these men were former Whigs and reluctant secessionists and that they recognized the need to modernize the South. Once in power, however, these "moderate" southern leaders faced agonizing choices. In their recognition of the need to compromise with northern authorities, they exposed themselves to intense criticism from more reactionary constituents. Aware of the need for modernization, they sometimes clashed with conservative planter elites who hoped to reconstitute the antebellum system.

Cimbala, Paul A. *Under the Guardianship of the Nation: The Freedmen's Bureau and the Reconstruction of Georgia, 1865–1870*. Athens: University of Georgia Press, 1997.

This book provides a detailed examination of the Freedmen's Bureau in Georgia and offers an assessment of the agency's role in the larger history of Reconstruction. Cimbala points out that the bureau agents varied considerably in terms of their competence and racial views, but he argues that the agency's inability to effect long-term change in the South resulted more from persistent underfunding and intense political hostility than from personal failings. Based on voluminous correspondence of bureau agents, this book provides significant insight into the challenging conditions these men faced in the rural South. Often isolated and subjected to threats from local whites, even the most committed agents struggled to protect former slaves against exploitation and intimidation.

Cimbala, Paul A., and Randall M. Miller, eds. *The Freedmen's Bureau and Reconstruction: Reconsiderations*. New York: Fordham University Press, 1999.

This collection of scholarly essays explores and assesses the role of the Freedmen's Bureau in the Reconstruction South. Examining the bureau's policy in a variety of locations and contexts throughout the region, the authors contend that its mandate to protect freedpeople against various forms of coercion was often compromised by the imperative of rebuilding the southern economic system. At the same time, however, the book shows that freedpeople responded well to the bureau's educational policies, which were often underwritten by nongovernmental organizations such as the American Missionary Association. Ultimately, however, the authors contend that the effectiveness of the Freedmen's Bureau must be assessed in the context of chronic understaffing and underfunding, a condition made worse by President Andrew Johnson's intense hostility to its underlying purpose.

Cimbala, Paul A., and Randall M. Miller, eds. *The Great Task Remaining Before Us: Reconstruction as America's Continuing Civil War*. New York: Fordham University Press, 2010.

This collection of scholarly essays explores a rich array of political, social, and cultural issues in the Reconstruction era. Of particular interest are articles dealing with questions of community and loyalty in the postwar South. Several authors note that in a population scarred by war and often bitterly divided along racial, political, and class lines, Reconstruction required the formation of new social and political relationships and a redefinition of the South as a cultural region. At the same time, the essays provide an important collective reminder that even though the formal military aspects of the Civil War ended in 1865, the conflict's central themes continued to dominate the life of the nation in the postwar period.

Current, Richard Nelson. *Those Terrible Carpetbaggers: A Reinterpretation*. New York: Oxford University Press, 1988.

In this study Current corrects the caricatured image of carpetbaggers as corrupt scoundrels and self-seekers who manipulated African Americans for their own gain. He offers a biographical study of 10 leading carpetbaggers and explores their varied motives for moving south and entering politics. Current concludes that most northern Republicans who settled in the South arrived before Congressional Reconstruction and as a result could have had little hope of political advancement. In addition, Current suggests that as a group, carpetbaggers were no more likely to be corrupt than other politicians of the age. Instead of creating flat images of heroes or villains, he presents a rich portrait of politically ambitious men who operated during this tumultuous time in American history.

Davis, Hugh. *"We Will Be Satisfied with Nothing Less": The African American Struggle for Equal Rights in the North during Reconstruction.* Ithaca, NY: Cornell University Press, 2011.

Hugh Davis examines the role of African American activists in combating racism, arguing for equal rights, and desegregating schools and transit systems in the North. As a result, he broadens our understanding of Reconstruction, presenting it as a national and not simply southern event. Beginning with the Civil War era and then moving forward to 1880, Davis explores how the ideal of emancipation affected the North. Organizations like the Equal Rights League mobilized African Americans and emphasized the importance of equal access to public education and voting rights. By examining a range of states, Davis demonstrates the extent of segregation in the North during the nineteenth century and the resistance of many whites to the Fourteenth and Fifteenth Amendments.

Downs, Jim. *Sick From Freedom: African-American Illness and Suffering during the Civil War and Reconstruction.* New York: Oxford University Press, 2012.

Jim Downs's *Sick From Freedom* focuses on the widespread illness and suffering of former slaves during and after the Civil War and also illuminates the tragic limitations of federal and state responses to the physical displacement that accompanied emancipation. Overlooked or avoided by historians of slavery whose recent emphasis has been on African American agency and autonomy, the chilling evidence in *Sick From Freedom* is a reminder that the African American struggle for freedom during Reconstruction confronted not only white supremacist violence, but also disease and physical illness.

Dray, Philip. *Capitol Men: The Epic Story of Reconstruction through the Lives of the First Black Congressmen.* New York: Houghton Mifflin, 2008.

This book explores the lives and public careers of 16 southern black men elected to national political office during the Reconstruction period. In a highly readable format designed for a popular audience, Dray shows that while some of these men had been slaves and others free before the war, their political lives were motivated by a common commitment to black freedom and equality. Although less well-known than white leaders such as Charles Sumner and Thaddeus Stevens, men like Robert Smalls, Francis Cardozo, and Richard Cain left a valuable legacy of black political leadership that remains important to the present day.

Egerton, Douglas R. *The Wars of Reconstruction: The Brief, Violent History of America's Most Progressive Era*. New York: Bloomsbury Press, 2014.

Rather than offering a sweeping narrative of national politics during Reconstruction, this work explores the day-to-day struggles of African Americans and their white allies to achieve political and social equality in the postwar South. Focusing on the work of black politicians, Freedmen's Bureau agents, and northern reformers who sought to educate and empower former slaves, the book narrates the bitter and often violent clash between advocates of equality and the defenders of white supremacy. The author argues that the failure of Reconstruction can be found at the outset of the period as President Andrew Johnson squandered a critical opportunity to demand important concessions from the defeated white South.

Epps, Garrett. *Democracy Reborn: The Fourteenth Amendment and the Fight for Civil Rights in Post-Civil War America*. New York: Holt, 2006.

Epps provides a clear, engaging narrative of the passage of the Fourteenth Amendment. In addition to exploring the individuals who wrote portions of the amendment, the book examines the heated debates in Congress over the precise wording of the amendment. The amendment is placed within its wider historical context so that a general reader can understand the beginning of Congressional Reconstruction.

Farmer-Kaiser, Mary. *Freedwomen and the Freedmen's Bureau: Race, Gender, and Public Policy in the Age of Emancipation*. New York: Fordham University Press, 2010.

This work revises earlier assessments of the Freedmen's Bureau and its connection to African American women as an agency of last resort. Farmer-Kaiser argues that freedwomen sought relief from the bureau on a daily basis to address both labor concerns and "domestic" issues like child custody, divorce, or violence. In her examination of the Freedmen's Bureau, Farmer-Kaiser concludes that agents and officials applied policies differently and less rigidly to women than to men.

Faulkner, Carol. *Women's Radical Reconstruction: The Freedmen's Aid Movement.* Philadelphia: University of Pennsylvania Press, 2004.

> Faulkner examines how northern white and black women of the Freedmen's Aid Movement attempted to influence the course of Reconstruction by arguing for universal suffrage as well as land confiscation and redistribution. Less wedded to wage labor as the solution to racial and economic inequalities in the South, women activists argued for government intervention to bring about equal rights.

Fitzgerald, Michael W. *Splendid Failure: Postwar Reconstruction in the American South.* Chicago, IL: Ivan R. Dee, 2007.

> Fitzgerald provides a short, readable overview of Reconstruction that is suitable for a general audience. Synthesizing recent scholarship on the period into one accessible volume, Fitzgerald covers national political events, like Andrew Johnson's Reconstruction policy, and the experiences of freedpeople on the local level. As the title indicates, Fitzgerald emphasizes that Reconstruction failed and he suggests that the root of that failure lay in the limited support in the North for racial justice.

Foner, Eric. *Forever Free: The Story of Emancipation and Reconstruction.* New York: Vintage, 2006.

> Written for general readers, *Forever Free* draws on the author's prize-winning work *Reconstruction* to provide a highly accessible introduction to the revisionist literature on the Civil War era. The narrative of the work focuses on African Americans' struggle to achieve a broad definition of freedom in the years before and after emancipation. It provides a wealth of evidence to show that enslaved people, abolitionists, black soldiers, and grass roots political movements played a central role both in the destruction of slavery and in the postwar struggle for freedom. In addition to a readable narrative, the book also contains a series of visual essays, which invite readers to view and analyze photographs, cartoons, illustrations, and other images from the period.

Foner, Eric. *Reconstruction: America's Unfinished Revolution 1863–1877.* New York: Harper & Row, 1988.

> Among the most important works on American history written in the twentieth century, this book redefined the study of Reconstruction for an entire generation of historians. Taking its cue from W. E. B. Du Bois's classic 1935 work *Black Reconstruction in America*, Foner's copiously researched study placed African American freedpeople at the center of the narrative and assessed Reconstruction in terms of its ability to realize the full freedom and equality of former slaves. Overturning the racially motivated criticism of

Reconstruction by early twentieth-century historians William Dunning and John Burgess, the book recognized the extraordinary egalitarian potential of the period while conceding that its great promise ultimately went unfulfilled. In Foner's interpretive framework, abolitionists and radical Republicans were critical, if flawed allies of the freedpeople, creating a coalition that achieved landmark constitutional change while falling short of remaking the nation in the image of its highest ideals.

Foster, Gaines M. *Ghosts of the Confederacy: Defeat, the Lost Cause, and the Emergence of the New South, 1865 to 1913.* New York: Oxford University Press, 1987.
This book examines the tradition of southern historical and memorial writing known as the Lost Cause, which was forged in the aftermath of the region's defeat in the Civil War. A response to the dishonor and "trauma" of military defeat, the Lost Cause tradition was also a way for southern whites to reenter American life with their dignity intact. While it described southern defeat as inevitable, it also insisted upon the honor of the cause and the integrity and bravery of the men who fought for it.

Franklin, John Hope. *Reconstruction after the Civil War.* Chicago, IL: University of Chicago Press, 2013. Originally published 1961.
Published more than 50 years ago, *Reconstruction After the Civil War* remains a valuable, readable introduction to the period written by one of the foremost historians of nineteenth-century America. Franklin exposed the weaknesses in the old views of Reconstruction that romanticized the Ku Klux Klan and attacked radical Republicans as vindictively making the South suffer under military despotism. In Franklin's work, we see a different picture of Reconstruction, one in which the Klan was a terrorist organization and Republican state governments, though marred by corruption, also made lasting achievements. Though elements of the work are dated, countless scholars have built on the foundation that Franklin created.

Gillette, William. *Retreat From Reconstruction 1869–1879.* Baton Rouge: Louisiana State University, 1979.
Gillette offers a carefully researched narrative of the political events of Reconstruction at the national level beginning in 1869. Shifting the focus from Andrew Johnson, where the preponderance of scholarship lies, to the Grant administration, Gillette suggests that the Republicans had the best chance to implement their Reconstruction policy after 1868 because the party no longer confronted the opposition of the president to its positions. Yet Gillette found that the commitment to remaking the South was in fact quite limited in the 1870s. He was critical of Grant's policy toward the South,

suggesting that it was inconsistent, and of Republicans in Congress, emphasizing the need for greater radicalism. Gillette presents the retreat by Republicans from their earlier commitment to racial equality as in place long before the formal end of Reconstruction in 1877.

Glymph, Thavolia. *Out of the House of Bondage: The Transformation of the Plantation Household*. New York: Cambridge University Press, 2008.
Presenting the perspective of both black and white women, this book examines the changes to the plantation household from slavery to emancipation. In the prewar household, white women held a position of privilege and upheld it through violent enforcement of the slave system. For the postwar period, Glymph places the unsuccessful efforts of white women to retain their prewar status within the context of black women's resistance to authority. Freedwomen made demands of their new employers, expressed their preference for flexible schedules, and quit if they did not like the terms offered. As a result, white women confronted a confusing new environment in which both their identity and their racial privilege were irrevocably challenged. Glymph's book incorporates poignant individual experiences with cogent analysis of important historiographical debates.

Goldstone, Lawrence. *Inherently Unequal: The Betrayal of Equal Rights by the Supreme Court, 1865–1903*. New York: Walker & Company, 2011.
Goldstone examines the political context for postbellum Supreme Court decisions that limited or invalidated Reconstruction-era amendments and legislation. The court decided that the federal government had only limited power to protect civil and political rights, and it accepted that states could institute poll taxes that disfranchised African Americans and create segregated facilities. As a result, a system of racial segregation supported by violence emerged in the South. Instead of focusing on the constitutional arguments in a vacuum, Goldstone juxtaposes the decisions and their impact on society.

Gordon-Reed, Annette. *Andrew Johnson*. New York: Henry Holt, 2011.
In this brief, readable biography, Pulitzer prize-winning historian Annette Gordon-Reed examines the life of the 17th president of the United States. Gordon-Reed clearly presents Johnson's ascent from humble beginnings to the height of American politics. Yet Johnson became president at a crucial juncture in American history, and she argues that his leadership style and temperament made him ill-suited to address the problems that confronted the nation after the assassination of Lincoln. In particular, Gordon-Reed emphasizes that his stubbornness created unnecessary conflict with Congress and that his overt racism led him to reject a broad understanding of freedom.

Hahn, Steven. *A Nation Under Our Feet: Black Political Struggles in the Rural South from Slavery to the Great Migration.* Cambridge, MA: Harvard University Press, 2003.
  In his Pulitzer prize-winning work, Hahn explores black political mobilization in the rural South over a 50-year period. This broad scope allows him to start with slavery and then move forward into and beyond Reconstruction. Unlike many works that focus heavily on urban blacks who were free before the war, Hahn concentrates his attention on the countryside. He examines how grass roots political activism emerged out of black communities in slavery and freedom. Kinship ties were at the core of the resistance to slavery and were heavily represented in the political organizations freedmen joined after the war. Hahn offers a synthetic examination of African Americans' struggle for self-governance.

Hahn, Steven. *The Roots of Southern Populism: Yeoman Farmers and the Transformation of the Georgia Upcountry, 1850–1890.* New York: Oxford University Press, 1983.
  This path-breaking work explores the economic and social changes that destroyed the independence of yeomen in upcountry Georgia during the second half of the nineteenth century. While upcountry families had largely shunned cotton production and market orientation before the war, economic changes accelerated by military conflict transformed the region. As these communities became dependent upon the production of cash crops to survive the dislocations of war and Reconstruction, they were increasingly divided into classes of landowners and tenants, creditors and debtors. Hahn's book is an important reminder to students of Reconstruction that the failure of comprehensive land reform negatively affected the economic independence of poor whites as well as former slaves.

Hahn, Steven, Steven F. Miller, Susan E. O'Donovan, John C. Rodrigue, and Leslie S. Rowland, eds. *Freedom: A Documentary History of Emancipation, 1861–1867,* series 3, volume 1: *Land and Labor, 1865.* Chapel Hill: University of North Carolina Press, 2008; Hayden, Rene, Anthony E. Kaye, Kate Masur, Steven F. Miller, Susan E. O'Donovan, Leslie S. Rowland, and Stephen A. West. *Freedom: A Documentary History of Emancipation, 1861–1867,* series 3, volume 2: *Land and Labor, 1866–1867.* Chapel Hill: University of North Carolina Press, 2013.
  These two volumes are part of the Freedmen and Southern Society Project that provides a documentary history of emancipation from the extensive collections of the National Archives and Records Administration. Organized both thematically and chronologically, these two volumes include documents related to land and labor in the three years after the Civil War. Lengthy introductions to the sources are provided, as well as cross-references to other volumes that make it possible to follow themes across

time. These volumes are a marvelous resource for those interested in exploring the meaning of freedom and accessing the perspectives of freedpeople.

Hogue, James K. *Uncivil War: Five New Orleans Street Battles and the Rise and Fall
of Radical Reconstruction*. Baton Rouge: Louisiana State University Press, 2011.
    Hogue starts with the premise that the Civil War did not end with the surrender
    at Appomattox but continued during Reconstruction under a different name.
    Covering five episodes in New Orleans, from the infamous 1866 riot through
    the coup in 1877 that ended the Republican rule, he convincingly demon-
    strated that violence was endemic to Louisiana politics. Organized paramilitary
    groups destabilized the Republican Party and forced them to rely on Union
    troops to remain in power. Hogue's readable account of five street battles dem-
    onstrates the connection between force and politics during Reconstruction.

Hume, Richard L., and Jerry B. Gough. *Blacks, Carpetbaggers, and Scalawags: The
Constitutional Conventions of Radical Reconstruction*. Baton Rouge: Louisiana State
University Press, 2008.
    The authors provide a detailed study of the 10 southern state constitutional
    conventions held between 1867 and 1869 and the constitutions that were
    drafted. The book includes a biographical overview of the more than 1,000
    delegates who attended the conventions, and it utilizes a wealth of quantita-
    tive data to analyze their voting behavior on issues ranging from suffrage to
    public education and office holding. Identifying the key features of each state
    convention, the book considers the relative strength of scalawags, carpetbag-
    gers, and blacks in defining the issues that would dominate the conventions.

Keith, LeeAnna. *The Colfax Massacre: The Untold Story of Black Power, White Terror, and the Death of Reconstruction*. New York: Oxford University Press, 2008.
    Keith's work focuses on the events of April 3, 1873, in Colfax, Louisiana,
    which left approximately 150 people dead. The Colfax Massacre is the largest
    outbreak of political violence during Reconstruction, but it was misremem-
    bered for decades as a riot caused by African Americans. Keith rejects this
    version of events and instead presents a compelling narrative of a massacre
    of blacks defending the Colfax courthouse. Keith explains that after the
    courthouse was set on fire, blacks fled the blaze, surrendered, and then were
    executed. This volume is suited for a general audience and provides helpful
    context for the massacre and a sense of its larger significance. In particular,
    Keith examines *U.S. v. Cruikshank*, the Supreme Court case that emerged
    from the prosecution of the perpetrators of the massacre. The decision
    resulted in the limiting of federal power to enforce the Fourteenth and Fif-
    teenth Amendments and marked the retreat from Reconstruction.

Lemann, Nicholas. *Redemption: The Last Battle of the Civil War*. New York: Farrar, Straus and Giroux, 2006.

> Lemann examines the role of violence in bringing about an end to Republican control of the state of Mississippi in 1875. This dramatic story offers readers the opportunity to explore the intersection of local and state action plans with the national policy considerations of the Grant administration. Designed for a general audience, *Redemption* powerfully presents the violent actions of white Mississippians and the seeming indifference of Northerners to the stories of murder and arson. At the center of this story is Lucius Q. C. Lamar, an avid secessionist who so successfully recast his image as a supporter of reconciliation that John F. Kennedy included him in his 1956 volume, *Profiles in Courage*. Lemann counteracts the myths about Redemption and offers a much more disturbing vision.

Litwack, Leon F. *Been in the Storm So Long: The Aftermath of Slavery*. New York: Vintage, 1979.

> In this Pulitzer prize-winning study, Leon Litwack explores the dramatic transition from slavery to freedom in the South. He examines what this process meant to both slaveholders and former slaves. In the process, Litwack uses a wealth of individual examples to create a composite portrait of how slavery was perceived and experienced. The perspective of slaveholders who confronted the end of slavery is detailed in the countless letters and diaries that convey their sense of confusion, loss, and anger. To present the African American perspective, Litwack uses statements made by freedpeople to Freedmen's Bureau agents and Union troops as well as the Federal Writers Project interviews with former slaves conducted during the 1930s. The result is a compelling story of the struggle to reconstruct families, lives, and economic opportunity.

McFeely, William S. *Yankee Stepfather: General O.O. Howard and the Freedmen*. New Haven, CT: Yale University Press, 1968.

> In *Yankee Stepfather*, McFeely revises positive assessments of General O. O. Howard and critically reexamines his role as commissioner of the Freedmen's Bureau. He argues that Howard was well meaning but naïve and timid. As a result, McFeely concludes that Howard failed to be an effective advocate for African Americans. When faced with a president who was hostile to the mission of the Freedmen's Bureau, Howard repeatedly made concessions to Johnson. Over land confiscation, in particular, McFeely suggests that Howard failed to fight for an issue that he understood to be important for freedpeople. In addition, McFeely presents Howard as disloyal to those subordinates like Rufus Saxton, an assistant commissioner for the bureau, who would not compromise his principles and who was ultimately removed by the president.

Middleton, Stephen. *Black Congressmen during Reconstruction: A Documentary Sourcebook*. Westport, CT: Greenwood Press, 2002.

Middleton's book is a helpful resource for examining the lives and speeches of 22 African Americans who served in the House and Senate, 1870–1901. For each entry, a brief biographical summary of the life of the black congressman is included along with primary sources that reveal political views and issues.

Rable, George C. *But There Was No Peace: The Role of Violence in the Politics of Reconstruction*. Athens: University of Georgia Press, 2007.

Rable analyzes the violence directed against white Republicans and blacks during Reconstruction. In particular, this book examines the 1866 race riots in New Orleans and Memphis as well as Klan violence against Republican voters and officeholders. Rable argues that white Southerners who opposed the federal government's "revolutionary" attempts to reconstruct the South used violence as a "counterrevolutionary" measure to intimidate local Republicans and overthrow state Republican parties.

Richardson, Heather Cox. *The Death of Reconstruction: Race, Labor, and Politics in the Post–Civil War North, 1865–1901*. Cambridge, MA: Harvard University Press, 2001.

Richardson explores why northern Republican support for the rights of freedpeople diminished during Reconstruction. She argues that while racism was certainly a factor, attitudes also changed because of broader concerns about labor unrest. Republicans believed in the "free labor ideology" that posited a harmony of interests between workers and owners. In the aftermath of the war, northern Republicans became increasingly concerned that this harmony of interests was breaking down. Using newspapers and magazines, Richardson documented rising fears that the emerging labor movement in the North was a sign of class conflict. Northern Republicans similarly interpreted events in South Carolina in the 1870s as evidence that economic radicalism was taking hold in the black community. African American politicians in the state, they argued, employed corrupt practices to victimize property owners in the interest of those without property. As a result, Northerners came to tolerate policies, most notably disfranchisement and segregation, which they had earlier opposed.

Richardson, Heather Cox. *West from Appomattox: The Reconstruction of America after the Civil War*. New Haven, CT: Yale University Press, 2007.

This book explores the role of the West in the remaking of American national identity from Reconstruction into the early twentieth century. The author argues that historians have concentrated too exclusively on North-South sectionalism without placing that conflict in the context of western expansion. Richardson shows that the conquest and settlement of the West created an image of American individualism that has been a dominant element in the culture of the United States ever since. As Americans in both the North and South consumed romantic images of self-reliant cowboys and rugged western settlers, they became less sympathetic to those, like former slaves, who claimed special protection from government. Richardson's analysis provides an important cultural explanation for the retreat from robust Reconstruction policies that included vigorous enforcement of Civil Rights laws.

Roark, James L. *Masters without Slaves: Southern Planters in the Civil War and Reconstruction*. New York: W. W. Norton, 1977.

In this classic study of the social transformation that followed the end of slavery, Roark explores the changes from the perspective of slaveholders, using the letters and diaries of planters to present their ideas and attitudes. At the center of the story are the white planters who were committed to retaining slavery, even as it disintegrated around them. In the process they lost their wealth and their mastery over those who labored for them. After the abolition of slavery, planters remained hostile to social change, deeply suspicious of free labor, and acutely aware of their own powerlessness. New mechanisms to control labor emerged, and most African Americans remained in agricultural labor, but the world of the antebellum plantation was destroyed.

Rodrigue, John C. *Lincoln and Reconstruction*. Carbondale: Southern Illinois University Press, 2013.

In this clear, concise volume, Rodrigue examines the evolution of Abraham Lincoln's views on Reconstruction. Lincoln did not have just one plan but instead his position changed as the military conflict was transformed from a limited war to preserve the Union to a war to end slavery. Initially Lincoln's views focused on the restoration of the southern states without any social, legal, or economic changes to the South. Once Union victory was linked to emancipation, however, Lincoln's understanding of Reconstruction broadened and he was forced to consider how Southern society would be remade. Rodrigue emphasizes that the limits of Lincoln's attitudes are visible less on racial issues than economic ones. As an ardent supporter of the sanctity of private property, he argues, Lincoln would not have been able to sanction land confiscation or other mechanisms to transform Southern society on a broad scale.

Rodrigue, John C. *Reconstruction in the Cane Fields: From Slavery to Free Labor in Louisiana's Sugar Parishes, 1862–1882*. Baton Rouge: Louisiana State University Press, 2001.

This work is part of a large body of scholarship that examines the emergence of a free labor system in the South after emancipation. Focusing on the sugar region of Louisiana, Rodrigue analyzes how work was reorganized, arguing that former slaves had the ability to negotiate effectively with planters over hours, wages, and conditions. He explains that the leverage freedpeople possessed to define the meaning of free labor emerged because of the heavy requirements of sugar production. Growing and processing sugar involved large groups of workers who possessed knowledge of the process—circumstances that helped former slaves to reorganize labor in line with their own ideas of freedom.

Saville, Julie. *The Work of Reconstruction: From Slave to Wage Laborer in South Carolina, 1860–1870*. Cambridge: Cambridge University Press, 1996.

This scholarly work explores the ways in which African Americans in the lowcountry of South Carolina experienced the complex transition from slavery to freedom. The author argues that freedpeople in this region sought to shape their freedom in ways that rejected both the control of their former owners and the attempt by northern reformers to impose capitalist work discipline on their daily labor. Having worked out a modicum of autonomy before emancipation through the "task system" of plantation management, freedpeople in the South Carolina Sea Islands were unwilling to accept an hourly wage system that treated them as individual employees rather than as members of families or communities. Saville provides a fascinating examination of labor relations in an important region of the Deep South.

Schwalm, Leslie A. *A Hard Fight for We: Women's Transition from Slavery to Freedom in South Carolina*. Urbana: University of Illinois Press, 1997.

In her study of the lowcountry of South Carolina, Schwalm explores the transition from slavery to freedom from the vantage point of black women. Covering three periods, Schwalm explores the work of enslaved women on rice plantations, their role in accelerating the collapse of slavery, and their efforts to reconstruct southern life after the war. In particular she presents evidence of black women's resistance to the demands of employers after the war. Defining the meaning of free labor for themselves, these women challenged the power of planters and the Freedmen's Bureau to determine the nature of their work and its hours.

Simpson, Brooks D. *The Reconstruction Presidents*. Lawrence: University Press of Kansas, 1998.

Simpson's work is a political history of Reconstruction, focusing on the policies of four presidents: Abraham Lincoln, Andrew Johnson, Ulysses S. Grant, and Rutherford B. Hayes. He offers a traditional approach to Reconstruction centering on national politics and the political leaders who shaped policy. In the chapters devoted to each of the four presidents, Simpson blends original research with a synthesis of longer biographical studies. As a result, the work offers readers the opportunity to understand the significance of specific policies and to make comparisons among the four presidents' response to Reconstruction.

Slap, Andrew L. *The Doom of Reconstruction: The Liberal Republicans in the Civil War Era.* New York: Fordham University Press, 2006.

In *The Doom of Reconstruction,* Andrew Slap studies 23 Liberal Republicans, including politicians like Carl Schurz and editors like E. L. Godkin of *The Nation.* Though they have often been criticized as politically inept and elitist, Slap presents a more sympathetic image of the Liberal Republicans, emphasizing their commitment to limited government, free trade, and civil service reform. Slap distinguishes between the liberal republican movement rooted in the antebellum era and the Liberal Republican Party that nominated Horace Greeley in the 1872 presidential election. During the campaign, the Liberal Republicans turned their back on their roots, and anti-Grantism replaced free trade and civil service reform as the central issue of their movement.

Stewart, David O. *Impeached: The Trial of President Andrew Johnson and the Fight for Lincoln's Legacy.* New York: Simon & Schuster, 2009.

This book provides a narrative history of Andrew Johnson's impeachment that is rich in detail and clear in analysis. Stewart demonstrates the many ways that Johnson alienated Congress and narrates the dogged attempts by Republican representatives like Thaddeus Stevens to find the grounds to impeach him. The trial itself is engagingly presented, including allegations that fraud played a key role in keeping Johnson in office. Stewart's training in the law makes him well-suited to explain the constitutional basis for the proceedings against President Johnson.

Stowell, Daniel W. *Rebuilding Zion: The Religious Reconstruction of the South, 1863–1877.* New York: Oxford University Press, 1998.

If the political institutions of Reconstruction have received intense scrutiny from historians, religious institutions have not. *Rebuilding Zion* addresses this gap by exploring the ways in which southern churches recovered from the spiritual and physical destruction of the Civil War. The author contends that while black and white churches were committed equally to the strengthening of denominational structures, their spiritual goals differed quite fundamentally. Committed to reconstructing the prewar order, white churches reaffirmed the honor and moral legitimacy of the defeated Confederate cause. Black churches, on the other hand, became important spiritual and political resources for a beleaguered but resilient community in its struggle for freedom and equality.

Trefousse, Hans L. *The Radical Republicans: Lincoln's Vanguard for Racial Justice.* New York: Knopf, 1969.

In this readable narrative history, Trefousse studies approximately 30 leading radical Republicans. He replaces negative portrayals of the radicals with a positive one, arguing that men like Thaddeus Stevens, Charles Sumner, and George Julian were leaders of the struggle for civil and political equality. For Trefousse, the radicals were ahead of Abraham Lincoln on issues like emancipation and racial justice but sought to work in partnership with him. Trefousse suggests that the Reconstruction amendments were the result of efforts by radicals to push moderates and conservatives into accepting more substantive changes to American political life after the Civil War.

Trefousse, Hans L. *Thaddeus Stevens: Nineteenth-Century Egalitarian.* Chapel Hill: University of North Carolina Press, 1997.

Thaddeus Stevens has often been attacked for forcing his radical and supposedly mean-spirited plans on the South. Hans Trefousse argues that Stevens's power in the House of Representatives has been exaggerated. Trefousse shows that the radical Republican failed to achieve his major policies, most notably land confiscation, during Reconstruction. Stevens was an important member of the House of Representatives, serving on the House Ways and Means committee and the Joint Committee of Fifteen during Reconstruction, but his authority was never dictatorial. Stevens supported civil and political equality, but he was also a pragmatic politician who would take the best deal he could get. Trefousse offers a short, readable biography of an important figure in Reconstruction.

Trelease, Allen W. *White Terror: The Ku Klux Klan Conspiracy and Southern Reconstruction.* New York: Harper & Row, 1971.

Trelease examines the impact of violence on Southern society during Reconstruction, and in the process, his book demolishes older, romanticized images of the Klan. He explores in particular the role political violence played in returning control of the region to the Democratic Party. Trelease focused on the Klan and not other white supremacist organizations and he ended in 1871, after the federal government targeted the Klan using the enforcement acts. A growing body of scholarship, including the work of George Rable, Richard Zuczek, and James Hogue, has built on the path-breaking work of Trelease, extending beyond the Klan and 1871.

Wang, Xi. *The Trial of Democracy: Black Suffrage and Northern Republicans, 1860–1910.* Athens: University of Georgia Press, 1997.

This book examines the passage and implementation of voting rights laws in the nineteenth century. Wang's book is carefully researched and enhances our understanding of the role of the federal government in supporting suffrage. Between 1870 and 1872, Congress passed a series of laws to enforce the Fifteenth Amendment in the face of southern resistance, and Wang explores the debates within the Republican Party over this issue. He demonstrates that Republicans enforced voting rights for both principled and pragmatic reasons. Black male suffrage became the mechanism to guarantee equality before the law, and it was also politically expedient because most black voters supported the Republican Party. Going beyond the formal end of Reconstruction, Wang's book examines the limited enforcement of voting rights after the South returned to Democratic control in 1877.

Williamson, Joel. *After Slavery: The Negro in South Carolina during Reconstruction, 1861–1877*. Chapel Hill: University of North Carolina Press, 1965.
This is an important work of revisionist scholarship that remains a useful starting point for examining South Carolina during Reconstruction. South Carolina, the state with the highest percentage of African Americans, offers rich material to understand both economic and political change during the period. Making extensive use of manuscripts and newspapers, Williamson examines the political conflict and racial attitudes during the transition to freedom. In the process, he revises numerous assumptions about Reconstruction, presenting participants neither as villains nor as heroes. All subsequent studies of South Carolina have built on Williamson's work.

Zuczek, Richard. *State of Rebellion: Reconstruction in South Carolina*. Columbia: University of South Carolina Press, 1996.
Building on the work of George Rable, Zuczek examines the role of political violence in the defeat of Reconstruction. He argues that white conservatives in South Carolina did not accept defeat and instead waged a counterrevolution to limit the extent of political and social change. To regain control of the state, conservatives used violence regularly and not, as some have argued, as isolated incidents. Zuczek also contends that the Ku Klux Act of 1871 did not have as large an effect on suppressing terrorist activities as many have suggested. The book culminates with a careful examination of the tactics employed in the election of 1876 that resulted in the Democrats regaining power in South Carolina.

INDEX